MAN AND SUPERMAN

'He did his best in redressing the fateful unbalance between truth and reality, in lifting mankind to a higher rung of social maturity. He often pointed a scornful finger at human frailty, but his jests were never at the expense of humanity' Thomas Mann

'Shaw will not allow complacency; he hates second-hand opinions; he attacks fashion; he continually challenges and unsettles, questioning and provoking us even when he is making us laugh. And he is still at it. No cliché or truism of contemporary life is safe from him' Michael Holroyd

'In his works Shaw left us his mind ... Today we have no Shavian wizard to awaken us with clarity and paradox, and the loss to our national intelligence is immense' John Carey, *Sunday Times*

'An important writer and an interesting socialist and critic ... Thank God he lived' Peter Levi, *Independent*

'He was a Tolstoy with jokes, a modern Dr Johnson, a universal genius who on his own modest reckoning put even Shakespeare in the shade' John Campbell, *Independent*

'His plays were superb exercises in high-level argument on every issue under the sun, from feminism and God, to war and eternity, but they were also hits – and still are' Paul Johnson, *Daily Mail*

BERNARD SHAW was born in Dublin in 1856. Although essentially shy, he created the persona of G.B.S., the showman, satirist, controversialist, critic, pundit, wit, intellectual buffoon and dramatist. Commentators brought a new adjective into English: Shavian, a term used to embody all his brilliant qualities.

After his arrival in London in 1876 he became an active Socialist and a brilliant platform speaker. He wrote on many social aspects of the day: on *Common Sense about the War* (1914), *How to Settle the Irish Question* (1917) and *The Intelligent Woman's Guide to Socialism and Capitalism* (1928). He undertook his own education at the British Museum and consequently became keenly interested in cultural subjects. Thus his prolific output included music, art and theatre reviews, which were collected into several volumes, such as *Music In London 1890–1894* (3 vols., 1931), *Pen Portraits and Reviews* (1931); and *Our Theatres in the Nineties* (23 vols., 1931). He also wrote five novels, including *Cashel Byron's Profession* (published by Penguin), and a collection of shorter works issued as *A Black Girl in Search of God and Some Lesser Tales* (also in Penguin).

Shaw conducted a strong attack on the London Theatre and was closely associated with the intellectual revival of British Theatre. His many plays (the full canon runs to 52) fall into several categories: 'Plays Pleasant'; 'Plays Unpleasant'; 'Plays for Puritans'; political plays; chronicle plays; 'metabiological Pentateuch' (*Back to Methuselah*) in five plays; extravaganzas; romances; and fables. He died in 1950.

STANLEY WEINTRAUB is Evan Pugh Professor Emeritus of Arts and Humanities at the Pennsylvania State University. He is the author and editor of nearly fifty books. Of these, twenty are about, or by, Bernard Shaw, including *Private Shaw and Public Shaw, Bernard Shaw 1914–1918: Journey to Heartbreak* and *Shaw's People*. He has edited Shaw's diaries and his art criticism, was editor of *The Annual of Bernard Shaw Studies* until 1990 and wrote the Shaw entry in the New Dictionary of National Biography.

DAN H. LAURENCE, editor of Shaw's *Collected Letters*, his *Collected Plays with their Prefaces*, *Shaw's Music* and (with Daniel Leary) *The Complete Prefaces*, was Literary Adviser to the Shaw Estate until his retirement in 1990. He is Series Editor for the works of Shaw in Penguin.

BERNARD SHAW

MAN AND SUPERMAN

A COMEDY AND A PHILOSOPHY

Definitive text under the editorial supervision of
DAN H. LAURENCE
with an Introduction by STANLEY WEINTRAUB

PENGUIN BOOKS

PENGUIN BOOKS

Published by the Penguin Group
Penguin Books Ltd, 80 Strand, London WC2R 0RL, England
Penguin Putnam Inc., 375 Hudson Street, New York, New York 10014, USA
Penguin Books Australia Ltd, 250 Camberwell Road, Camberwell, Victoria 3124, Australia
Penguin Books Canada Ltd, 10 Alcorn Avenue, Toronto, Ontario, Canada M4V 3B2
Penguin Books India (P) Ltd, 11 Community Centre, Panchsheel Park, New Delhi – 110 017, India
Penguin Books (NZ) Ltd, Cnr Rosedale and Airborne Roads, Albany, Auckland, New Zealand
Penguin Books (South Africa) (Pty) Ltd, 24 Sturdee Avenue, Rosebank 2196, South Africa

Penguin Books Ltd, Registered Offices: 80 Strand, London WC2R 0RL, England

www.penguin.com

First published 1903
The play (without the Don Juan in Hell scene) first
produced in London and New York in 1905
Don Juan in Hell first produced in 1907
The play in its entirety first performed in 1915 (Edinburgh)
Published in Penguin Books 26 July 1946
Reprinted with a new Introduction in Penguin Classics 2000

6

Printed in England by Clays Ltd, St Ives plc
Set in Monotype Baskerville

*All business connected with Bernard Shaw's plays is in the hands of the Society of Authors,
84 Drayton Gardens, London SW10 9SB (Telephone 020-7373-6642), to which all inquiries
and applications for licences to perform should be addressed and performing fees paid.
Dates and places of contemplated performances must be precisely specified in all
applications.*

*Applications for permission to give stock and amateur performances of Bernard Shaw's
plays in the United States of America and Canada should be made to Samuel French Inc.,
45 West 25th Street, New York, 10010. In all other cases, whether for stage, radio, or
television, applications should be made to The Society of Authors, 84 Drayton Gardens,
London SW10 9SB, England.*

CONTENTS

INTRODUCTION

In a cartoon by Max Beerbohm about *Man and Superman*, the Danish critic Georg Brandes asks Bernard Shaw what he would take for his motley clothes, and Shaw answers, 'Immortality.' The sophisticated Brandes scoffs, 'Come, I've handled these same goods before! Coat, Mr. Schopenhauer's; waistcoat, Mr. Ibsen's; trousers, Mr. Nietzche's...'

'Ah,' counters Shaw, 'but look at the patches!' And the patches are a collection of other influential writers to whom Shaw was allegedly indebted. Beerbohm's mockery failed to disturb Shaw. He would write, in the preface to another play, 'I did not cut these cerebral capers in mere inconsiderate exuberance. I did it because the worst convention of the criticism of the theatre current at that time was that intellectual seriousness is out of place on the stage .... My answer to all this was to put all my intellectual goods in the shop window under the sign of Man and Superman. By good luck and acting, the comedy triumphed on the stage ...'

He began the scenario in July 1901, determined not only to write a play that would be for all seasons, but one that would encapsulate the new century's intellectual inheritance. 'Accordingly,' he wrote, '... I took the legend of Don Juan in its Mozartian form and made it a dramatic parable.' He also took some of his Don Juan from Lord Byron's verse satire, where the alleged philanderer is not the pursuer, but the pursued, a concept Shaw also attributed to 'Shakespearean law,' where 'the woman always takes the initiative.' From the Victorian comedy fashionable in Shaw's earliest days he took the twin themes of love and money, giving one heroine an inheritance but not the man she wants to share it with her, and the other the man, but not the money his father wants to withhold if he marries the wrong woman.

'I should make formal acknowledgment,' he wrote in his preface to the play, 'to the authors I have pillaged in the following pages if I could recollect them all.' His 'brigand–

poetaster' was owed to Arthur Conan Doyle; his 'motor engineer and New Man' was from H. G. Wells. His 'servant who knows more than his masters' he conceded to James Barrie. He took his Octavius 'unaltered from Mozart,' but neglected to note that the same character is also 'Ricky-Ticky-Tavy,' from Rudyard Kipling. After watching a production of the medieval *Everyman*, he asked himself, 'Why not Everywoman?' – and confessed, 'Ann was the result: every woman is not Ann, but Ann is Everywoman.'

Readers and playgoers will find that the feast of overt and covert sources in *Man and Superman* adds continuing dimensions to the comedy. There are many more. Shaw even mined his own earlier and little-known writings. As a failed novelist in his twenties, Shaw began a satirical novel he intended to call *The Heartless Man* but eventually titled *An Unsocial Socialist* (1883). Its hero is an analogue of John Tanner in the later play, and the novel's ineffectual poe-tasting suitor is a precursor to Octavius. Its 'duel of sex' at the conclusion recalls Congreve's elegant comedy of manners *The Way of the World* (1700) and anticipates the witty, ironic last scene of Shaw's play. Even less known is Shaw's 1887 short story 'Don Giovanni Explains', rejected by editors who sensed scandal. In this, his first working out of the Don Juan legend, the narrator – the Don himself – confides that he had been initiated in sex by an amorous widow. Two years before, that had actually happened to Shaw, who noted in his diary that he had celebrated his birthday 'by a new experience.' (Shaw finally published the story in his Collected Edition in 1932, when he was seventy-six.)

Even the four figments of a dream in the almost-independent Interlude that makes up most of Act III are anticipated in 'Don Giovanni Explains', which opens with a young woman daydreaming on a train about the opera she has just seen, and then observing the Don sitting opposite her in his traditional Mozartian costume. When she startles, he advises her, 'Pray be quiet. You are alone. I am only what you call a ghost, and have not the slightest interest in meddling with you.' At that point the story turns into what

seems to be a preliminary scenario for 'Don Juan in Hell',
the dream interlude, with the Lady, an equivalent to Dona
Ana, who finds herself at the opening of the interlude face-
to-face with an equally ethereal Don Juan.

Even more striking is the resemblance of the concepts of
Heaven and Hell in the Shavian short story to those in the
Hell Scene. The principals of the Hell Scene – all four are
equivalents to characters in the frame-play – learn that the
frontier separating Heaven from Hell is 'only the difference
between two ways of looking at things,' and Ana is told that
they 'see each other as bodies only because we learnt to think
about one another under that aspect when we were alive.'
The Don of the story had told the Lady, 'If I speak of [Hell]
as a place at all, I do so in order to make my narrative comprehensible, just as I express myself to you phenomenally as
a gentleman in hat, cloak, and boots, although such things
are no part of the category to which I belong.' The Hell of
the play is a place for gross satisfaction of the senses, and the
Devil is the leader of its best society. The Don acknowledges
the Devil's intellectual and debating gifts, but resents his
insufferable cordiality. In the story, the Don confides to the
Lady, 'I found society there composed chiefly of the vulgar,
hysterical, brutish, weak, good-for-nothing people, all well-
intentioned, who kept up the reputation of the place by
making themselves and each other as unhappy as they were
capable of being. They wearied and disgusted me; and I dis-
concerted them beyond measure. The Prince of Darkness is
not a gentleman. His knowledge and insight are remarkable as far as they go; ... and I was polite to him.' Each
Don, in both the early story and the mature play, is a sub-
versive whose austere vision of life is unsuitable for the
Shavian Hell.

To integrate play and play-within-the-play, Shaw would
identify his hero, John Tanner, as a distant relative of the
legendary Don Juan Tenorio – thus his echo of a surname.
Throughout the romantic misadventures and misunder-
standings with which the play abounds are echoes of dreams
and references to dreams, even, in Ann/Ana's words 'an

echo from a former existence which always seems to me such a striking proof that we have immortal souls.' Toward the close, Tanner wonders, 'When did all this happen to me before? Are we two dreaming?'

Shaw calls the phenomenon which disturbs John Tanner the Life Force, and explains it at length in the preface which he dedicated ironically and extravagantly to Arthur Bingham Walkley, the most influential theatre critic of the day. Drama reviewer for *The Times*, Walkley loathed Shaw's plays and wished none of them well. He failed to appreciate the wry comedy of manners which Shaw had wrapped around his philosophical romp (produced at first without the interlude in Hell), and was at a loss to explain why the play worked. When it was first performed at the Royal Court Theatre in Sloane Square in 1904, Walkley began his critique by comparing Shaw to Shakespeare and putting his ambitious contemporary down. 'On the one hand a born dramatist, and that the greatest,' he wrote of the Bard; 'on the other [hand] a man who is no dramatist at all.' Yet Walkley felt forced to confess that there was something peculiar about what he had seen. 'When I venture to say that Mr Shaw is no dramatist I do not mean that he fails to interest and stimulate and amuse us in the theatre. Many of us find him more entertaining than any other living writer for the stage. There are many things in his plays that give us far keener thrills of delight ... than many things in Shakespeare's plays.'

Walkley and most other critics could not make sense of Shaw's coupling of newness and tradition in what was the first great twentieth century English play. It was even more difficult for the London critical fraternity to comprehend it in its book form. 'I decorated it,' Shaw blamed himself later, 'too brilliantly and too lavishly. I surrounded it with a comedy of which it formed only one act, and that act was so completely episodical (it was a dream that did not affect the action of the piece) that the comedy could be detached and played by itself. Also I supplied the published work with an imposing framework consisting of a preface, an appendix called 'The Revolutionist's Handbook' [supposedly written by John Tanner], and a final display of [Tanner's] aphoristic fireworks.' It was all too much for the critics, who had never seen anything like it before. They dismissed it. Somehow he and theatre critic William Archer remained friends despite Archer's smug dismissal that Shaw 'is not, and never will be, a great dramatist; but he is something rarer, if not better – a philosophic humorist, with the art of expressing himself in dramatic form'. The *Daily Telegraph* agreed that there was no play, not even a story, in *Man and Superman*, but, its reviewer conceded, 'let us frankly admit that it is one of the most amusing pieces of work which ... the Court Theatre has ever put upon the stage.'

Shaw subtitled his pairing of play and dream 'a comedy and a philosophy.' When the third act, largely John Tanner's dream, is performed with the frame-play, the performance can run five hours – no longer than the uncut *Hamlet*, Shaw reminded contemporaries. (It was first given in full in 1915.) In its entirety it is a vivid evocation of his ideas about male–female relations and the inner forces that dominate them. Playing it in its Edwardian setting does not diminish that impact. Performed without the dream interlude, as audiences first experienced it in 1905, *Man and Superman* is buoyant, romantic theatre with a satirical edge. Performed separately as 'Don Juan in Hell' in 1907, and often, still, performed independently, the dream-interlude proved to be a lively conversation, a quartet for voices that aspires to the condition of music, yet given dramatic tension by a thread of plot: which alternative, Heaven or Hell, will Juan and Ana each choose? Whether the characters are only opinions in costume, or mythic figures brought to near-life, remains Shaw's challenge to directors, players, audiences – and, even, readers.

As the play closes, with the heroines having snared their prey, we realize that Shaw's plays are open-ended, like life. Is the power of biological purpose, which both Juan and his Edwardian successor, John Tanner, consider unscrupulous, enough to keep the sexes together for a lifetime? The 'true joy of life', Shaw contends in his rhetorical feat of a preface, is 'being used for a purpose recognized by yourself as a mighty one; the being thoroughly worn out [in fulfilling it] before you are thrown on the scrap heap; the being a force of Nature instead of a feverish selfish little clod of ailments complaining that the world will not devote itself to making you happy.' If so, is *Man and Superman*, for all its effervescence, a comedy after all?

The Royal Court Theatre, managed and directed then by John Vedrenne and Harley Granville Barker, used the repertory system, making long runs impossible, but the public demanded more opportunities to see *Man and Superman*. Through 1907 the Court revived it three times, for a total of 176 performances. That success was too much for the still-influential quarterly, *Blackwood's*, which sneered that Shaw had enjoyed a 'peculiar triumph', and predicted unhappily that 'henceforth there is no extravagance which will not be permitted to him' while he 'wrap[ped] up a genuine talent in the rags of charlatanry ... under the inspiration of that demented professor, Friedrich Nietzsche'. Shaw did not believe in wasting his writing energy on anger, and waited until 1910 to put a collection of critics into a comedy. In *Fanny's First Play*, Walkley is the critic 'Trotter', who reviews the play-within-the-play ostensibly written by Fanny O'Dowda. Waiting for the curtain to go up, 'Trotter' rails against an unnamed playwright, clearly Shaw, who 'resorts to the dastardly subterfuge of calling [his work for the stage] conversation pieces, discussions, and so forth.' To 'Trotter' they were, of course, not plays. But play or nay, *Fanny* would run for 622 performances, one of the longest-running hits of the time.

By putting recognizable critics on stage in the frame-play, Shaw was taking a step farther toward what Bertolt Brecht would later call the 'alienation effect' – the audience recognition that the play being seen and heard was not a representation of reality but a presentation by a playwright that required, beyond possible empathy with its characters, a stepping back to consider the play as a play. While a Shakespeare or a Dryden had created a 'Chorus' figure to step forward and ask the audience (as in *Henry V*) to 'entertain conjecture of a time', Shaw created as early as *Man and Superman* the player who is both actor and character in the same person – the self-conscious character, or actor directly aware of his audience. In 'Don Juan in Hell' he combined two of the most primitive, yet basic, elements of the self-conscious theatre – the platform of the philosopher and the ring of the clown. In post-Shavian refinements the technique would sweep across the century. When the Devil, exasperated by Juan's long speeches, challenges, 'Let us go on for another hour if you like,' and Don Juan agrees, 'Good: let us,' the perceptible groans amid the laughter make it clear that the audience knows it is at a play. When the Statue (of the Commander) carps, 'I begin to doubt whether you will ever finish, my friend. You are extremely fond of hearing yourself talk,' the audience recognizes Shaw's tongue in his cheek, a perception reinforced by Juan's response, 'True; but since you have endured so much, you may as well endure to the end.'

That a playwright can misunderstand the implications of his words has energized critics since the dawn of drama reviewing. Shaw, then, may have been mistaken in his contention, quoted earlier, that the dispensable dream scene does not affect the action of the frame-play. Indeed it seems otherwise. Readers and audiences may find John Tanner's collapse of resistance to betrothal related to his experience as the dreamer, for in the dream scene Don Juan encounters the inevitability of the Life Force, 'the universal creative energy, of which the parties are both the helpless agents, [which] overrides and sweeps away all personal considerations', and which throws potential sexual partners 'into one another's arms at the exchange of a glance.' Whether or not Ann has long plotted her moves, and Tanner has long resisted even the thought of them, his subconscious, in the grip of his dream, prepares him for the inevitable. Tanner recognizes that he is doomed to happiness and to what Francis Bacon, in his Shakespeare-era essay on marriage, had called 'hostages to fortune'. Despite pages of paradoxes,

Shaw had, in the end, recognized the realities of the box-office, without which there is no theatre. Thus *Man and Superman* plays on, and on, and on.

Stanley Weintraub

MAN AND SUPERMAN

CONTENTS

TO ARTHUR BINGHAM WALKLEY

My dear Walkley

You once asked me why I did not write a Don Juan play. The levity with which you assumed this frightful responsibility has probably by this time enabled you to forget it; but the day of reckoning has arrived: here is your play! I say your play, because *qui facit per alium facit per se*. Its profits, like its labor, belong to me: its morals, its manners, its philosophy, its influence on the young, are for you to justify. You were of mature age when you made the suggestion; and you knew your man. It is hardly fifteen years since, as twin pioneers of the New Journalism of that time, we two, cradled in the same new sheets, began an epoch in the criticism of the theatre and the opera house by making it the pretext for a propaganda of our own views of life. So you cannot plead ignorance of the character of the force you set in motion. You meant me to épater le bourgeois; and if he protests, I hereby refer him to you as the accountable party.

I warn you that if you attempt to repudiate your responsibility, I shall suspect you of finding the play too decorous for your taste. The fifteen years have made me older and graver. In you I can detect no such becoming change. Your levities and audacities are like the loves and comforts prayed for by Desdemona: they increase, even as your days do grow. No mere pioneering journal dares meddle with them now: the stately Times itself is alone sufficiently above suspicion to act as your chaperone; and even The Times must sometimes thank its stars that new plays are not produced every day, since after each such event its gravity is compromised, its platitude turned to epigram, its portentousness to wit, its propriety to elegance, and even its decorum into naughtiness by criticisms which the traditions of the paper do not allow you to sign at the end, but which you take care to sign with the most extravagant flourishes between the lines. I am not sure that this is not a portent of Revolution. In

7

XVIII century France the end was at hand when men bought the Encyclopedia and found Diderot there. When I buy The Times and find you there, my prophetic ear catches a rattle of XX century tumbrils.

However, that is not my present anxiety. The question is, will you not be disappointed with a Don Juan play in which not one of that hero's *mille e tre* adventures is brought upon the stage? To propitiate you, let me explain myself. You will retort that I never do anything else: it is your favorite jibe at me that what I call drama is nothing but explanation. But you must not expect me to adopt your inexplicable, fantastic, petulant, fastidious ways: you must take me as I am, a reasonable, patient, consistent, apologetic, laborious person, with the temperament of a schoolmaster and the pursuits of a vestryman. No doubt that literary knack of mine which happens to amuse the British public distracts attention from my character; but the character is there none the less, solid as bricks. I have a conscience; and conscience is always anxiously explanatory. You, on the contrary, feel that a man who discusses his conscience is much like a woman who discusses her modesty. The only moral force you condescend to parade is the force of your wit: the only demand you make in public is the demand of your artistic temperament for symmetry, elegance, style, grace, refinement, and the cleanliness which comes next to godliness if not before it. But my conscience is the genuine pulpit article: it annoys me to see people comfortable when they ought to be uncomfortable; and I insist on making them think in order to bring them to conviction of sin. If you dont like my preaching you must lump it. I really cannot help it.

In the preface to my Plays for Puritans I explained the predicament of our contemporary English drama, forced to deal almost exclusively with cases of sexual attraction, and yet forbidden to exhibit the incidents of that attraction or even to discuss its nature. Your suggestion that I should write a Don Juan play was virtually a challenge to me to treat this subject myself dramatically. The challenge was difficult enough to be worth accepting, because, when you come to think of it, though we have plenty of dramas with heroes and heroines who are in love and must accordingly marry or perish at the end of the play, or about people whose relations with one another have been complicated by the marriage laws, not to mention the looser sort of plays which trade on the tradition that illicit love affairs are at once vicious and delightful, we have no modern English plays in which the natural attraction of the sexes for one another is made the mainspring of the action. That is why we insist on beauty in our performers, differing herein from the countries our friend William Archer holds up as examples of seriousness to our childish theatres. There the Juliets and Isoldes, the Romeos and Tristans, might be our mothers and fathers. Not so the English actress. The heroine she impersonates is not allowed to discuss the elemental relations of men and women: all her romantic twaddle about noveletmade love, all her purely legal dilemmas as to whether she was married or 'betrayed', quite miss our hearts and worry our minds. To console ourselves we must just look at her. We do so; and her beauty feeds our starving emotions. Sometimes we grumble ungallantly at the lady because she does not act as well as she looks. But in a drama which, with all its preoccupation with sex, is really void of sexual interest, good looks are more desired than histrionic skill.

Let me press this point on you, since you are too clever to raise the fool's cry of paradox whenever I take hold of a stick by the right instead of the wrong end. Why are our occasional attempts to deal with the sex problem on the stage so repulsive and dreary that even those who are most determined that sex questions shall be held open and their discussion kept free, cannot pretend to relish these joyless attempts at social sanitation? Is it not because at bottom they are utterly sexless? What is the usual formula for such plays? A woman has, on some past occasion, been brought into conflict with the law which regulates the relations of the sexes. A man, by falling in love with her, or marrying her, is brought into conflict with the social convention which discountenances the woman. Now the conflicts of individuals with law and convention can be dramatized like all other human conflicts; but they are purely judicial; and the fact that we are much more curious about the suppressed relations between the man and the woman than about the relations between both and our courts of law and private juries of matrons, produces that sensation of evasion, of dissatisfaction, of fundamental irrelevance, of shallowness, of useless disagreeableness, of total failure to edify and partial failure to interest, which is as familiar to you in the theatres as it was to me when I, too, frequented those uncomfortable buildings, and found our popular playwrights in the mind to (as they thought) emulate Ibsen.

I take it that when you asked me for a Don Juan play you did not want that sort of thing. Nobody does: the successes such plays sometimes obtain are due to the incidental conventional melodrama with which the experienced popular author instinctively saves himself from failure. But what did you want? Owing to your unfortunate habit – you now, I hope, feel its inconvenience – of not explaining yourself, I have had to discover this for myself. First, then, I have had to ask myself, what is a Don Juan? Vulgarly, a libertine. But your dislike of vulgarity is pushed to the length of a defect (universality of character is impossible without a share of vulgarity); and even if you could acquire the taste, you would find yourself overfed from ordinary sources without troubling me. So I took it that you demanded a Don Juan in the philosophic sense.

Philosophically, Don Juan is a man who, though gifted enough to be exceptionally capable of distinguishing between good and evil, follows his own instincts without regard to the common, statute, or canon law; and therefore, whilst gaining the ardent sympathy of our rebellious instincts (which are flattered by the brilliancies with which Don Juan associates them) finds himself in mortal conflict with existing institutions, and defends himself by fraud and force as unscrupulously as a farmer defends his crops by the same means against vermin. The prototypic Don Juan, invented early in the XVI century by a Spanish monk, was

presented, according to the ideas of that time, as the enemy
of God, the approach of whose vengeance is felt throughout
the drama, growing in menace from minute to minute. No
anxiety is caused on Don Juan's account by any minor antagonist: he easily eludes the police, temporal and spiritual;
and when an indignant father seeks private redress with the
sword, Don Juan kills him without an effort. Not until the
slain father returns from heaven as the agent of God, in the
form of his own statue, does he prevail against his slayer and
cast him into hell. The moral is a monkish one: repent and
reform now; for tomorrow it may be too late. This is really
the only point on which Don Juan is sceptical; for he is a
devout believer in an ultimate hell, and risks damnation
only because, as he is young, it seems so far off that repentance can be postponed until he has amused himself to his
heart's content.

But the lesson intended by an author is hardly ever the
lesson the world chooses to learn from his book. What at-
tracts and impresses us in El Burlador de Sevilla is not the
immediate urgency of repentance, but the heroism of daring
to be the enemy of God. From Prometheus to my own
Devil's Disciple, such enemies have always been popular.
Don Juan became such a pet that the world could not bear
his damnation. It reconciled him sentimentally to God in a
second version, and clamored for his canonization for a
whole century, thus treating him as English journalism has
treated that comic foe of the gods, Punch. Molière's Don
Juan casts back to the original in point of impenitence;
but in piety he falls off greatly. True, he also proposes
to repent; but in what terms! '*Oui, ma foi! il faut s'amender.
Encore vingt ou trente ans de cette vie-ci, et puis nous songerons à
nous.*' After Molière comes the artist-enchanter, the master
beloved by masters, Mozart, revealing the hero's spirit in
magical harmonies, elfin tones, and elate darting rhythms
as of summer lightning made audible. Here you have freedom in love and in morality mocking exquisitely at slavery
to them, and interesting you, attracting you, tempting you,
inexplicably forcing you to range the hero with his enemy

the statue on a transcendent plane, leaving the prudish daughter and her priggish lover on a crockery shelf below to live piously ever after.

After these completed works Byron's fragment does not count for much philosophically. Our vagabond libertines are no more interesting from that point of view than the sailor who has a wife in every port; and Byron's hero is, after all, only a vagabond libertine. And he is dumb: he does not discuss himself with a Sganarelle-Leporello or with the fathers or brothers of his mistresses: he does not even, like Casanova, tell his own story. In fact he is not a true Don Juan at all; for he is no more an enemy of God than any romantic and adventurous young sower of wild oats. Had you and I been in his place at his age, who knows whether we might not have done as he did, unless indeed your fastidiousness had saved you from the empress Catherine. Byron was as little of a philosopher as Peter the Great: both were instances of that rare and useful, but unedifying variation, an energetic genius born without the prejudices or superstitions of his contemporaries. The resultant unscrupulous freedom of thought made Byron a bolder poet than Wordsworth just as it made Peter a bolder king than George III; but as it was, after all, only a negative qualification, it did not prevent Peter from being an appalling blackguard and an arrant poltroon, nor did it enable Byron to become a religious force like Shelley. Let us, then, leave Byron's Don Juan out of account. Mozart's is the last of the true Don Juans; for by the time he was of age, his cousin Faust had, in the hands of Goethe, taken his place and carried both his warfare and his reconciliation with the gods far beyond mere lovemaking into politics, high art, schemes for reclaiming new continents from the ocean, and recognition of an eternal womanly principle in the universe. Goethe's Faust and Mozart's Don Juan were the last words of the XVIII century on the subject; and by the time the polite critics of the XIX century, ignoring William Blake as superficially as the XVIII had ignored Hogarth or the XVII Bunyan, had got past the Dickens-Macaulay Dumas-Guizot stage and the Stendhal-

Meredith-Turgenieff stage, and were confronted with philosophic fiction by such pens as Ibsen's and Tolstoy's, Don Juan had changed his sex and become Doña Juana, breaking out of the Doll's House and asserting herself as an individual instead of a mere item in a moral pageant.

Now it is all very well for you at the beginning of the XX century to ask me for a Don Juan play; but you will see from the foregoing survey that Don Juan is a full century out of date for you and for me; and if there are millions of less literate people who are still in the XVIII century, have they not Molière and Mozart, upon whose art no human hand can improve? You would laugh at me if at this time of day I dealt in duels and ghosts and 'womanly' women. As to mere libertinism, you would be the first to remind me that the Festin de Pierre of Molière is not a play for amorists, and that one bar of the voluptuous sentimentality of Gounod or Bizet would appear as a licentious stain on the score of Don Giovanni. Even the more abstract parts of the Don Juan play are dilapidated past use: for instance, Don Juan's supernatural antagonist hurled those who refuse to repent into lakes of burning brimstone, there to be tormented by devils with horns and tails. Of that antagonist, and of that conception of repentance, how much is left that could be used in a play by me dedicated to you? On the other hand, those forces of middle class public opinion which hardly existed for a Spanish nobleman in the days of the first Don Juan, are now triumphant everywhere. Civilized society is one huge bourgeoisie: no nobleman dares now shock his greengrocer. The women, 'marchesane, principesse, cameriere, cittadine' and all, are become equally dangerous: the sex is aggressive, powerful: when women are wronged they do not group themselves pathetically to sing '*Protegga il giusto cielo*': they grasp formidable legal and social weapons, and retaliate. Political parties are wrecked and public careers undone by a single indiscretion. A man had better have all the statues in London to supper with him, ugly as they are, than be brought to the bar of the Nonconformist Conscience by Donna Elvira. Excommunication has become almost as serious a business as it was in the tenth century.

As a result, Man is no longer, like Don Juan, victor in the duel of sex. Whether he has ever really been may be doubted: at all events the enormous superiority of Woman's natural position in this matter is telling with greater and greater force. As to pulling the Nonconformist Conscience by the beard as Don Juan plucked the beard of the Commandant's statue in the convent of San Francisco, that is out of the question nowadays: prudence and good manners alike forbid it to a hero with any mind. Besides, it is Don Juan's own beard that is in danger of plucking. Far from relapsing into hypocrisy, as Sganarelle feared, he has unexpectedly discovered a moral in his immorality. The growing recognition of his new point of view is heaping responsibility on him. His former jests he has had to take as seriously as I have had to take some of the jests of Mr W. S. Gilbert. His scepticism, once his least tolerated quality, has now triumphed so completely that he can no longer assert himself by witty negations, and must, to save himself from cipherdom, find an affirmative position. His thousand and three affairs of gallantry, after becoming, at most, two immature intrigues, leading to sordid and prolonged complications and humiliations, have been discarded altogether as unworthy of his philosophic dignity and compromising to his newly acknowledged position as the founder of a school. Instead of pretending to read Ovid he does actually read Schopenhauer and Nietzsche, studies Westernmarck, and is concerned for the future of the race instead of for the freedom of his own instincts. Thus his profligacy and his dare-devil airs have gone the way of his sword and mandoline into the rag shop of anachronisms and superstitions. In fact, he is now more Hamlet than Don Juan; for though the lines put into the actor's mouth to indicate to the pit that Hamlet is a philosopher are for the most part mere harmonious platitude which, with a little debasement of the word-music, would be properer to Pecksniff, yet if you separate the real hero, inarticulate and unintelligible to himself except in flashes of inspiration, from the performer who has to talk at any cost through five acts; and if you also do what you must always do in Shakespear's tragedies: that is, dissect out the absurd sensational incidents and physical violences of the borrowed story from the genuine Shakespearian tissue, you will get a true Promethean foe of the gods, whose instinctive attitude towards women much resembles that to which Don Juan is now driven. From this point of view Hamlet was a developed Don Juan whom Shakespear palmed off as a reputable man just as he palmed poor Macbeth off as a murderer. Today the palming off is no longer necessary (at least on your plane and mine) because Don Juanism is no longer misunderstood as mere Casanovism. Don Juan himself is almost ascetic in his desire to avoid that misunderstanding; and so my attempt to bring him up to date by launching him as a modern Englishman into a modern English environment has produced a figure superficially quite unlike the hero of Mozart.

And yet I have not the heart to disappoint you wholly of another glimpse of the Mozartian *dissoluto punito* and his antagonist the statue. I feel sure you would like to know more of that statue – to draw him out when he is off duty, so to speak. To gratify you, I have resorted to the trick of the strolling theatrical manager who advertizes the pantomime of Sinbad the Sailor with a stock of second-hand picture posters designed for Ali Baba. He simply thrusts a few oil jars into the valley of diamonds, and so fulfils the promise held out by the hoardings to the public eye. I have adapted this easy device to our occasion by thrusting into my perfectly modern three-act play a totally extraneous act in which my hero, enchanted by the air of the Sierra, has a dream in which his Mozartian ancestor appears and philosophizes at great length in a Shavio-Socratic dialogue with the lady, the statue, and the devil.

But this pleasantry is not the essence of the play. Over this essence I have no control. You propound a certain social substance, sexual attraction to wit, for dramatic distillation; and I distil it for you. I do not adulterate the product with aphrodisiacs nor dilute it with romance and water; for I am merely executing your commission, not producing a popular play for the market. You must therefore (unless, like most wise men, you read the play first and the preface afterwards) prepare yourself to face a trumpery story of modern London life, a life in which, as you know, the ordinary man's main business is to get means to keep up the position and habits of a gentleman, and the ordinary woman's business is to get married. In 9,999 cases out of 10,000 you can count on their doing nothing, whether noble or base, that conflicts with these ends; and that assurance is what you rely on as their religion, their morality, their principles, their patriotism, their reputation, their honor and so forth.

On the whole, this is a sensible and satisfactory foundation for society. Money means nourishment and marriage means children; and that men should put nourishment first and women children first is, broadly speaking, the law of Nature and not the dictate of personal ambition. The secret of the prosaic man's success, such as it is, is the simplicity with which he pursues these ends: the secret of the artistic man's failure, such as that is, is the versatility with which he strays in all directions after secondary ideals. The artist is either a poet or a scallawag; as poet, he cannot see, as the prosaic man does, that chivalry is at bottom only romantic suicide: as scallawag, he cannot see that it does not pay to spunge and beg and lie and brag and neglect his person. Therefore do not misunderstand my plain statement of the fundamental constitution of London society as an Irishman's reproach to your nation. From the day I first set foot on this foreign soil I knew the value of the prosaic qualities of which Irishmen teach Englishmen to be ashamed as well as I knew the vanity of the poetic qualities of which Englishmen teach Irishmen to be proud. For the Irishman instinctively disparages the quality which makes the Englishman dangerous to him; and the Englishman instinctively flatters the fault that makes the Irishman harmless and amusing to him. What is wrong with the prosaic Englishman is what is wrong with the prosaic men of all countries: stupidity. The vitality which places nourishment and children first, heaven and hell a somewhat remote second, and the health

of society as an organic whole nowhere, may muddle successfully through the comparatively tribal stages of gre-
gariousness; but in XIX century nations and XX century
commonwealths the resolve of every man to be rich at all
costs, and of every woman to be married at all costs, must,
without a highly scientific social organization, produce
a ruinous development of poverty, celibacy, prostitution,
infant mortality, adult degeneracy, and everything that wise
men most dread. In short, there is no future for men, however brimming with crude vitality, who are neither intelligent nor politically educated enough to be Socialists. So do
not misunderstand me in the other direction either: if I
appreciate the vital qualities of the Englishman as I appreciate the vital qualities of the bee, I do not guarantee the
Englishman against being, like the bee (or the Canaanite)
smoked out and unloaded of his honey by beings inferior to
himself in simple acquisitiveness, combativeness, and fecundity, but superior to him in imagination and cunning.

The Don Juan play, however, is to deal with sexual
attraction, and not with nutrition, and to deal with it in a
society in which the serious business of sex is left by men to
women, as the serious business of nutrition is left by women
to men. That the men, to protect themselves against a too
aggressive prosecution of the women's business, have set up
a feeble romantic convention that the initiative in sex business must always come from the man, is true; but the pretence is so shallow that even in the theatre, that last sanctuary of unreality, it imposes only on the inexperienced. In
Shakespear's plays the woman always takes the initiative.
In his problem plays and his popular plays alike the love
interest is the interest of seeing the woman hunt the man
down. She may do it by charming him, like Rosalind, or by
strategem, like Mariana; but in every case the relation
between the woman and the man is the same: she is the
pursuer and contriver, he the pursued and disposed of.
When she is baffled, like Ophelia, she goes mad and com-
mits suicide; and the man goes straight from her funeral to a
fencing match. No doubt Nature, with very young creatures,

may save the woman the trouble of scheming; Prospero knows that he has only to throw Ferdinand and Miranda together and they will mate like a pair of doves; and there is no need for Perdita to capture Florizel as the lady doctor in All's Well That Ends Well (an early Ibsenite heroine) captures Bertram. But the mature cases all illustrate the Shakespearian law. The one apparent exception, Petruchio, is not a real one: he is most carefully characterized as a purely commercial matrimonial adventurer. Once he is assured that Katherine has money, he undertakes to marry her before he has seen her. In real life we find not only Petruchios, but Mantalinis and Dobbins who pursue women with appeals to their pity or jealousy or vanity, or cling to them in a romantically infatuated way. Such effeminates do not count in the world scheme: even Bunsby dropping like a fascinated bird into the jaws of Mrs MacStinger is by comparison a true tragic object of pity and terror. I find in my own plays that Woman, projecting herself dramatically by my hands (a process over which I assure you I have no more real control than I have over my wife), behaves just as Woman did in the plays of Shakespear.

And so your Don Juan has come to birth as a stage projection of the tragi-comic love chase of the man by the woman; and my Don Juan is the quarry instead of the huntsman. Yet he is a true Don Juan, with a sense of reality that disables convention, defying to the last the fate which finally overtakes him. The woman's need of him to enable her to carry on Nature's most urgent work, does not prevail against him until his resistance gathers her energy to a climax at which she dares to throw away her customary exploitations of the conventional affectionate and dutiful poses, and claim him by natural right for a purpose that far transcends their mortal personal purposes.

Among the friends to whom I have read this play in manuscript are some of our own sex who are shocked at the 'unscrupulousness,' meaning the utter disregard of masculine fastidiousness, with which the woman pursues her purpose. It does not occur to them that if women were as

fastidious as men, morally or physically, there would be an
end of the race. Is there anything meaner than to throw
necessary work upon other people and then disparage it as
unworthy and indelicate. We laugh at the haughty American nation because it makes the negro clean its boots and
then proves the moral and physical inferiority of the negro
by the fact that he is a shoeblack; but we ourselves throw
the whole drudgery of creation on one sex, and then imply
that no female of any womanliness or delicacy would initiate
any effort in that direction. There are no limits to male
hypocrisy in this matter. No doubt there are moments when
man's sexual immunities are made acutely humiliating to
him. When the terrible moment of birth arrives, its supreme
importance and its superhuman effort and peril, in which
the father has no part, dwarf him into the meanest insignifi-
cance: he slinks out of the way of the humblest petticoat,
happy if he be poor enough to be pushed out of the house
to outface his ignominy by drunken rejoicings. But when
the crisis is over he takes his revenge, swaggering as the
breadwinner, and speaking of Woman's 'sphere' with con-
descension, even with chivalry, as if the kitchen and the
nursery were less important than the office in the city. When
his swagger is exhausted he drivels into erotic poetry or
sentimental uxoriousness; and the Tennysonian King Arthur posing at Guinevere becomes Don Quixote grovelling
before Dulcinea. You must admit that here Nature beats
Comedy out of the field: the wildest hominist or feminist
farce is insipid after the most commonplace 'slice of life'.
The pretence that women do not take the initiative is part of
the farce. Why, the whole world is strewn with snares, traps,
gins, and pitfalls for the capture of men by women. Give
women the vote, and in five years there will be a crushing
tax on bachelors. Men, on the other hand, attach penalties
to marriage, depriving women of property, of the franchise,
of the free use of their limbs, of that ancient symbol of
immortality, the right to make oneself at home in the house
of God by taking off the hat, of everything that he can force
Woman to dispense with without compelling himself to

dispense with her. All in vain. Woman must marry because the race must perish without her travail: if the risk of death and the certainty of pain, danger, and unutterable discomforts cannot deter her, slavery and swaddled ankles will not. And yet we assume that the force that carries women through all these perils and hardships, stops abashed before the primnesses of our behaviour for young ladies. It is assumed that the woman must wait, motionless, until she is wooed. Nay, she often does wait motionless. That is how the spider waits for the fly. But the spider spins her web. And if the fly, like my hero, shews a strength that promises to extricate him, how swiftly does she abandon her pretence of passiveness, and openly fling coil after coil about him until he is secured for ever!

If the really impressive books and other art-works of the world were produced by ordinary men, they would express more fear of women's pursuit than love of their illusory beauty. But ordinary men cannot produce really impressive art-works. Those who can are men of genius: that is, men selected by Nature to carry on the work of building up an intellectual consciousness of her own instinctive purpose. Accordingly, we observe in the man of genius all the unscrupulousness and all the 'self-sacrifice' (the two things are the same) of Woman. He will risk the stake and the cross; starve, when necessary, in a garret all his life; study women and live on their work and care as Darwin studied worms and lived upon sheep; work his nerves into rags without payment, a sublime altruist in his disregard of himself, an atrocious egotist in his disregard of others. Here Woman meets a purpose as impersonal, as irresistible as her own; and the clash is sometimes tragic. When it is complicated by the genius being a woman, then the game is one for a king of critics: your George Sand becomes a mother to gain experience for the novelist and to develop her, and gobbles up men of genius, Chopins, Mussets and the like, as mere hors d'œuvres.

I state the extreme case, of course; but what is true of the great man who incarnates the philosophic consciousness of

Life and the woman who incarnates its fecundity, is true in some degree of all geniuses and all women. Hence it is that the world's books get written, its pictures painted, its statues modelled, its symphonies composed, by people who are free from the otherwise universal dominion of the tyranny of sex. Which leads us to the conclusion, astonishing to the vulgar, that art, instead of being before all things the expression of the normal sexual situation, is really the only department in which sex is a superseded and secondary power, with its consciousness so confused and its purpose so perverted, that its ideas are mere fantasy to common men. Whether the artist becomes poet or philosopher, moralist or founder of a religion, his sexual doctrine is nothing but a barren special pleading for pleasure, excitement, and knowledge when he is young, and for contemplative tranquillity when he is old and satiated. Romance and Asceticism, Amorism and Puritanism are equally unreal in the great Philistine world. The world shewn us in books, whether the books be confessed epics or professed gospels, or in codes, or in political orations, or in philosophic systems, is not the main world at all: it is only the self-consciousness of certain abnormal people who have the specific artistic talent and temperament. A serious matter this for you and me, because the man whose consciousness does not correspond to that of the majority is a madman; and the old habit of worshipping madmen is giving way to the new habit of locking them up. And since what we call education and culture is for the most part nothing but the substitution of reading for experience, of literature for life, of the obsolete fictitious for the contemporary real, education, as you no doubt observed at Oxford, destroys, by supplantation, every mind that is not strong enough to see through the imposture and to use the great Masters of Arts as what they really are and no more: that is, patentees of highly questionable methods of thinking, and manufacturers of highly questionable, and for the majority but half valid representations of life. The schoolboy who uses his Homer to throw at his fellow's head makes perhaps the safest and most rational use of him; and I observe with reassurance that you occasionally do the same, in your prime, with your Aristotle.

Fortunately for us, whose minds have been so overwhelmingly sophisticated by literature, what produces all these treatises and poems and scriptures of one sort or another is the struggle of Life to become divinely conscious of itself instead of blindly stumbling hither and thither in the line of least resistance. Hence there is a driving towards truth in all books on matters where the writer, though exceptionally gifted, is normally constituted, and has no private axe to grind. Copernicus had no motive for misleading his fellowmen as to the place of the sun in the solar system: he looked for it as honestly as a shepherd seeks his path in a mist. But Copernicus would not have written love stories scientifically. When it comes to sex relations, the man of genius does not share the common man's danger of capture, nor the woman of genius the comman woman's overwhelming specialization. And that is why our scriptures and other art works, when they deal with love, turn from honest attempts at science in physics to romantic nonsense, erotic ecstasy, or the stern asceticism of satiety ('the road of excess leads to the palace of wisdom' said William Blake; for 'you never know what is enough unless you know what is more than enough').

There is a political aspect of this sex question which is too big for my comedy, and too momentous to be passed over without culpable frivolity. It is impossible to demonstrate that the initiative in sex transactions remains with Woman, and has been confirmed to her, so far, more and more by the suppression of rapine and discouragement of importunity, without being driven to very serious reflections on the fact that this initiative is politically the most important of all the initiatives, because our political experiment of democracy, the last refuge of cheap misgovernment, will ruin us if our citizens are ill bred.

When we two were born, this country was still dominated by a selected class bred by political marriages. The commercial class had not then completed the first twentyfive

years of its new share of political power; and it was itself
selected by money qualification, and bred, if not by political
marriage, at least by a pretty rigorous class marriage. Aristocracy and plutocracy still furnish the figureheads of politics; but they are now dependent on the votes of the
promiscuously bred masses. And this, if you please, at the
very moment when the political problem, having suddenly
ceased to mean a very limited and occasional interference,
mostly by way of jobbing public appointments, in the mis-
management of a tight but parochial little island, with
occasional meaningless prosecution of dynastic wars, has
become the industrial reorganization of Britain, the construction of a practically international Commonwealth, and
the partition of the whole of Africa and perhaps the whole of
Asia by the civilized Powers. Can you believe that the
people whose conceptions of society and conduct, whose
power of attention and scope of interest, are measured by
the British theatre as you know it today, can either handle
this colossal task themselves, or understand and support the
sort of mind and character that is (at least comparatively)
capable of handling it? For remember: what our voters are
in the pit and gallery they are also in the polling booth. We
are all now under what Burke called 'the hoofs of the swinish
multitude'. Burke's language gave great offence because the
implied exceptions to its universal application made it a
class insult; and it certainly was not for the pot to call the
kettle black. The aristocracy he defended, in spite of the
political marriages by which it tried to secure breeding for
itself, had its mind undertrained by silly schoolmasters and
governesses, its character corrupted by gratuitous luxury,
its self-respect adulterated to complete spuriousness by flat-
tery and flunkeyism. It is no better today and never will be
any better: our very peasants have something morally hard-
ier in them that culminates occasionally in a Bunyan, a
Burns, or a Carlyle. But observe, this aristocracy, which was
overpowered from 1832 to 1885 by the middle class, has
come back to power by the votes of 'the swinish multitude'.
Tom Paine has triumphed over Edmund Burke; and the

swine are now courted electors. How many of their own
class have these electors sent to parliament? Hardly a dozen
out of 670, and these only under the persuasion of conspicuous personal qualifications and popular eloquence. The
multitude thus pronounces judgment on its own units: it
admits itself unfit to govern, and will vote only for a man
morphologically and generically transfigured by palatial
residence and equipage, by transcendent tailoring, by the
glamour of aristocratic kinship. Well, we two know these
transfigured persons, these college passmen, these well
groomed monocular Algys and Bobbies, these cricketers to
whom age brings golf instead of wisdom, these plutocratic
products of 'the nail and sarspan business as he got his
money by.' Do you know whether to laugh or cry at the
notion that they, poor devils! will drive a team of continents
as they drive a four-in-hand; turn a jostling anarchy of
casual trade and speculation into an ordered productivity;
and federate our colonies into a world-Power of the first
magnitude? Give these people the most perfect political
constitution and the soundest political program that benevolent omniscience can devise for them, and they will
interpret it into mere fashionable folly or canting charity as
infallibly as a savage converts the philosophical theology of
a Scotch missionary into crude African idolatry.

I do not know whether you have any illusions left on the
subject of education, progress, and so forth. I have none.
Any pamphleteer can shew the way to better things; but
when there is no will there is no way. My nurse was fond of
remarking that you cannot make a silk purse out of a sow's
ear; and the more I see of the efforts of our churches and
universities and literary sages to raise the mass above its own
level, the more convinced I am that my nurse was right.
Progress can do nothing but make the most of us all as we
are, and that most would clearly not be enough even if those
who are already raised out of the lowest abysses would allow
the others a chance. The bubble of Heredity has been
pricked: the certainty that acquirements are negligible as
elements in practical heredity has demolished the hopes of

the educationists as well as the terrors of the degeneracy mongers; and we know now that there is no hereditary 'governing class' any more than a hereditary hooliganism. We must either breed political capacity or be ruined by Democracy, which was forced on us by the failure of the older alternatives. Yet if Despotism failed only for want of a capable benevolent despot, what chance has Democracy, which requires a whole population of capable voters: that is, of political critics who, if they cannot govern in person for lack of spare energy or specific talent for administration, can at least recognize and appreciate capacity and benevolence in others, and so govern through capably benevolent representatives? Where are such voters to be found today? Nowhere. Plutocratic inbreeding has produced a weakness of character that is too timid to face the full stringency of a thoroughly competitive struggle for existence and too lazy and petty to organize the commonwealth co-operatively. Being cowards, we defeat natural selection under cover of philanthropy: being sluggards, we neglect artificial selection under cover of delicacy and morality.

Yet we must get an electorate of capable critics or collapse as Rome and Egypt collapsed. At this moment the Roman decadent phase of *panem et circenses* is being inaugurated under our eyes. Our newspapers and melodramas are blustering about our imperial destiny; but our eyes and hearts turn eagerly to the American millionaire. As his hand goes down to his pocket, our fingers go up to the brims of our hats by instinct. Our ideal prosperity is not the prosperity of the industrial north, but the prosperity of the Isle of Wight, of Folkestone and Ramsgate, of Nice and Monte Carlo. That is the only prosperity you see on the stage, where the workers are all footmen, parlormaids, comic lodging-letters, and fashionable professional men, whilst the heroes and heroines are miraculously provided with unlimited dividends and eat gratuitously, like the knights in Don Quixote's books of chivalry. The city papers prate of the competition of Bombay with Manchester and the like. The real competition is the competition of Regent Street with the Rue de Rivoli, of

Brighton and the south coast with the Riviera, for the spending money of the American Trusts. What is all this growing love of pageantry, this effusive loyalty, this officious rising and uncovering at a wave from a flag or a blast from a brass band? Imperialism? Not a bit of it. Obsequiousness, servility, cupidity roused by the prevailing smell of money. When Mr Carnegie rattled his millions in his pockets all England became one rapacious cringe. Only, when Rhodes (who had probably been reading my Socialism for Millionaires) left word that no idler was to inherit his estate, the bent backs straightened mistrustfully for a moment. Could it be that the Diamond King was no gentleman after all? However, it was easy to ignore a rich man's solecism. The ungentlemanly clause was not mentioned again; and the backs soon bowed themselves back into their natural shape.

But I hear you asking me in alarm whether I have actually put all this tub thumping into a Don Juan comedy. I have not. I have only made my Don Juan a political pamphleteer, and given you his pamphlet in full by way of appendix. You will find it at the end of the book. I am sorry to say that it is a common practice with romancers to announce their hero as a man of extraordinary genius, and then leave his works entirely to the reader's imagination; so that at the end of the book you whisper to yourself ruefully that but for the author's solemn preliminary assurance you should hardly have given the gentleman credit for ordinary good sense. You cannot accuse me of this pitiable barrenness, this feeble evasion. I not only tell you that my hero wrote a revolutionists' handbook: I give you the handbook at full length for your edification if you care to read it. And in that handbook you will find the politics of the sex question as I conceive Don Juan's descendant to understand them. Not that I disclaim the fullest responsibility for his opinions and for those of all my characters, pleasant and unpleasant. They are all right from their several points of view; and their points of view are, for the dramatic moment, mine also. This may puzzle the people who believe that there is such a thing as an absolutely right point of view, usually their own. It may seem to them that nobody who doubts this can be in a state of grace. However that may be, it is certainly true that nobody who agrees with them can possibly be a dramatist, or indeed anything else that turns upon a knowledge of mankind. Hence it has been pointed out that Shakespear had no conscience. Neither have I, in that sense.

You may, however, remind me that this digression of mine into politics was preceded by a very convincing demonstration that the artist never catches the point of view of the common man on the question of sex, because he is not in the same predicament. I first prove that anything I write on the relation of the sexes is sure to be misleading; and then I proceed to write a Don Juan play. Well, if you insist on asking me why I behave in this absurd way, I can only reply that you asked me to, and that in any case my treatment of the subject may be valid for the artist, amusing to the amateur, and at least intelligible and therefore possibly suggestive to the Philistine. Every man who records his illusions is providing data for the genuinely scientific psychology which the world still waits for. I plank down my view of the existing relations of men to women in the most highly civilized society for what it is worth. It is a view like any other view and no more, neither true nor false, but, I hope, a way of looking at the subject which throws into the familiar order of cause and effect a sufficient body of fact and experience to be interesting to you, if not to the playgoing public of London. I have certainly shewn little consideration for that public in this enterprise; but I know that it has the friendliest disposition towards you and me as far as it has any consciousness of our existence, and quite understands that what I write for you must pass at a considerable height over its simple romantic head. It will take my books as read and my genius for granted, trusting me to put forth work of such quality as shall bear out its verdict. So we may disport ourselves on our own plane to the top of our bent; and if any gentleman points out that neither this epistle dedicatory nor the dream of Don Juan in the third act of the ensuing comedy is suitable for immediate production at a popular theatre we need not contradict him. Napoleon provided Talma with a pit of kings, with what effect on Talma's acting is not recorded. As for me, what I have always wanted is a pit of philosophers; and this is a play for such a pit.

I should make formal acknowledgment to the authors whom I have pillaged in the following pages if I could recollect them all. The theft of the brigand-poetaster from Sir Arthur Conan Doyle is deliberate; and the metamorphosis of Leporello into Enry Straker, motor engineer and New Man, is an intentional dramatic sketch of the contemporary embryo of Mr H. G. Wells's anticipation of the efficient engineering class which will, he hopes, finally sweep the jabberers out of the way of civilization. Mr Barrie has also, whilst I am correcting my proofs, delighted London with a servant who knows more than his masters. The conception of Mendoza Limited I trace back to a certain West Indian colonial secretary, who, at a period when he and I and Mr Sidney Webb were sowing our political wild oats as a sort of Fabian Three Musketeers, without any prevision of the surprising respectability of the crop that followed, recommended Webb, the encyclopedic and inexhaustible, to form himself into a company for the benefit of the shareholders. Octavius I take over unaltered from Mozart; and I hereby authorize any actor who impersonates him, to sing '*Dalla sua pace*' (if he can) at any convenient moment during the representation. Ann was suggested to me by the XV century Dutch morality called Everyman, which Mr William Poel has lately resuscitated so triumphantly. I trust he will work that vein further, and recognize that Elizabethan Renascence fustian is no more bearable after medieval poesy than Scribe after Ibsen. As I sat watching Everyman at the Charterhouse, I said to myself Why not Everywoman? Ann was the result: every woman is not Ann; but Ann is Everywoman.

That the author of Everyman was no mere artist, but an artist-philosopher, and that the artist-philosophers are the only sort of artists I take quite seriously, will be no news to you. Even Plato and Boswell, as the dramatists who invented Socrates and Dr Johnson, impress me more deeply than the romantic playwrights. Ever since, as a boy, I first breathed the air of the transcendental regions at a performance of Mozart's Zauberflöte, I have been proof against the garish splendors and alcoholic excitements of the ordinary stage combinations of Tappertitian romance with the police intelligence. Bunyan, Blake, Hogarth, and Turner (these four apart and above all the English classics), Goethe, Shelley, Schopenhauer, Wagner, Ibsen, Morris, Tolstoy, and Nietzsche are among the writers whose peculiar sense of the world I recognize as more or less akin to my own. Mark the word peculiar. I read Dickens and Shakespear without shame or stint; but their pregnant observations and demonstrations of life are not co-ordinated into any philosophy or religion: on the contrary, Dickens's sentimental assumptions are violently contradicted by his observations; and Shakespear's pessimism is only his wounded humanity. Both have the specific genius of the fictionist and the common sympathies of human feeling and thought in pre-eminent degree. They are often saner and shrewder than the philosophers just as Sancho Panza was often saner and shrewder than Don Quixote. They clear away vast masses of oppressive gravity by their sense of the ridiculous, which is at bottom a combination of sound moral judgment with lighthearted good humor. But they are concerned with the diversities of the world instead of with its unities: they are so irreligious that they exploit popular religion for professional purposes without delicacy or scruple (for example, Sydney Carton and the ghost in Hamlet!): they are anarchical, and cannot balance their exposures of Angelo and Dogberry, Sir Leicester Dedlock and Mr Tite Barnacle, with any portrait of a prophet or a worthy leader: they have no constructive ideas: they regard those who have them as dangerous fanatics: in all their fictions there is no leading thought or inspiration for which any man could conceivably risk the spoiling of his hat in a shower, much less his life. Both are alike forced to borrow motives for the more strenuous actions of their personages from the common stockpot of melodramatic plots; so that Hamlet has to be stimulated by the prejudices of a policeman and Macbeth by the cupidities of a bushranger. Dickens, without the excuse of having to manufacture motives for Hamlets and Macbeths, superfluously punts his crew down the stream of his monthly parts by mechanical devices which I leave you to describe, my own memory being quite baffled by the simplest question as to Monks in Oliver Twist, or the long lost parentage of Smike, or the relations between the Dorrit and Clennam families so inopportunely discovered by Monsieur Rigaud Blandois. The truth is, the world was to Shakespear a great 'stage of fools' on which he was utterly bewildered. He could see no sort of sense in living at all; and Dickens saved himself from the despair of the dream in The Chimes by taking the world for granted and busying himself with its details. Neither of them could do anything with a serious positive character: they could place a human figure before you with perfect verisimilitude; but when the moment came for making it live and move, they found, unless it made them laugh, that they had a puppet on their hands, and had to invent some artificial external stimulus to make it work. This is what is the matter with Hamlet all through: he has no will except in his bursts of temper. Foolish Bardolaters make a virtue of this after their fashion: they declare that the play is the tragedy of irresolution; but all Shakespear's projections of the deepest humanity he knew have the same defect: their characters and manners are lifelike; but their actions are forced on them from without, and the external force is grotesquely inappropriate except when it is quite conventional, as in the case of Henry V. Falstaff is more vivid than any of these serious reflective characters, because he is self-acting: his motives are his own appetites and instincts and humors. Richard III, too, is delightful as the whimsical comedian who stops a funeral to make love to the corpse's son's widow; but when, in the next act, he is replaced by a stage villain who smothers babies and offs with people's heads, we are revolted at the imposture and repudiate the changeling. Faulconbridge, Coriolanus, Leontes are admirable descriptions of instinctive temperaments: indeed the play of Coriolanus is the greatest of Shakespear's comedies; but description is not philosophy; and comedy neither compromises the author nor reveals him. He must be judged by those characters into which he puts what he knows of himself, his Hamlets and Macbeths and Lears and Prosperos. If these characters are agonizing in a void about factitious melodramatic murders and revenges and the like, whilst the comic characters walk with their feet on solid ground, vivid and amusing, you know that the author has much to shew and nothing to teach. The comparison between Falstaff and Prospero is like the comparison between Micawber and David Copperfield. At the end of the book you know Micawber, whereas you only know what has happened to David, and are not interested enough in him to wonder what his politics or religion might be if anything so stupendous as a religious or political idea, or a general idea of any sort, were to occur to him. He is tolerable as a child; but he never becomes a man, and might be left out of his own biography altogether but for his usefulness as a stage confidant, a Horatio or 'Charles his friend': what they call on the stage a feeder.

Now you cannot say this of the works of the artist-philosophers. You cannot say it, for instance, of The Pilgrim's Progress. Put your Shakespearian hero and coward, Henry V and Pistol or Parolles, beside Mr Valiant and Mr Fearing, and you have a sudden revelation of the abyss that lies between the fashionable author who could see nothing in the world but personal aims and the tragedy of their disappointment or the comedy of their incongruity, and the field preacher who achieved virtue and courage by identifying himself with the purpose of the world as he understood it. The contrast is enormous: Bunyan's coward stirs your blood more than Shakespear's hero, who actually leaves you cold and secretly hostile. You suddenly see that Shakespear, with all his flashes and divinations, never understood virtue and courage, never conceived how any man who was not a fool could, like Bunyan's hero, look back from the brink of the river of death over the strife and labor of his pilgrimage, and say 'yet do I not repent me'; or, with the panache of a millionaire, bequeath 'my sword to him that shall succeed me in my pilgrimage, and my courage and skill to him that can get it.' This is the true joy in life, the being used for a purpose recognized by yourself as a mighty one; the being thoroughly worn out before you are thrown on the scrap heap; the being a force of Nature instead of a feverish selfish little clod of ailments and grievances complaining that the world will not devote itself to making you happy. And also the only real tragedy in life is the being used by personally minded men for purposes which you recognize to be base. All the rest is at worst mere misfortune or mortality: this alone is misery, slavery, hell on earth; and the revolt against it is the only force that offers a man's work to the poor artist, whom our personally minded rich people would so willingly employ as pandar, buffoon, beauty monger, sentimentalizer and the like.

It may seem a long step from Bunyan to Nietzsche; but the difference between their conclusions is merely formal. Bunyan's perception that righteousness is filthy rags, his scorn for Mr Legality in the village of Morality, his defiance of the Church as the supplanter of religion, his insistence on courage as the virtue of virtues, his estimate of the career of the conventionally respectable and sensible Worldly Wiseman as no better at bottom than the life and death of Mr Badman: all this, expressed by Bunyan in the terms of a tinker's theology, is what Nietzsche has expressed in terms of post-Darwin, post-Schopenhauer philosophy; Wagner in terms of polytheistic mythology; and Ibsen in terms of mid-XIX century Parisian dramaturgy. Nothing is new in these matters except their novelties: for instance, it is a novelty to call Justification by Faith 'Wille', and Justification by Works 'Vorstellung'. The sole use of the novelty is that you and I buy and read Schopenhauer's treatise on Will and Representation when we should not dream of buying a set of sermons on Faith versus Works. At bottom the controversy is the same, and the dramatic results are the same.

Bunyan makes no attempt to present his pilgrims as more sensible or better conducted than Mr Worldly Wiseman. Mr W. W.'s worst enemies, Mr Embezzler, Mr Never-go-to-Church-on-Sunday, Mr Bad Form, Mr Murderer, Mr Burglar, Mr Co-respondent, Mr Blackmailer, Mr Cad, Mr Drunkard, Mr Labor Agitator and so forth, can read The Pilgrim's Progress without finding a word said against them; whereas the respectable people who snub them and put them in prison, such as Mr W. W. himself and his young friend Civility; Formalist and Hypocrisy; Wildhead, Inconsiderate, and Pragmatick (who were clearly young university men of good family and high feeding); that brisk lad Ignorance, Talkative, By-ends of Fairspeech and his mother-in-law Lady Feigning, and other reputable gentlemen and citizens, catch it very severely. Even Little Faith, though he gets to heaven at last, is given to understand that it served him right to be mobbed by the brothers Faint Heart, Mistrust, and Guilt, all three recognized members of respectable society and veritable pillars of the law. The whole allegory is a consistent attack on morality and respectability, without a word that one can remember against vice and crime. Exactly what is complained of in Nietzsche and Ibsen, is it not? And also exactly what would be complained of in all the literature which is great enough and old enough to have attained canonical rank, officially or unofficially, were it not that books are admitted to the canon by a compact which confesses their greatness in consideration of abrogating their meaning; so that the reverend rector can agree with the prophet Micah as to his inspired style without being committed to any complicity in Micah's furiously Radical opinions. Why, even I, as I force myself, pen in hand, into recognition and civility, find all the force of my onslaught destroyed by a simple policy of non-resistance. In vain do I redouble the violence of the language in which I proclaim my heterodoxies. I rail at the theistic credulity of Voltaire, the amoristic superstition of Shelley, the revival of tribal soothsaying and idolatrous rites which Huxley called Science and mistook for an advance on the Pentateuch, no less than at the welter of ecclesiastical and professional humbug which saves the face of the stupid system of violence and robbery which we call Law and Industry. Even atheists reproach me with infidelity and anarchists with nihilism because I cannot endure their moral tirades. And yet, instead of exclaiming 'Send this inconceivable Satanist to the stake,' the respectable newspapers pith me by announcing 'another book by this brilliant and thoughtful writer.' And the ordinary citizen, knowing that an author who is well spoken of by a respectable newspaper must be all right, reads me, as he reads Micah, with undisturbed edification from his own point of view. It is narrated that in the eighteenseventies an old lady, a very devout Methodist, moved from Colchester to a house in the neighborhood of the City Road, in London, where, mistaking the Hall of Science for a chapel, she sat at the feet of Charles Bradlaugh for many years, entranced by his eloquence, without questioning his orthodoxy or moulting a feather of her faith. I fear I shall be defrauded of my just martyrdom in the same way.

However, I am digressing, as a man with a grievance always does. And, after all, the main thing in determining the artistic quality of a book is not the opinions it propagates, but the fact that the writer has opinions. The old lady from Colchester was right to sun her simple soul in the energetic radiance of Bradlaugh's genuine beliefs and disbeliefs rather than in the chill of such mere painting of light and heat as elocution and convention can achieve. My contempt for *belles lettres*, and for amateurs who become the heroes of the fanciers of literary virtuosity, is not founded on any illusion of mine as to the permanence of those forms of thought (call them opinions) by which I strive to communicate my bent to my fellows. To younger men they are already outmoded; for though they have no more lost their logic than an eighteenth century pastel has lost its drawing or its color, yet, like the pastel, they grow indefinably shabby, and will grow shabbier until they cease to count at all, when my books will either perish, or, if the world is still poor enough to want them, will have to stand, with Bunyan's, by quite amor-

phous qualities of temper and energy. With this conviction
I cannot be a bellettrist. No doubt I must recognize, as even
the Ancient Mariner did, that I must tell my story enter-
tainingly if I am to hold the wedding guest spellbound in
spite of the siren sounds of the loud bassoon. But 'for art's
sake' alone I would not face the toil of writing a single sentence. I know that there are men who, having nothing to
say and nothing to write, are nevertheless so in love with
oratory and with literature that they delight in repeating as
much as they can understand of what others have said or
written aforetime. I know that the leisurely tricks which
their want of conviction leaves them free to play with the
diluted and misapprehended message supply them with a
pleasant parlor game which they call style. I can pity their
dotage and even sympathize with their fancy. But a true
original style is never achieved for its own sake: a man may
pay from a shilling to a guinea, according to his means, to
see, hear, or read another man's act of genius; but he will
not pay with his whole life and soul to become a mere vir-
tuoso in literature, exhibiting an accomplishment which
will not even make money for him, like fiddle playing.
Effectiveness of assertion is the Alpha and Omega of style.
He who has nothing to assert has no style and can have
none: he who has something to assert will go as far in power
of style as its momentousness and his conviction will carry
him. Disprove his assertion after it is made, yet its style remains. Darwin has no more destroyed the style of Job nor of
Handel than Martin Luther destroyed the style of Giotto.
All the assertions get disproved sooner or later; and so we
find the world full of a magnificent débris of artistic fossils,
with the matter-of-fact credibility gone clean out of them,
but the form still splendid. And that is why the old masters
play the deuce with our mere susceptibles. Your Royal Aca-
demician thinks he can get the style of Giotto without
Giotto's beliefs, and correct his perspective into the bargain.
Your man of letters thinks he can get Bunyan's or Shakespear's style without Bunyan's conviction or Shakespear's
apprehension, especially if he takes care not to split his

infinitives. And so with your Doctors of Music, who, with their collections of discords duly prepared and resolved or retarded or anticipated in the manner of the great composers, think they can learn the art of Palestrina from Cherubini's treatise. All this academic art is far worse than the trade in sham antique furniture; for the man who sells me an oaken chest which he swears was made in the XIII century, though as a matter of fact he made it himself only yesterday, at least does not pretend that there are any modern ideas in it; whereas your academic copier of fossils offer them to you as the latest outpouring of the human spirit, and, worst of all, kidnaps young people as pupils and persuades them that his limitations are rules, his observances dexterities, his timidities good taste, and his emptinesses purities. And when he declares that art should not be didactic, all the people who have nothing to teach and all the people who dont want to learn agree with him emphatically.

I pride myself on not being one of these susceptibles. If you study the electric light with which I supply you in that Bumbledonian public capacity of mine over which you make merry from time to time, you will find that your house contains a great quantity of highly susceptible copper wire which gorges itself with electricity and gives you no light whatever. But here and there occurs a scrap of intensely insusceptible, intensely resistant material; and that stubborn scrap grapples with the current and will not let it through until it has made itself useful to you as those two vital qualities of literature, light and heat. Now if I am to be no mere copper wire amateur but a luminous author, I must also be a most intensely refractory person, liable to go out and to go wrong at inconvenient moments, and with incendiary possibilities. These are the faults of my qualities; and I assure you that I sometimes dislike myself so much that when some irritable reviewer chances at that moment to pitch into me with zest, I feel unspeakably relieved and obliged. But I never dream of reforming, knowing that I must take myself as I am and get what work I can out of myself. All this you will understand; for there is community of material between us: we are both critics of life as well as of art; and you have perhaps said to yourself when I have passed your windows 'There, but for the grace of God, go I.' An awful and chastening reflection, which shall be the closing cadence of this immoderately long letter from yours faithfully,

G. BERNARD SHAW

Woking, 1903

P.S. – Amid unprecedented critical cerebration over this book of ours – alas! that your own voice should be dedicated to silence! – I find myself warned to prepare a new edition. I take the opportunity to correct a slip or two. You may have noticed (nobody else has, by the way) that I fitted you with a quotation from Othello, and then unconsciously referred it to A Winter's Tale. I correct this with regret; for half its appropriateness goes with Florizel and Perdita: still, one must not trifle with Shakespear; so I have given Desdemona back her property.

On the whole, the book has done very well. The strong critics are impressed; the weak intimidated; the connoisseurs tickled by my literary bravura (put in to please you): the humorists alone, oddly enough, sermonize me, scared out of their profession into the quaintest tumults of conscience. Not all my reviewers have understood me: like Englishmen in France, confidently uttering their own island diphthongs as good French vowels, many of them offer, as samples of the Shavian philosophy, the likest article from their own stock. Others are the victims of association of ideas: they call me Pessimist because my remarks wound their self-complacency, and Renegade because I would have my mob all Caesars instead of Toms, Dicks, and Harrys. Worst of all, I have been accused of preaching a Final Ethical Superman: no other, in fact, than our old friend the Just Man made Perfect! This misunderstanding is so galling that I lay down my pen without another word lest I should be tempted to make the postscript longer even than the letter.

POSTSCRIPT 1933. The evolutionary theme of the third

act of Man and Superman was resumed by me twenty years later in the preface to Back to Methuselah, where it is developed as the basis of the religion of the near future.

MAN AND SUPERMAN

A COMEDY AND A PHILOSOPHY

1901–2

ACT ONE

Roebuck Ramsden is in his study, opening the morning's letters. The study, handsomely and solidly furnished, proclaims the man of means. Not a speck of dust is visible: it is clear that there are at least two housemaids and a parlormaid downstairs, and a house-keeper upstairs who does not let them spare elbow-grease. Even the top of Roebuck's head is polished: on a sunshiny day he could helio-graph his orders to distant camps by merely nodding. In no other respect, however, does he suggest the military man. It is in active civil life that men get his broad air of importance, his dignified expectation of deference, his determinate mouth disarmed and refined since the hour of his success by the withdrawal of opposition and the concession of comfort and precedence and power. He is more than a highly respectable man: he is marked out as a president of highly respectable men, a chairman among directors, an alderman among councillors, a mayor among aldermen. Four tufts of iron-grey hair, which will soon be as white as isinglass, and are in other respects not at all unlike it, grow in two symmetrical pairs above his ears and at the angles of his spreading jaws. He wears a black frock coat, a white waistcoat (it is bright spring weather), and trousers, neither black nor perceptibly blue, of one of those indefinitely mixed hues which the modern clothier has produced to harmonize with the religions of res-pectable men. He has not been out of doors yet today; so he still wears his slippers, his boots being ready for him on the hearthrug. Surmising that he has no valet, and seeing that he has no secretary with a short-hand notebook and a typewriter, one meditates on how little our great burgess domesticity has been disturbed by new fashions and methods, or by the enterprise of the railway and hotel companies which sell you a Saturday to Monday of life at Folkestone as a real gentleman for two guineas, first class fares both ways included.

How old is Roebuck? The question is important on the threshold of a drama of ideas; for under such circumstances everything depends on whether his adolescence belonged to the sixties or to the eighties. He was born, as a matter of fact, in 1839, and was a Unitarian and Free Trader from his boyhood, and an Evolutionist from the

41

publication of the Origin of Species. Consequently he has always classed himself as an advanced thinker and fearlessly outspoken reformer.

Sitting at his writing table, he has on his right the windows giving on Portland Place. Through these, as through a proscenium, the curious spectator may contemplate his profile as well as the blinds will permit. On his left is the inner wall, with a stately bookcase, and the door not quite in the middle, but somewhat further from him. Against the wall opposite him are two busts on pillars: one, to his left, of John Bright; the other, to his right, of Mr Herbert Spencer. Between them hang an engraved portrait of Richard Cobden; enlarged photographs of Martineau, Huxley, and George Eliot; autotypes of allegories by Mr G. F. Watts (for Roebuck believes in the fine arts with all the earnestness of a man who does not understand them), and an impression of Dupont's engraving of Delaroche's Beaux Arts hemicycle, representing the great men of all ages. On the wall behind him, above the mantelshelf, is a family portrait of impenetrable obscurity.

A chair stands near the writing table for the convenience of business visitors. Two other chairs are against the wall between the busts.

A parlormaid enters with a visitor's card. Roebuck takes it, and nods, pleased. Evidently a welcome caller.

RAMSDEN: Shew him in.

[*The parlormaid goes out and returns with the visitor.*]
THE MAID: Mr Robinson.

[*Mr Robinson is really an uncommonly nice looking young fellow. He must, one thinks, be the jeune premier; for it is not in reason to suppose that a second such attractive male figure should appear in one story. The slim, shapely frame, the elegant suit of new mourning, the small head and regular features, the pretty little moustache, the frank clear eyes, the wholesome bloom on the youthful complexion, the well brushed glossy hair, not curly, but of fine texture and good dark color, the arch of good nature in the eyebrows, the erect forehead and neatly pointed chin, all announce the man who will love and suffer later on. And that he will not do so without sympathy is guaranteed by an engaging sincerity and eager modest service-*

ableness which stamp him as a man of amiable nature. The moment he appears, Ramsden's face expands into fatherly liking and welcome, an expression which drops into one of decorous grief as the young man approaches him with sorrow in his face as well as in his black clothes. Ramsden seems to know the nature of the bereavement. As the visitor advances silently to the writing table, the old man rises and shakes his hand across it without a word: a long, affectionate shake which tells the story of a recent sorrow common to both.]

RAMSDEN [*concluding the handshake and cheering up*]: Well, well, Octavius, it's the common lot. We must all face it some day. Sit down.

[*Octavius takes the visitor's chair. Ramsden replaces himself in his own.*]

OCTAVIUS: Yes: we must face it, Mr Ramsden. But I owed him a great deal. He did everything for me that my father could have done if he had lived.

RAMSDEN: He had no son of his own, you see.

OCTAVIUS: But he had daughters; and yet he was as good to my sister as to me. And his death was so sudden! I always intended to thank him – to let him know that I had not taken all his care of me as a matter of course, as any boy takes his father's care. But I waited for an opportunity; and now he is dead – dropped without a moment's warning. He will never know what I felt. [*He takes out his handkerchief and cries unaffectedly.*]

RAMSDEN: How do we know that, Octavius? He may know it: we cannot tell. Come! dont grieve. [*Octavius masters himself and puts up his handkerchief.*] Thats right. Now let me tell you something to console you. The last time I saw him – it was in this very room – he said to me: 'Tavy is a generous lad and the soul of honor; and when I see how little consideration other men get from their sons, I realize how much better than a son he's been to me.' There! Doesnt that do you good?

OCTAVIUS: Mr Ramsden: he used to say to me that he had met only one man in the world who was the soul of honor, and that was Rocbuck Ramsden.

RAMSDEN: Oh, that was his partiality: we were very old friends, you know. But there was something else he used to say about you. I wonder whether I ought to tell you or not!

OCTAVIUS: You know best.

RAMSDEN: It was something about his daughter.

OCTAVIUS [*eagerly*]: About Ann! Oh, do tell me that, Mr Ramsden.

RAMSDEN: Well, he said he was glad, after all, you were not his son, because he thought that someday Annie and you – [*Octavius blushes vividly*]. Well, perhaps I shouldnt have told you. But he was in earnest.

OCTAVIUS: Oh, if only I thought I had a chance! You know, Mr Ramsden, I dont care about money or about what people call position; and I cant bring myself to take an interest in the business of struggling for them. Well, Ann has a most exquisite nature; but she is so accustomed to be in the thick of that sort of thing that she thinks a man's character incomplete if he is not ambitious. She knows that if she married me she would have to reason herself out of being ashamed of me for not being a big success of some kind.

RAMSDEN [*getting up and planting himself with his back to the fireplace*]: Nonsense, my boy, nonsense! Youre too modest. What does she know about the real value of men at her age? [*More seriously*] Besides, she's a wonderfully dutiful girl. Her father's wish would be sacred to her. Do you know that since she grew up to years of discretion, I dont believe she has ever once given her own wish as a reason for doing anything or not doing it. It's always 'Father wishes me to,' or 'Mother wouldnt like it.' It's really almost a fault in her. I have often told her she must learn to think for herself.

OCTAVIUS [*shaking his head*]: I couldnt ask her to marry me because her father wished it, Mr Ramsden.

RAMSDEN: Well, perhaps not. No: of course not. I see that. No: you certainly couldnt. But when you win her on your own merits, it will be a great happiness to her to

44

fulfil her father's desire as well as her own. Eh? Come! youll ask her, wont you?

OCTAVIUS [*with sad gaiety*]: At all events I promise you I shall never ask anyone else.

RAMSDEN: Oh, you shant need to. She'll accept you, my boy – although [*here he suddenly becomes very serious indeed*] you have one great drawback.

OCTAVIUS [*anxiously*]: What drawback is that, Mr Ramsden? I should rather say which of my many drawbacks?

RAMSDEN: I'll tell you, Octavius. [*He takes from the table a book bound in red cloth.*] I have in my hand a copy of the most infamous, the most scandalous, the most mischievous, the most blackguardly book that ever escaped burning at the hands of the common hangman. I have not read it: I would not soil my mind with such filth; but I have read what the papers say of it. The title is quite enough for me. [*He reads it.*] The Revolutionist's Handbook and Pocket Companion. By John Tanner, M.I.R.C., Member of the Idle Rich Class.

OCTAVIUS [*smiling*]: But Jack –

RAMSDEN [*testily*]: For goodness' sake, dont call him Jack under my roof [*he throws the book violently down on the table. Then, somewhat relieved, he comes past the table to Octavius, and addresses him at close quarters with impressive gravity*]. Now, Octavius, I know that my dead friend was right when he said you were a generous lad. I know that this man was your schoolfellow, and that you feel bound to stand by him because there was a boyish friendship between you. But I ask you to consider the altered circumstances. You were treated as a son in my friend's house. You lived there; and your friends could not be turned from the door. This man Tanner was in and out there on your account almost from his childhood. He addresses Annie by her Christian name as freely as you do. Well, while her father was alive, that was her father's business, not mine. This man Tanner was only a boy to him: his opinions were something to be laughed at, like a man's hat on a child's head. But now Tanner is a grown man and Annie a grown woman. And her father is gone. We dont as yet know the exact terms of his will; but he often talked it over with me; and I have no more doubt than I have that youre sitting there that the will appoints me Annie's trustee and guardian. [*Forcibly*] Now I tell you, once for all, I cant and I wont have Annie placed in such a position that she must, out of regard for you, suffer the intimacy of this fellow Tanner. It's not fair: it's not right: it's not kind. What are you going to do about it?

OCTAVIUS: But Ann herself has told Jack that whatever his opinions are, he will always be welcome because he knew her dear father.

RAMSDEN [*out of patience*]: That girl's mad about her duty to her parents. [*He starts off like a goaded ox in the direction of John Bright, in whose expression there is no sympathy for him. As he speaks he fumes down to Herbert Spencer, who receives him still more coldly.*] Excuse me, Octavius; but there are limits to social toleration. You know that I am not a bigoted or prejudiced man. You know that I am plain Roebuck Ramsden when other men who have done less have got handles to their names, because I have stood for equality and liberty of conscience while they were truckling to the Church and to the aristocracy. Whitefield and I lost chance after chance through our advanced opinions. But I draw the line at Anarchism and Free Love and that sort of thing. If I am to be Annie's guardian, she will have to learn that she has a duty to me. I wont have it: I will not have it. She must forbid John Tanner the house; and so must you.

The parlormaid returns.

OCTAVIUS: But –

RAMSDEN [*calling his attention to the servant*]: Ssh! Well?

THE MAID: Mr Tanner wishes to see you, sir.

RAMSDEN: Mr Tanner!

OCTAVIUS: Jack!

RAMSDEN: How dare Mr Tanner call on me! Say I cannot see him.

OCTAVIUS [*hurt*]: I am sorry you are turning my friend from your door like that.

THE MAID [*calmly*]: He's not at the door, sir. He's upstairs in the drawing room with Miss Ramsden. He came with Mrs Whitefield and Miss Ann and Miss Robinson, sir.

Ramsden's feelings are beyond words.

OCTAVIUS [*grinning*]: Thats very like Jack, Mr Ramsden. You must see him, even if it's only to turn him out.

RAMSDEN [*hammering out his words with suppressed fury*]: Go upstairs and ask Mr Tanner to be good enough to step down here. [*The parlormaid goes out; and Ramsden returns to the fireplace, as to a fortified position.*] I must say that of all the confounded pieces of impertinence – well, if these are Anarchist manners, I hope you like them. And Annie with him! Annie! A – [*he chokes*].

OCTAVIUS: Yes: thats what surprises me. He's so desperately afraid of Ann. There must be something the matter.

[*Mr John Tanner suddenly opens the door and enters. He is too young to be described simply as a big man with a beard. But it is already plain that middle life will find him in that category. He has still some of the slimness of youth; but youthfulness is not the effect he aims at: his frock coat would befit a prime minister; and a certain high chested carriage of the shoulders, a lofty pose of the head, and the Olympian majesty with which a mane, or rather a huge whisp, of hazel colored hair is thrown back from an imposing brow, suggest Jupiter rather than Apollo. He is prodigiously fluent of speech, restless, excitable (mark the snorting nostril and the restless blue eye, just the thirty-secondth of an inch too wide open), possibly a little mad. He is carefully dressed, not from the vanity that cannot resist finery, but from a sense of the importance of everything he does which leads him to make as much of paying a call as other men do of getting married or laying a foundation stone. A sensitive, susceptible, exaggerative, earnest man: a megolmaniac, who would be lost without a sense of humor.*

Just at present the sense of honor is in abeyance. To say that he is excited is nothing: all his moods are phases of excitement. He is now in the panic-stricken phase; and he walks straight up to Ramsden as if with the fixed intention of shooting him on his own hearthrug. But what he pulls from his breast pocket is not a pistol, but a foolscap document which he thrusts under the indignant nose of Ramsden as he exclaims.]

TANNER: Ramsden: do you know what this is?

RAMSDEN [*loftily*]: No, sir.

TANNER: It's a copy of Whitefield's will. Ann got it this morning.

RAMSDEN: When you say Ann, you mean, I presume, Miss Whitefield.

TANNER: I mean our Ann, your Ann, Tavy's Ann, and now, Heaven help me, my Ann!

OCTAVIUS [*rising, very pale*]: What do you mean?

TANNER: Mean! [*He holds up the will.*] Do you know who is appointed Ann's guardian by this will?

RAMSDEN [*coolly*]: I believe I am.

TANNER: You! You and I, man. I! I!! I!!! Both of us! [*He flings the will down on the writing table.*]

RAMSDEN: You! Impossible.

TANNER: It's only too hideously true. [*He throws himself into Octavius's chair.*] Ramsden: get me out of it somehow. You dont know Ann as well as I do. She'll commit every crime a respectable woman can; and she'll justify every one of them by saying that it was the wish of her guardians. She'll put everything on us; and we shall have no more control over her than a couple of mice over a cat.

OCTAVIUS: Jack, I wish you wouldnt talk like that about Ann.

TANNER: This chap's in love with her: thats another complication. Well, she'll either jilt him and say I didnt approve of him, or marry him and say you ordered her to. I tell you, this is the most staggering blow that has ever fallen on a man of my age and temperament.

RAMSDEN: Let me see that will, sir. [*He goes to the writing table and picks it up.*] I cannot believe that my old friend Whitefield would have shewn such a want of confidence in me as to associate me with – [*His countenance falls as he reads*].

TANNER: It's all my own doing: thats the horrible irony of it. He told me one day that you were to be Ann's guardian; and like a fool I began arguing with him about the folly of leaving a young woman under the control of an old man with obsolete ideas.

RAMSDEN [*stupended*]: My ideas obsolete !!!!!!!

TANNER: Totally. I had just finished an essay called Down with Government by the Greyhaired; and I was full of arguments and illustrations. I said the proper thing was to combine the experience of an old hand with the vitality of a young one. Hang me if he didnt take me at my word and alter his will – it's dated only a fortnight after that conversation – appointing me as joint guardian with you !

RAMSDEN [*pale and determined*]: I shall refuse to act.

TANNER: Whats the good of that? Ive been refusing all the way from Richmond; but Ann keeps on saying that of course she's only an orphan; and that she cant expect the people who were glad to come to the house in her father's time to trouble much about her now. Thats the latest game. An orphan ! It's like hearing an ironclad talk about being at the mercy of the wind and waves.

OCTAVIUS: This is not fair, Jack. She is an orphan. And you ought to stand by her.

TANNER: Stand by her ! What danger is she in? She has the law on her side; she has popular sentiment on her side; she has plenty of money and no conscience. All she wants with me is to load up all her moral responsibilities on me, and do as she likes at the expense of my character. I cant control her; and she can compromise me as much as she likes. I might as well be her husband.

RAMSDEN: You can refuse to accept the guardianship. *I* shall certainly refuse to hold it jointly with you.

TANNER: Yes; and what will she say to that? what does she say to it? Just that her father's wishes are sacred to her, and that she shall always look up to me as her guardian whether I care to face the responsibility or not. Refuse ! You might as well refuse to accept the embraces of a boa constrictor when once it gets round your neck.

OCTAVIUS: This sort of talk is not kind to me, Jack.

TANNER [*rising and going to Octavius to console him, but still lamenting*]: If he wanted a young guardian, why didnt he appoint Tavy?

RAMSDEN: Ah! why indeed?

OCTAVIUS: I will tell you. He sounded me about it; but I refused the trust because I loved her. I had no right to let myself be forced on her as a guardian by her father. He spoke to her about it; and she said I was right. You know I love her, Mr Ramsden; and Jack knows it too. If Jack loved a woman, I would not compare her to a boa constrictor in his presence, however much I might dislike her [*he sits down between the busts and turns his face to the wall*].

RAMSDEN: I do not believe that Whitefield was in his right senses when he made that will. You have admitted that he made it under your influence.

TANNER: You ought to be pretty well obliged to me for my influence. He leaves you two thousand five hundred for your trouble. He leaves Tavy a dowry for his sister and five thousand for himself.

OCTAVIUS [*his tears flowing afresh*]: Oh, I cant take it. He was too good to us.

TANNER: You wont get it, my boy, if Ramsden upsets the will.

RAMSDEN: Ha! I see. You have got me in a cleft stick.

TANNER: He leaves me nothing but the charge of Ann's morals, on the ground that I have already more money than is good for me. That shews that he had his wits about him, doesnt it?

RAMSDEN [*grimly*]: I admit that.

OCTAVIUS [*rising and coming from his refuge by the wall*]: Mr Ramsden: I think you are prejudiced against Jack. He is a man of honor, and incapable of abusing –

TANNER: Dont, Tavy: youll make me ill. I am not a man of honor: I am a man struck down by a dead hand. Tavy: you must marry her after all and take her off my hands. And I had my heart set on saving you from her!

OCTAVIUS: Oh, Jack, you talk of saving me from my highest happiness.

TANNER: Yes, a lifetime of happiness. If it were only the first half hour's happiness, Tavy, I would buy it for you with my last penny. But a lifetime of happiness! No man alive could bear it: it would be hell on earth.

RAMSDEN [*violently*]: Stuff, sir. Talk sense; or else go and waste someone else's time: I have something better to do than listen to your fooleries [*he positively kicks his way to his table and resumes his seat*].

TANNER: You hear him, Tavy! Not an idea in his head later than eighteensixty. We cant leave Ann with no other guardian to turn to.

RAMSDEN: I am proud of your contempt for my character and opinions, sir. Your own are set forth in that book, I believe.

TANNER [*eagerly going to the table*]: What! Youve got my book! What do you think of it?

RAMSDEN: Do you suppose I would read such a book, sir?

TANNER: Then why did you buy it?

RAMSDEN: I did not buy it, sir. It has been sent me by some foolish lady who seems to admire your views. I was about to dispose of it when Octavius interrupted me. I shall do so now, with your permission. [*He throws the book into the waste-paper basket with such vehemence that Tanner recoils under the impression that it is being thrown at his head.*]

TANNER: You have no more manners than I have myself. However, that saves ceremony between us. [*He sits down again.*] What do you intend to do about this will?

OCTAVIUS: May I make a suggestion?

RAMSDEN: Certainly, Octavius.

OCTAVIUS: Arnt we forgetting that Ann herself may have some wishes in this matter?

RAMSDEN: I quite intend that Annie's wishes shall be consulted in every reasonable way. But she is only a woman, and a young and inexperienced woman at that.

TANNER: Ramsden: I begin to pity you.

RAMSDEN [*hotly*]: I dont want to know how you feel towards me, Mr Tanner.

TANNER: Ann will do just exactly what she likes. And whats more, she'll force us to advise her to do it; and she'll put the blame on us if it turns out badly. So, as Tavy is longing to see her –

OCTAVIUS [*shyly*]: I am not, Jack.

TANNER: You lie, Tavy: you are. So lets have her down from the drawing room and ask her what she intends us to do. Off with you, Tavy, and fetch her. [*Tavy turns to go.*] And dont be long; for the strained relations between myself and Ramsden will make the interval rather painful. [*Ramsden compresses his lips, but says nothing.*]

OCTAVIUS: Never mind him, Mr Ramsden. He's not serious. [*He goes out.*]

RAMSDEN [*very deliberately*]: Mr Tanner: you are the most impudent person I have ever met.

TANNER [*seriously*]: I know it, Ramsden. Yet even I cannot wholly conquer shame. We live in an atmosphere of shame. We are ashamed of everything that is real about us; ashamed of ourselves, of our relatives, of our incomes, of our accents, of our opinions, of our experience, just as we are ashamed of our naked skins. Good Lord, my dear Ramsden, we are ashamed to walk, ashamed to ride in an omnibus, ashamed to hire a hansom instead of keeping a carriage, ashamed of keeping one horse instead of two and a groom-gardener instead of a coachman and footman. The more things a man is ashamed of, the more respectable he is. Why, youre ashamed to buy my book, ashamed to read it: the only thing youre not ashamed of is to judge me for it without having read it; and even that only means that youre ashamed to have heterodox opinions. Look at the effect I produce because my fairy godmother withheld from me this gift of shame. I have every possible virtue that a man can have except –

RAMSDEN: I am glad you think so well of yourself.

TANNER: All you mean by that is that you think I ought to be ashamed of talking about my virtues. You dont mean

that I havnt got them: you know perfectly well that I am
as sober and honest a citizen as yourself, as truthful personally, and much more truthful politically and morally.

RAMSDEN [*touched on his most sensitive point*]: I deny that. I
will not allow you or any man to treat me as if I were a
mere member of the British public. I detest its prejudices;
I scorn its narrowness; I demand the right to think for
myself. You pose as an advanced man. Let me tell you
that I was an advanced man before you were born.

TANNER: I knew it was a long time ago.

RAMSDEN: I am as advanced as ever I was. I defy you to
prove that I have ever hauled down the flag. I am more
advanced than ever I was. I grow more advanced every
day.

TANNER: More advanced in years, Polonius.

RAMSDEN: Polonius! So you are Hamlet, I suppose.

TANNER: No: I am only the most impudent person youve
ever met. Thats your notion of a thoroughly bad character. When you want to give me a piece of your mind,
you ask yourself, as a just and upright man, what is the
worst you can fairly say of me. Thief, liar, forger, adult-
erer, perjurer, glutton, drunkard? Not one of these
names fit me. You have to fall back on my deficiency in
shame. Well, I admit it. I even congratulate myself; for if
I were ashamed of my real self, I should cut as stupid a
figure as any of the rest of you. Cultivate a little impud-
ence, Ramsden; and you will become quite a remarkable
man.

RAMSDEN: I have no —

TANNER: You have no desire for that sort of notoriety.
Bless you, I knew that answer would come as well as I
know that a box of matches will come out of an automatic
machine when I put a penny in the slot: you would be
ashamed to say anything else.

[*The crushing retort for which Mr Ramsden has been visibly
collecting his forces is lost for ever; for at this point Octavius
returns with Miss Ann Whitefield and her mother; and Ramsden springs up and hurries to the door to receive them. Whether*

Ann is good-looking or not depends upon your taste; also and perhaps chiefly on your age and sex. To Octavius she is an enchantingly beautiful woman, in whose presence the world becomes transfigured, and the puny limits of individual consciousness are suddenly made infinite by a mystic memory of the whole life of the race to its beginnings in the east, or even back to the paradise from which it fell. She is to him the reality of romance, the inner good sense of nonsense, the unveiling of his eyes, the freeing of his soul, the abolition of time, place, and circumstance, the etherealization of his blood into rapturous rivers of the very water of life itself, the revelation of all the mysteries and the sanctification of all the dogmas. To her mother she is, to put it as moderately as possible, nothing whatever of the kind. Not that Octavius's admiration is in any way ridiculous or discreditable. Ann is a well formed creature, as far as that goes; and she is perfectly ladylike, graceful, and comely, with ensnaring eyes and hair. Besides, instead of making herself an eyesore, like her mother, she has devised a mourning costume of black and violet silk which does honor to her late father and reveals the family tradition of brave unconventionality by which Ramsden sets such store.

But all this is beside the point as an explanation of Ann's charm. Turn up her nose, give a cast to her eye, replace her black and violet confection by the apron and feathers of a flower girl, strike all the aitches out of her speech, and Ann would still make men dream. Vitality is as common as humanity; but, like humanity, it sometimes rises to genius; and Ann is one of the vital geniuses. Not at all, if you please, an oversexed person: that is a vital defect, not a true excess. She is a perfectly respectable, perfectly self-controlled woman, and looks it; though her pose is fashionably frank and impulsive. She inspires confidence as a person who will do nothing she does not mean to do; also some fear, perhaps, as a woman who will probably do everything she means to do without taking more account of other people than may be necessary and what she calls right. In short, what the weaker of her own sex sometimes call a cat.

Nothing can be more decorous than her entry and her reception by Ramsden, whom she kisses. The late Mr Whitefield would be gratified almost to impatience by the long faces of the men (except Tanner, who is fidgety), the silent handgrasps, the sympathetic placing of chairs, the sniffing of the widow, and the liquid eye of the daughter, whose heart, apparently, will not let her control her tongue to speech. Ramsden and Octavius take the two chairs from the wall, and place them for the two ladies; but Ann comes to Tanner and takes his chair, which he offers with a brusque gesture, subsequently relieving his irritation by sitting down on the corner of the writing table with studied indecorum. Octavius gives Mrs Whitefield a chair next Ann, and himself takes the vacant one which Ramsden has placed under the nose of the effigy of Mr Herbert Spencer.

Mrs Whitefield, by the way, is a little woman, whose faded flaxen hair looks like straw on an egg. She has an expression of muddled shrewdness, a squeak of protest in her voice, and an odd air of continually elbowing away some larger person who is crushing her into a corner. One guesses her as one of those women who are conscious of being treated as silly and negligible, and who, without having strength enough to assert themselves effectually, at any rate never submit to their fate. There is a touch of chivalry in Octavius's scrupulous attention to her, even whilst his whole soul is absorbed by Ann.

Ramsden goes solemnly back to his magisterial seat at the writing table, ignoring Tanner, and opens the proceedings.]

RAMSDEN: I am sorry, Annie, to force business on you at a sad time like the present. But your poor dear father's will has raised a very serious question. You have read it, I believe?

[*Ann assents with a nod and a catch of her breath, too much affected to speak.*]

I must say I am surprised to find Mr Tanner named as joint guardian and trustee with myself of you and Rhoda. [*A pause. They all look portentous; but they have nothing to say. Ramsden, a little ruffled by the lack of any response, continues*] I dont know that I can consent to act under such conditions. Mr Tanner has, I understand, some objection also; but I do not profess to understand its nature: he will

55

no doubt speak for himself. But we are agreed that we can decide nothing until we know your views. I am afraid I shall have to ask you to choose between my sole guardianship and that of Mr Tanner; for I fear it is impossible for us to undertake a joint arrangement.

ANN [*in a low musical voice*]: Mamma –

MRS WHITEFIELD [*hastily*]: Now, Ann, I do beg you not to put it on me. I have no opinion on the subject; and if I had, it would probably not be attended to. I am quite content with whatever you three think best.

[*Tanner turns his head and looks fixedly at Ramsden, who angrily refuses to receive this mute communication.*]

ANN [*resuming in the same gentle voice, ignoring her mother's bad taste*]: Mamma knows that she is not strong enough to bear the whole responsibility for me and Rhoda without some help and advice. Rhoda must have a guardian; and though I am older, I do not think any young unmarried woman should be left quite to her own guidance. I hope you agree with me, Granny?

TANNER [*starting*]: Granny! Do you intend to call your guardians Granny?

ANN: Dont be foolish, Jack. Mr Ramsden has always been Grandpapa Roebuck to me: I am Granny's Annie; and he is Annie's Granny. I christened him so when I first learned to speak.

RAMSDEN [*sarcastically*]: I hope you are satisfied, Mr Tanner. Go on, Annie: I quite agree with you.

ANN: Well, if I am to have a guardian, can I set aside anybody whom my dear father appointed for me?

RAMSDEN [*biting his lip*]: You approve of your father's choice, then?

ANN: It is not for me to approve or disapprove. I accept it. My father loved me and knew best what was good for me.

RAMSDEN: Of course I understand your feeling, Annie. It is what I should have expected of you; and it does you credit. But it does not settle the question so completely as you think. Let me put a case to you. Suppose you were to discover that I had been guilty of some disgraceful action

– that I was not the man your poor dear father took me for! Would you still consider it right that I should be Rhoda's guardian?

ANN: I cant imagine you doing anything disgraceful, Granny.

TANNER [to Ramsden]: You havnt done anything of the sort, have you?

RAMSDEN [indignantly]: No, sir.

MRS WHITEFIELD [placidly]: Well, then, why suppose it?

ANN: You see, Granny, Mamma would not like me to suppose it.

RAMSDEN [much perplexed]: You are both so full of natural and affectionate feeling in these family matters that it is very hard to put the situation fairly before you.

TANNER: Besides, my friend, you are not putting the situation fairly before them.

RAMSDEN [sulkily]: Put it yourself, then.

TANNER: I will. Ann: Ramsden thinks I am not fit to be your guardian; and I quite agree with him. He considers that if your father had read my book, he wouldnt have appointed me. That book is the disgraceful action he has been talking about. He thinks it's your duty for Rhoda's sake to ask him to act alone and to make me withdraw. Say the word; and I will.

ANN: But I havnt read your book, Jack.

TANNER [diving at the waste-paper basket and fishing the book out for her]: Then read it at once and decide.

RAMSDEN [vehemently]: If I am to be your guardian, I positively forbid you to read that book, Annie. [He smites the table with his fist and rises.]

ANN: Of course not if you dont wish it. [She puts the book on the table.]

TANNER: If one guardian is to forbid you to read the other guardian's book, how are we to settle it? Suppose I order you to read it! What about your duty to me?

ANN [gently]: I am sure you would never purposely force me into a painful dilemma, Jack.

RAMSDEN [irritably]: Yes, yes, Annie: this is all very well, and, as I said, quite natural and becoming. But you must make a choice one way or the other. We are as much in a dilemma as you.

ANN: I feel that I am too young, too inexperienced, to decide. My father's wishes are sacred to me.

MRS WHITEFIELD: If you two men wont carry them out I must say it is rather hard that you should put the responsibility on Ann. It seems to me that people are always putting things on other people in this world.

RAMSDEN: I am sorry you take it in that way.

ANN [*touchingly*]: Do you refuse to accept me as your ward, Granny?

RAMSDEN: No: I never said that. I greatly object to act with Mr Tanner: thats all.

MRS WHITEFIELD: Why? What's the matter with poor Jack?

TANNER: My views are too advanced for him.

RAMSDEN [*indignantly*]: They are not. I deny it.

ANN: Of course not. What nonsense! Nobody is more advanced than Granny. I am sure it is Jack himself who has made all the difficulty. Come, Jack! be kind to me in my sorrow. You dont refuse to accept me as your ward, do you?

TANNER [*gloomily*]: No. I let myself in for it; so I suppose I must face it. [*He turns away to the bookcase, and stands there, moodily studying the titles of the volumes.*]

ANN [*rising and expanding with subdued but gushing delight*]: Then we are all agreed; and my dear father's will is to be carried out. You dont know what a joy that is to me and to my mother! [*She goes to Ramsden and presses both his hands, saying*] And I shall have my dear Granny to help and advise me. [*She casts a glance at Tanner over her shoulder.*] And Jack the Giant Killer. [*She goes past her mother to Octavius*] And Jack's inseparable friend Ricky-ticky-tavy [*he blushes and looks inexpressibly foolish*].

MRS WHITEFIELD [*rising and shaking her widow's weeds straight*]: Now that you are Ann's guardian, Mr Ramsden, I wish you would speak to her about her habit of giving

58

people nicknames. They cant be expected to like it. [*She moves towards the door.*]

ANN: How can you say such a thing, Mamma! [*Glowing with affectionate remorse*] Oh, I wonder can you be right! Have I been inconsiderate? [*She turns to Octavius, who is sitting astride his chair with his elbows on the back of it. Putting her hand on his forehead she turns his face up suddenly.*] Do you want to be treated like a grown-up man? Must I call you Mr Robinson in future?

OCTAVIUS [*earnestly*]: Oh please call me Ricky-ticky-tavy. 'Mr Robinson' would hurt me cruelly.

ANN [*laughs and pats his cheek with her finger; then comes back to Ramsden.*] You know I'm beginning to think that Granny is rather a piece of impertinence. But I never dreamt of its hurting you.

RAMSDEN [*breezily, as he pats her affectionately on the back*]: My dear Annie, nonsense. I insist on Granny. I wont answer to any other name than Annie's Granny.

ANN [*gratefully*]: You all spoil me, except Jack.

TANNER [*over his shoulder, from the bookcase*]: I think you ought to call me Mr Tanner.

ANN [*gently*]: No you dont, Jack. Thats like the things you say on purpose to shock people: those who know you pay no attention to them. But, if you like, I'll call you after your famous ancestor Don Juan.

RAMSDEN: Don Juan!

ANN [*innocently*]: Oh, is there any harm in it? I didnt know. Then I certainly wont call you that. May I call you Jack until I can think of something else?

TANNER: Oh, for Heaven's sake dont try to invent anything worse. I capitulate. I consent to Jack. I embrace Jack. Here endeth my first and last attempt to assert my authority.

ANN: You see, Mamma, they all really like to have pet names.

MRS WHITEFIELD: Well, I think you might at least drop them until we are out of mourning.

ANN [*reproachfully, stricken to the soul*]: Oh, how could you remind me, mother? [*She hastily leaves the room to conceal her emotion.*]

MRS WHITEFIELD: Of course. My fault as usual! [*She follows Ann.*]

TANNER [*coming from the bookcase*]: Ramsden: we're beaten – smashed – nonentitized, like her mother.

RAMSDEN: Stuff, sir. [*He follows Mrs Whitefield out of the room.*]

TANNER [*left alone with Octavius, stares whimsically at him*]: Tavy: do you want to count for something in the world?

OCTAVIUS: I want to count for something as a poet: I want to write a great play.

TANNER: With Ann as the heroine?

OCTAVIUS: Yes: I confess it.

TANNER: Take care, Tavy. The play with Ann as the heroine is all right; but if youre not very careful, by Heaven she'll marry you.

OCTAVIUS [*sighing*]: No such luck, Jack!

TANNER: Why, man, your head is in the lioness's mouth: you are half swallowed already – in three bites – Bite One, Ricky; Bite Two, Ticky; Bite Three, Tavy; and down you go.

OCTAVIUS: She is the same to everybody, Jack: you know her ways.

TANNER: Yes: she breaks everybody's back with the stroke of her paw; but the question is, which of us will she eat? My own opinion is that she means to eat you.

OCTAVIUS [*rising, pettishly*]: It's horrible to talk like that about her when she is upstairs crying for her father. But I do so want her to eat me that I can bear your brutalities because they give me hope.

TANNER: Tavy: thats the devilish side of a woman's fascination: she makes you will your own destruction.

OCTAVIUS: But it's not destruction: it's fulfilment.

TANNER: Yes, of her purpose; and that purpose is neither her happiness nor yours, but Nature's. Vitality in a woman is a blind fury of creation. She sacrifices herself to it: do you think she will hesitate to sacrifice you?

OCTAVIUS: Why, it is just because she is self-sacrificing that she will not sacrifice those she loves.

TANNER: That is the profoundest of mistakes, Tavy. It is the self-sacrificing women that sacrifice others most recklessly. Because they are unselfish, they are kind in little things. Because they have a purpose which is not their own purpose, but that of the whole universe, a man is nothing to them but an instrument of that purpose.

OCTAVIUS: Dont be ungenerous, Jack. They take the tenderest care of us.

TANNER: Yes, as a soldier takes care of his rifle or a musician of his violin. But do they allow us any purpose or freedom of our own? Will they lend us to one another? Can the strongest man escape from them when once he is appropriated? They tremble when we are in danger, and weep when we die; but the tears are not for us, but for a father wasted, a son's breeding thrown away. They accuse us of treating them as a mere means to our pleasure; but how can so feeble and transient a folly as a man's selfish pleasure enslave a woman as the whole purpose of Nature embodied in a woman can enslave a man?

OCTAVIUS: What matter, if the slavery makes us happy?

TANNER: No matter at all if you have no purpose of your own, and are, like most men, a mere breadwinner. But you, Tavy, are an artist: that is, you have a purpose as absorbing and as unscrupulous as a woman's purpose.

OCTAVIUS: Not unscrupulous.

TANNER: Quite unscrupulous. The true artist will let his wife starve, his children go barefoot, his mother drudge for his living at seventy, sooner than work at anything but his art. To women he is half vivisector, half vampire. He gets into intimate relations with them to study them, to strip the mask of convention from them, to surprise their inmost secrets, knowing that they have the power to rouse his deepest creative energies, to rescue him from his cold reason, to make him see visions and dream dreams, to inspire him, as he calls it. He persuades women that they may do this for their own purpose whilst he really means them to do it for his. He steals the mother's milk and blackens it to make printers' ink to scoff at her and glorify ideal women with. He pretends to spare her the pangs of child-bearing so that he may have for himself the tenderness and fostering that belong of right to her children. Since marriage began, the great artist has been known as a bad husband. But he is worse: he is a child-robber, a bloodsucker, a hypocrite, and a cheat. Perish the race and wither a thousand women if only the sacrifice of them enable him to act Hamlet better, to paint a finer picture, to write a deeper poem, a greater play, a profounder philosophy! For mark you, Tavy, the artist's work is to shew us ourselves as we really are. Our minds are nothing but this knowledge of ourselves; and he who adds a jot to such knowledge creates new mind as surely as any woman creates new men. In the rage of that creation he is as ruthless as the woman, as dangerous to her as she to him, and as horribly fascinating. Of all human struggles there is none so treacherous and remorseless as the struggle between the artist man and the mother woman. Which shall use up the other? that is the issue between them. And it is all the deadlier because, in your romanticist cant, they love one another.

OCTAVIUS: Even if it were so – and I dont admit it for a moment – it is out of the deadliest struggles that we get the noblest characters.

TANNER: Remember that the next time you meet a grizzly bear or a Bengal tiger, Tavy.

OCTAVIUS: I meant where there is love, Jack.

TANNER: Oh, the tiger will love you. There is no love sincerer than the love of food. I think Ann loves you that way: she patted your cheek as if it were a nicely underdone chop.

OCTAVIUS: You know, Jack, I should have to run away from you if I did not make it a fixed rule not to mind anything you say. You come out with perfectly revolting things sometimes.

[*Ramsden returns, followed by Ann. They come in quickly,*

*with their former leisurely air of decorous grief changed to one
of genuine concern, and, on Ramsden's part, of worry. He comes
between the two men, intending to address Octavius, but pulls
himself up abruptly as he sees Tanner.*]

RAMSDEN: I hardly expected to find you still here, Mr
Tanner.

TANNER: Am I in the way? Good morning, fellow guardian
[*he goes towards the door*].

ANN: Stop, Jack. Granny: he must know, sooner or
later.

RAMSDEN: Octavius: I have a very serious piece of news
for you. It is of the most private and delicate nature – of
the most painful nature too, I am sorry to say. Do you
wish Mr Tanner to be present whilst I explain?

OCTAVIUS [*turning pale*]: I have no secrets from Jack.

RAMSDEN: Before you decide that finally, let me say that
the news concerns your sister, and that it is terrible
news.

OCTAVIUS: Violet! What has happened? Is she – dead?

RAMSDEN: I am not sure that it is not even worse than
that.

OCTAVIUS: Is she badly hurt? Has there been an accident?

RAMSDEN: No: nothing of that sort.

TANNER: Ann: will you have the common humanity to tell
us what the matter is?

ANN [*half whispering*]: I cant. Violet has done something
dreadful. We shall have to get her away somewhere. [*She
flutters to the writing table and sits in Ramsden's chair, leaving
the three men to fight it out between them.*]

OCTAVIUS [*enlightened*]: Is that what you meant, Mr Ramsden?

RAMSDEN: Yes. [*Octavius sinks upon a chair, crushed.*] I am
afraid there is no doubt that Violet did not really go to
Eastbourne three weeks ago when we thought she was
with the Parry Whitefields. And she called on a strange
doctor yesterday with a wedding ring on her finger. Mrs
Parry Whitefield met her there by chance; and so the
whole thing came out.

OCTAVIUS [*rising with his fists clenched*]: Who is the scoundrel?

ANN: She wont tell us.

OCTAVIUS [*collapsing into the chair again*]: What a frightful thing!

TANNER [*with angry sarcasm*]: Dreadful. Appalling. Worse than death, as Ramsden says. [*He comes to Octavius.*] What would you not give, Tavy, to turn it into a railway accident, with all her bones broken, or something equally respectable and deserving of sympathy?

OCTAVIUS: Dont be brutal, Jack.

TANNER: Brutal! Good Heavens, man, what are you crying for? Here is a woman we all supposed to be making bad water color sketches, practising Grieg and Brahms, gadding about to concerts and parties, wasting her life and her money. We suddenly learn that she has turned from these sillinesses to the fulfilment of her highest purpose and greatest function – to increase, multiply, and replenish the earth. And instead of admiring her courage and rejoicing in her instinct; instead of crowning the completed womanhood and raising the triumphal strain of 'Unto us a child is born: unto us a son is given', here you are – you who have been as merry as grigs in your mourning for the dead – all pulling long faces and looking as ashamed and disgraced as if the girl had committed the vilest of crimes.

RAMSDEN [*roaring with rage*]: I will not have these abominations uttered in my house [*he smites the writing table with his fist*].

TANNER: Look here: if you insult me again I'll take you at your word and leave your house. Ann: where is Violet now?

ANN: Why? Are you going to her?

TANNER: Of course I am going to her. She wants help; she wants money; she wants respect and congratulation; she wants every chance for her child. She does not seem likely to get it from you: she shall from me. Where is she?

ANN: Dont be so headstrong, Jack. She's upstairs.

TANNER: What! Under Ramsden's sacred roof! Go and

do your miserable duty, Ramsden. Hunt her out into the street. Cleanse your threshold from her contamination. Vindicate the purity of your English home. I'll go for a cab.

ANN [*alarmed*]: Oh, Granny, you mustnt do that.

OCTAVIUS [*broken-heartedly, rising*]: I'll take her away, Mr Ramsden. She had no right to come to your house.

RAMSDEN [*indignantly*]: But I am only too anxious to help her. [*Turning on Tanner*] How dare you, sir, impute such monstrous intentions to me? I protest against it. I am ready to put down my last penny to save her from being driven to run to you for protection.

TANNER [*subsiding*]: It's all right, then. He's not going to act up to his principles. It's agreed that we all stand by Violet.

OCTAVIUS: But who is the man? He can make reparation by marrying her; and he shall, or he shall answer for it to me.

RAMSDEN: He shall, Octavius. There you speak like a man.

TANNER: Then you dont think him a scoundrel, after all?

OCTAVIUS: Not a scoundrel! He is a heartless scoundrel.

RAMSDEN: A damned scoundrel. I beg your pardon, Annie; but I can say no less.

TANNER: So we are to marry your sister to a damned scoundrel by way of reforming her character? On my soul, I think you are all mad.

ANN: Dont be absurd, Jack. Of course you are quite right, Tavy; but we dont know who he is: Violet wont tell us.

TANNER: What on earth does it matter who he is? He's done his part; and Violet must do the rest.

RAMSDEN [*beside himself*]: Stuff! lunacy! There is a rascal in our midst, a libertine, a villain worse than a murderer; and we are not to learn who he is! In our ignorance we are to shake him by the hand; to introduce him into our homes; to trust our daughters with him; to – to –

ANN [*coaxingly*]: There, Granny, dont talk so loud. It's most shocking: we must all admit that; but if Violet wont tell us, what can we do? Nothing. Simply nothing.

RAMSDEN: Hmph! I'm not so sure of that. If any man has paid Violet any special attention, we can easily find that out. If there is any man of notoriously loose principles among us –

TANNER: Ahem!

RAMSDEN [*raising his voice*]: Yes, sir, I repeat, if there is any man of notoriously loose principles among us –

TANNER: Or any man notoriously lacking in self-control.

RAMSDEN [*aghast*]: Do you dare to suggest that *I* am capable of such an act?

TANNER: My dear Ramsden, this is an act of which every man is capable. That is what comes of getting at cross purposes with Nature. The suspicion you have just flung at me clings to us all. It's the sort of mud that sticks to the judge's ermine or the cardinal's robe as fast as to the rags of the tramp. Come, Tavy! dont look so bewildered: it might have been me: it might have been Ramsden; just as it might have been anybody. If it had, what could we do but lie and protest – as Ramsden is going to protest.

RAMSDEN [*choking*]: I – I – I –

TANNER: Guilt itself could not stammer more confusedly. And yet you know perfectly well he's innocent, Tavy.

RAMSDEN [*exhausted*]: I am glad you admit that, sir. I admit, myself, that there is an element of truth in what you say, grossly as you may distort it to gratify your malicious humor. I hope, Octavius, no suspicion of me i⸗ possible in your mind.

OCTAVIUS: Of you! No, not for a moment.

TANNER [*drily*]: I think he suspects me just a little.

OCTAVIUS: Jack: you couldnt – you wouldnt –

TANNER: Why not?

OCTAVIUS [*appalled*]: Why not!

TANNER: Oh, well, I'll tell you why not. First, you would feel bound to quarrel with me. Second, Violet doesnt like me. Third, if I had the honor of being the father of Violet's child, I should boast of it instead of denying it. So be easy: our friendship is not in danger.

OCTAVIUS: I should have put away the suspicion with

horror if only you would think and feel naturally about it. I beg your pardon.

TANNER: My pardon! nonsense! And now lets sit down and have a family council. [*He sits down. The rest follow his example, more or less under protest.*] Violet is going to do the State a service; consequently she must be packed abroad like a criminal until it's over. Whats happening upstairs?

ANN: Violet is in the housekeeper's room – by herself, of course.

TANNER: Why not in the drawing room?

ANN: Dont be absurd, Jack. Miss Ramsden is in the drawing room with my mother, considering what to do.

TANNER: Oh! the housekeeper's room is the penitentiary, I suppose; and the prisoner is waiting to be brought before her judges. The old cats!

ANN: Oh, Jack!

RAMSDEN: You are at present a guest beneath the roof of one of the old cats, sir. My sister is the mistress of this house.

TANNER: She would put me in the housekeeper's room, too, if she dared, Ramsden. However, I withdraw cats. Cats would have more sense. Ann: as your guardian, I order you to go to Violet at once and be particularly kind to her.

ANN: I have seen her, Jack. And I am sorry to say I am afraid she is going to be rather obstinate about going abroad. I think Tavy ought to speak to her about it.

OCTAVIUS: How can I speak to her about such a thing [*he breaks down*].

ANN: Dont break down, Ricky. Try to bear it for all our sakes.

RAMSDEN: Life is not all plays and poems, Octavius. Come! face it like a man.

TANNER [*chafing again*]: Poor dear brother! Poor dear friends of the family! Poor dear Tabbies and Grimalkins! Poor dear everybody except the woman who is going to risk her life to create another life! Tavy: dont you be a selfish ass. Away with you and talk to Violet; and bring her down here if she cares to come. [*Octavius rises.*] Tell her we'll stand by her.

RAMSDEN [*rising*]: No, sir –

TANNER [*rising also and interrupting him*]: Oh, we understand: it's against your conscience; but still youll do it.

OCTAVIUS: I assure you all, on my word, I never meant to be selfish. It's so hard to know what to do when one wishes earnestly to do right.

TANNER: My dear Tavy, your pious English habit of regarding the world as a moral gymnasium built expressly to strengthen your character in, occasionally leads you to think about your own confounded principles when you should be thinking about other people's necessities. The need of the present hour is a happy mother and a healthy baby. Bend your energies on that; and you will see your way clearly enough.

[*Octavius, much perplexed, goes out.*]

RAMSDEN [*facing Tanner impressively*]: And Morality, sir? What is to become of that?

TANNER: Meaning a weeping Magdalen and an innocent child branded with her shame. Not in our circle, thank you. Morality can go to its father the devil.

RAMSDEN: I thought so, sir. Morality sent to the devil to please our libertines, male and female. That is to be the future of England, is it?

TANNER: Oh, England will survive your disapproval. Meanwhile, I understand that you agree with me as to the practical course we are to take?

RAMSDEN: Not in your spirit, sir. Not for your reasons.

TANNER: You can explain that if anybody calls you to account, here or hereafter. [*He turns away and plants himself in front of Mr Herbert Spencer, at whom he stares gloomily.*]

ANN [*rising and coming to Ramsden*]: Granny: hadnt you better go up to the drawing room and tell them what we intend to do?

RAMSDEN [*looking pointedly at Tanner*]: I hardly like to leave you alone with this gentleman. Will you not come with me?

ANN: Miss Ramsden would not like to speak about it before me, Granny. I ought not to be present.

RAMSDEN: You are right: I should have thought of that. You are a good girl, Annie.

[*He pats her on the shoulder. She looks up at him with beaming eyes; and he goes out, much moved. Having disposed of him, she looks at Tanner. His back being turned to her, she gives a moment's attention to her personal appearance, then softly goes to him and speaks almost into his ear.*]

ANN: Jack [*he turns with a start*]: are you glad that you are my guardian? You dont mind being made responsible for me, I hope.

TANNER: The latest addition to your collection of scape-goats, eh?

ANN: Oh, that stupid old joke of yours about me! Do please drop it. Why do you say things that you know must pain me? I do my best to please you, Jack: I suppose I may tell you so now that you are my guardian. You will make me so unhappy if you refuse to be friends with me.

TANNER [*studying her as gloomily as he studied the bust*]: You need not go begging for my regard. How unreal our moral judgments are! You seem to me to have absolutely no conscience – only hypocrisy; and you cant see the difference – yet there is a sort of fascination about you. I always attend to you, somehow. I should miss you if I lost you.

ANN [*tranquilly slipping her arm into his and walking about with him*]: But isnt that only natural, Jack? We have known each other since we were children. Do you remember –

TANNER [*abruptly breaking loose*]: Stop! I remember every-thing.

ANN: Oh, I daresay we were often very silly; but –

TANNER: I wont have it, Ann. I am no more that schoolboy now than I am the dotard of ninety I shall grow into if I live long enough. It is over: let me forget it.

ANN: Wasnt it a happy time? [*She attempts to take his arm again.*]

TANNER: Sit down and behave yourself. [*He makes her sit*

down in the chair next the writing table.] No doubt it was a happy time for you. You were a good girl and never compromised yourself. And yet the wickedest child that ever was slapped could hardly have had a better time. I can understand the success with which you bullied the other girls: your virtue imposed on them. But tell me this: did you ever know a good boy?

ANN: Of course. All boys are foolish sometimes; but Tavy was always a really good boy.

TANNER [*struck by this*] : Yes: youre right. For some reason you never tempted Tavy.

ANN: Tempted! Jack!

TANNER: Yes, my dear Lady Mephistopheles, tempted. You were insatiably curious as to what a boy might be capable of, and diabolically clever at getting through his guard and surprising his inmost secrets.

ANN: What nonsense! All because you used to tell me long stories of the wicked things you had done – silly boy's tricks! And you call such things inmost secrets! Boys' secrets are just like men's; and you know what they are!

TANNER [*obstinately*]: No, I dont. What are they, pray?

ANN: Why, the things they tell everybody, of course.

TANNER: Now I swear I told you things I told no one else. You lured me into a compact by which we were to have no secrets from one another. We were to tell one another everything. I didnt notice that you never told me anything.

ANN: You didnt want to talk about me, Jack. You wanted to talk about yourself.

TANNER: Ah, true, horribly true. But what a devil of a child you must have been to know that weakness and to play on it for the satisfaction of your own curiosity! I wanted to brag to you, to make myself interesting. And I found myself doing all sorts of mischievous things simply to have something to tell you about. I fought with boys I didnt hate; I lied about things I might just as well have told the truth about; I stole things I didnt want; I kissed little girls I didnt care for. It was all bravado: passionless and therefore unreal.

ANN: And I never told of you, Jack.

TANNER: No; but if you had wanted to stop me you would have told of me. You wanted me to go on.

ANN [*flashing out*]: Oh, thats not true: it's n o t true, Jack. I never wanted you to do those dull, disappointing, brutal, stupid, vulgar things. I always hoped that it would be something really heroic at last. [*Recovering herself*] Excuse me, Jack; but the things you did were never a bit like the things I wanted you to do. They often gave me great uneasiness; but I could not tell of you and get you into trouble. And you were only a boy. I knew you would grow out of them. Perhaps I was wrong.

TANNER [*sardonically*]: Do not give way to remorse, Ann. At least nineteen twentieths of the exploits I confessed to you were pure lies. I soon noticed that you didnt like the true stories.

ANN: Of course I knew that some of the things couldnt have happened. But –

TANNER: You are going to remind me that some of the most disgraceful ones did.

ANN [*fondly, to his great terror*]: I dont want to remind you of anything. But I knew the people they happened to, and heard about them.

TANNER: Yes; but even the true stories were touched up for telling. A sensitive boy's humiliations may be very good fun for ordinary thickskinned grown-ups; but to the boy himself they are so acute, so ignominious, that he cannot confess them – cannot but deny them passionately. However, perhaps it was as well for me that I romanced a bit; for, on the one occasion when I told you the truth, you threatened to tell of me.

ANN: Oh, never. Never once.

TANNER: Yes, you did. Do you remember a dark-eyed girl named Rachel Rosetree? [*Ann's brows contract for an instant involuntarily.*] I got up a love affair with her; and we met one night in the garden and walked about very uncomfortably with our arms round one another, and kissed at parting, and were most conscientiously romantic. If that love affair had gone on, it would have bored me to death; but it didnt go on; for the next thing that happened was that Rachel cut me because she found out that I had told you. How did she find it out? From you. You went to her and held the guilty secret over her head, leading her a life of abject terror and humiliation by threatening to tell on her.

ANN: And a very good thing for her, too. It was my duty to stop her misconduct; and she is thankful to me for it now.

TANNER: Is she?

ANN: She ought to be, at all events.

TANNER: It was not your duty to stop my misconduct, I suppose.

ANN: I did stop it by stopping her.

TANNER: Are you sure of that? You stopped my telling you about my adventures; but how do you know that you stopped the adventures?

ANN: Do you mean to say that you went on in the same way with other girls?

TANNER: No. I had enough of that sort of romantic tomfoolery with Rachel.

ANN [*unconvinced*]: Then why did you break off our confidences and become quite strange to me?

TANNER [*enigmatically*]: It happened just then that I got something that I wanted to keep all to myself instead of sharing it with you.

ANN: I am sure I shouldnt have asked for any of it if you had grudged it.

TANNER: It wasnt a box of sweets, Ann. It was something youd never have let me call my own.

ANN [*incredulously*]: What?

TANNER: My soul.

ANN: Oh, do be sensible, Jack. You know youre talking nonsense.

TANNER: The most solemn earnest, Ann. You didnt notice at that time that you were getting a soul too. But you were. It was not for nothing that you suddenly found you had a moral duty to chastise and reform Rachel. Up to that time you had traded pretty extensively in being a good child; but you had never set up a sense of duty to others. Well, I set one up too. Up to that time I had played the boy buccaneer with no more conscience than a fox in a poultry farm. But now I began to have scruples, to feel obligations, to find that veracity and honor were no longer goody-goody expressions in the mouths of grown-up people, but compelling principle in myself.

ANN [*quietly*]: Yes, I suppose youre right. You were beginning to be a man, and I to be a woman.

TANNER: Are you sure it was not that we were beginning to be something more? What does the beginning of manhood and womanhood mean in most people's mouths? You know: it means the beginning of love. But love began long before that for me. Love played its part in the earliest dreams and follies and romances I can remember – may I say the earliest follies and romances we can remember? – though we did not understand it at the time. No: the change that came to me was the birth in me of moral passion; and I declare that according to my experience moral passion is the only real passion.

ANN: All passions ought to be moral, Jack.

TANNER: Ought! Do you think that anything is strong enough to impose oughts on a passion except a stronger passion still?

ANN: Our moral sense controls passion, Jack. Dont be stupid.

TANNER: Our moral sense! And is that not a passion? Is the devil to have all the passions as well as all the good tunes? If it were not a passion – if it were not the mightiest of the passions, all the other passions would sweep it away like a leaf before a hurricane. It is the birth of that passion that turns a child into a man.

ANN: There are other passions, Jack. Very strong ones.

TANNER: All the other passions were in me before; but they were idle and aimless – mere childish greedinesses

73

and cruelties, curiosities and fancies, habits and superstititions, grotesque and ridiculous to the mature intelligence. When they suddenly began to shine like newly lit flames it was by no light of their own, but by the radiance of the dawning moral passion. That passion dignified them, gave them conscience and meaning, found them a mob of appetites and organized them into an army of purposes and principles. My soul was born of that passion.

ANN: I noticed that you got more sense. You were a dreadfully destructive boy before that.

TANNER: Destructive! Stuff! I was only mischievous.

ANN: Oh, Jack, you were very destructive. You ruined all the young fir trees by chopping off their leaders with a wooden sword. You broke all the cucumber frames with your catapult. You set fire to the common: the police arrested Tavy for it because he ran away when he couldnt stop you. You –

TANNER: Pooh! pooh! pooh! these were battles, bombardments, stratagems to save our scalps from the red Indians. You have no imagination, Ann. I am ten times more destructive now than I was then. The moral passion has taken my destructiveness in hand and directed it to moral ends. I have become a reformer, and, like all reformers, an iconoclast. I no longer break cucumber frames and burn gorse bushes: I shatter creeds and demolish idols.

ANN [*bored*]: I am afraid I am too feminine to see any sense in destruction. Destruction can only destroy.

TANNER: Yes. That is why it is so useful. Construction cumbers the ground with institutions made by busybodies. Destruction clears it and gives us breathing space and liberty.

ANN: It's no use, Jack. No woman will agree with you there.

TANNER: Thats because you confuse construction and destruction with creation and murder. Theyre quite different: I adore creation and abhor murder. Yes: I adore it in tree and flower, in bird and beast, even in you. [*A flush of interest and delight suddenly chases the growing perplexity*

74

and boredom from her face.] It was the creative instinct that led you to attach me to you by bonds that have left their mark on me to this day. Yes, Ann: the old childish compact between us was an unconscious love compact –

ANN: Jack!

TANNER: Oh, dont be alarmed –

ANN: I am not alarmed.

TANNER [*whimsically*]: Then you ought to be: where are your principles?

ANN: Jack: are you serious or are you not?

TANNER: Do you mean about the moral passion?

ANN: No, no: the other one. [*Confused*] Oh! you are so silly: one never knows how to take you.

TANNER: You must take me quite seriously. I am your guardian; and it is my duty to improve your mind.

ANN: The love compact is over, then, is it? I suppose you grew tired of me?

TANNER: No; but the moral passion made our childish relations impossible. A jealous sense of my new individuality arose in me –

ANN: You hated to be treated as a boy any longer. Poor Jack!

TANNER: Yes, because to be treated as a boy was to be taken on the old footing. I had become a new person; and those who knew the old person laughed at me. The only man who behaved sensibly was my tailor: he took my measure anew every time he saw me, whilst all the rest went on with their old measurements and expected them to fit me.

ANN: You became frightfully self-conscious.

TANNER: When you go to heaven, Ann, you will be frightfully conscious of your wings for the first year or so. When you meet your relatives there, and they persist in treating you as if you were still a mortal, you will not be able to bear them. You will try to get into a circle which has never known you except as an angel.

ANN: So it was only your vanity that made you run away from us after all?

TANNER: Yes, only my vanity, as you call it.

ANN: You need not have kept away from me on that account.

TANNER: From you above all others. You fought harder than anybody against my emancipation.

ANN [*earnestly*]: Oh, how wrong you are! I would have done anything for you.

TANNER: Anything except let me get loose from you. Even then you had acquired by instinct that damnable woman's trick of heaping obligations on a man, of placing yourself so entirely and helplessly at his mercy that at last he dare not take a step without running to you for leave. I know a poor wretch whose one desire in life is to run away from his wife. She prevents him by threatening to throw herself in front of the engine of the train he leaves her in. That is what all women do. If we try to go where you do not want us to go there is no law to prevent us; but when we take the first step your breasts are under our foot as it descends: your bodies are under our wheels as we start. No woman shall ever enslave me in that way.

ANN: But, Jack, you cannot get through life without considering other people a little.

TANNER: Ay; but what other people? It is this consideration of other people – or rather this cowardly fear of them which we call consideration – that makes us the sentimental slaves we are. To consider you, as you call it, is to substitute your will for my own. How if it be a baser will than mine? Are women taught better than men or worse? Are mobs of voters taught better than statesmen or worse? Worse, of course, in both cases. And then what sort of world are you going to get, with its public men considering its voting mobs, and its private men considering their wives? What does Church and State mean nowadays? The Woman and the Ratepayer.

ANN [*placidly*]: I am so glad you understand politics, Jack: it will be most useful to you if you go into parliament [*he collapses like a pricked bladder*]. But I am sorry you thought my influence a bad one.

TANNER: I dont say it was a bad one. But bad or good, I

didnt choose to be cut to your measure. And I wont be cut to it.

ANN: Nobody wants you to, Jack. I assure you – really on my word – I dont mind your queer opinions one little bit. You know we have all been brought up to have advanced opinions. Why do you persist in thinking me so narrow minded?

TANNER: Thats the danger of it. I know you dont mind, because youve found out that it doesnt matter. The boa constrictor doesnt mind the opinions of a stag one little bit when once she has got her coils round it.

ANN [*rising in sudden enlightenment*]: O-o-o-o-oh! now I understand why you warned Tavy that I am a boa constrictor. Granny told me. [*She laughs and throws her boa round his neck.*] Doesnt it feel nice and soft, Jack?

TANNER [*in the toils*]: You scandalous woman, will you throw away even your hypocrisy?

ANN: I am never hypocritical with you, Jack. Are you angry? [*She withdraws the boa and throws it on a chair.*] Perhaps I shouldnt have done that.

TANNER [*contemptuously*]: Pooh, prudery! Why should you not, if it amuses you?

ANN [*shyly*]: Well, because – because I suppose what you really meant by the boa constrictor was this [*she puts her arms round his neck*].

TANNER [*staring at her*]: Magnificent audacity! [*She laughs and pats his cheeks.*] Now just to think that if I mentioned this episode not a soul would believe me except the people who would cut me for telling, whilst if you accused me of it nobody would believe my denial!

ANN [*taking her arms away with perfect dignity*]: You are incorrigible, Jack. But you should not jest about our affection for one another. Nobody could possibly misunderstand it. You do not misunderstand it, I hope.

TANNER: My blood interprets for me, Ann. Poor Ricky Ticky Tavy!

ANN [*looking quickly at him as if this were a new light*]: Surely you are not so absurd as to be jealous of Tavy.

TANNER: Jealous! Why should I be? But I dont wonder at your grip of him. I feel the coils tightening round my very self, though you are only playing with me.

ANN: Do you think I have designs on Tavy?

TANNER: I know you have.

ANN [*earnestly*]: Take care, Jack. You may make Tavy very unhappy if you mislead him about me.

TANNER: Never fear: he will not escape you.

ANN: I wonder are you really a clever man!

TANNER: Why this sudden misgiving on the subject?

ANN: You seem to understand all the things I dont understand; but you are a perfect baby in the things I do understand.

TANNER: I understand how Tavy feels for you, Ann: you may depend on that, at all events.

ANN: And you think you understand how I feel for Tavy, dont you?

TANNER: I know only too well what is going to happen to poor Tavy.

ANN: I should laugh at you, Jack, if it were not for poor papa's death. Mind! Tavy will be very unhappy.

TANNER: Yes; but he wont know it, poor devil. He is a thousand times too good for you. Thats why he is going to make the mistake of his life about you.

ANN: I think men make more mistakes by being too clever than by being too good [*she sits down, with a trace of contempt for the whole male sex in the elegant carriage of her shoulders*].

TANNER: Oh, I know you dont care very much about Tavy. But there is always one who kisses and one who only allows the kiss. Tavy will kiss; and you will only turn the cheek. And you will throw him over if anybody better turns up.

ANN [*offended*]: You have no right to say such things, Jack. They are not true, and not delicate. If you and Tavy choose to be stupid about me, that is not my fault.

TANNER [*remorsefully*]: Forgive my brutalities, Ann. They are levelled at this wicked world, not at you. [*She looks up at him, pleased and forgiving. He becomes cautious at once.*] All the same, I wish Ramsden would come back. I never feel safe with you: there is a devilish charm – or no: not a charm, a subtle interest [*she laughs*] – Just so: you know it: and you triumph in it. Openly and shamelessly triumph in it!

ANN: What a shocking flirt you are, Jack!

TANNER: A flirt!! I!!!

ANN: Yes, a flirt. You are always abusing and offending people; but you never really mean to let go your hold of them.

TANNER: I will ring the bell. This conversation has already gone further than I intended.

[*Ramsden and Octavius come back with Miss Ramsden, a hard-headed old maiden lady in a plain brown silk gown, with enough rings, chains, and brooches to shew that her plainness of dress is a matter of principle, not of poverty. She comes into the room very determinedly: the two men, perplexed and downcast, following her. Ann rises and goes eagerly to meet her. Tanner retreats to the wall between the busts and pretends to study the pictures. Ramsden goes to his table as usual; and Octavius clings to the neighborhood of Tanner.*]

MISS RAMSDEN [*almost pushing Ann aside as she comes to Mrs Whitefield's chair and plants herself there resolutely*]: I wash my hands of the whole affair.

OCTAVIUS [*very wretched*]: I know you wish me to take Violet away, Miss Ramsden. I will. [*He turns irresolutely to the door.*]

RAMSDEN: No, no –

MISS RAMSDEN: What is the use of saying no, Roebuck? Octavius knows that I would not turn any truly contrite and repentant woman from your doors. But when a woman is not only wicked, but intends to go on being wicked, she and I part company.

ANN: Oh, Miss Ramsden, what do you mean? What has Violet said?

RAMSDEN: Violet is certainly very obstinate. She wont leave London. I dont understand her.

MISS RAMSDEN: I do. It's as plain as the nose on your face, Roebuck, that she wont go because she doesnt want to be separated from this man, whoever he is.

ANN: Oh, surely, surely! Octavius: did you speak to her?

OCTAVIUS: She wont tell us anything. She wont make any arrangement until she has consulted somebody. It cant be anybody else than the scoundrel who has betrayed her.

TANNER [to Octavius]: Well, let her consult him. He will be glad enough to have her sent abroad. Where is the difficulty?

MISS RAMSDEN [taking the answer out of Octavius's mouth]: The difficulty, Mr Jack, is that when I offered to help her I didnt offer to become her accomplice in her wickedness. She either pledges her word never to see that man again, or else she finds some new friends; and the sooner the better.

> [The parlormaid appears at the door. Ann hastily resumes her seat, and looks as unconcerned as possible. Octavius instinctively imitates her.]

THE MAID: The cab is at the door, maam.

MISS RAMSDEN: What cab?

THE MAID: For Miss Robinson.

MISS RAMSDEN: Oh! [Recovering herself] All right. [The maid withdraws.] She has sent for a cab.

TANNER: I wanted to send for that cab half an hour ago.

MISS RAMSDEN: I am glad she understands the position she has placed herself in.

RAMSDEN: I dont like her going away in this fashion, Susan. We had better not do anything harsh.

OCTAVIUS: No: thank you again and again; but Miss Ramsden is quite right. Violet cannot expect to stay.

ANN: Hadnt you better go with her, Tavy?

OCTAVIUS: She wont have me.

MISS RAMSDEN: Of course she wont. She's going straight to that man.

TANNER: As a natural result of her virtuous reception here.

RAMSDEN [much troubled]: There, Susan! You hear! and theres some truth in it. I wish you could reconcile it with your principles to be a little patient with this poor girl. She's very young; and theres a time for everything.

MISS RAMSDEN: Oh, she will get all the sympathy she wants from the men. I'm surprised at you, Roebuck.

TANNER: So am I, Ramsden, most favourably.

[*Violet appears at the door. She is as impenitent and self-possessed a young lady as one would desire to see among the best behaved of her sex. Her small head and tiny resolute mouth and chin; her haughty crispness of speech and trimness of carriage; the ruthless elegance of her equipment, which includes a very smart hat with a dead bird in it, mark a personality which is as formidable as it is exquisitely pretty. She is not a siren, like Ann: admiration comes to her without any compulsion or even interest on her part; besides, there is some fun in Ann, but in this woman none, perhaps no mercy either: if anything restrains her, it is intelligence and pride, not compassion. Her voice might be the voice of a school-mistress addressing a class of girls who had disgraced themselves, as she proceeds with complete composure and some disgust to say what she has come to say.*]*

VIOLET: I have only looked in to tell Miss Ramsden that she will find her birthday present to me, the filagree bracelet, in the housekeeper's room.

TANNER: Do come in, Violet; and talk to us sensibly.

VIOLET: Thank you: I have had quite enough of the family conversation this morning. So has your mother, Ann: she has gone home crying. But at all events, I have found out what some of my pretended friends are worth. Goodbye.

TANNER: No, no: one moment. I have something to say which I beg you to hear. [*She looks at him without the slightest curiosity, but waits, apparently as much to finish getting her glove on as to hear what he has to say.*] I am altogether on your side in this matter. I congratulate you, with the sincerest respect, on having the courage to do what you have done. You are entirely in the right; and the family is entirely in the wrong.

[*Sensation. Ann and Miss Ramsden rise and turn towards the two. Violet, more surprised than any of the others, forgets her glove, and comes forward into the middle of the room, both puzzled and displeased. Octavius alone does not move nor raise his head: he is overwhelmed with shame.*]

ANN [*pleading to Tanner to be sensible*]: Jack!

MISS RAMSDEN [*outraged*]: Well, I must say!

VIOLET [*sharply to Tanner*]: Who told you?

TANNER: Why, Ramsden and Tavy of course. Why should they not?

VIOLET: But they dont know.

TANNER: Dont know what?

VIOLET: They dont know that I am in the right, I mean.

TANNER: Oh, they know it in their hearts, though they think themselves bound to blame you by their silly superstitions about morality and propriety and so forth. But I know, and the whole world really knows, though it dare not say so, that you were right to follow your instinct; that vitality and bravery are the greatest qualities a woman can have, and motherhood her solemn initiation into womanhood; and that the fact of your not being legally married matters not one scrap either to your own worth or to our real regard for you.

VIOLET [*flushing with indignation*]: Oh! You think me a wicked woman, like the rest. You think I have not only been vile, but that I share your abominable opinions. Miss Ramsden: I have borne your hard words because I knew you would be sorry for them when you found out the truth. But I wont bear such a horrible insult as to be complimented by Jack on being one of the wretches of whom he approves. I have kept my marriage a secret for my husband's sake. But now I claim my right as a married woman not to be insulted.

OCTAVIUS [*raising his head with inexpressible relief*]: You are married!

VIOLET: Yes; and I think you might have guessed it. What business had you all to take it for granted that I had no right to wear my wedding ring? Not one of you even asked me: I cannot forget that.

TANNER [*in ruins*]: I am utterly crushed. I meant well. I apologize – abjectly apologize.

VIOLET: I hope you will be more careful in future about the things you say. Of course one does not take them seriously; but they are very disagreeable, and rather in bad taste, I think.

TANNER [*bowing to the storm*]: I have no defence: I shall know better in future than to take any woman's part. We have all disgraced ourselves in your eyes, I am afraid, except Ann. She befriended you. For Ann's sake, forgive us.

VIOLET: Yes: Ann has been kind; but then Ann knew.

TANNER [*with a desperate gesture*]: Oh!!! Unfathomable deceit! Double crossed!

MISS RAMSDEN [*stiffly*]: And who, pray, is the gentleman who does not acknowledge his wife?

VIOLET [*promptly*]: That is my business, Miss Ramsden, and not yours. I have my reasons for keeping my marriage a secret for the present.

RAMSDEN: All I can say is that we are extremely sorry, Violet. I am shocked to think of how we have treated you.

OCTAVIUS [*awkwardly*]: I beg your pardon, Violet. I can say no more.

MISS RAMSDEN [*still loath to surrender*]: Of course what you say puts a very different complexion on the matter. All the same, I owe it to myself –

VIOLET [*cutting her short*]: You owe me an apology, Miss Ramsden: thats what you owe both to yourself and to me. If you were a married woman you would not like sitting in the housekeeper's room and being treated like a naughty child by young girls and old ladies without any serious duties and responsibilities.

TANNER: Dont hit us when we're down, Violet. We seem to have made fools of ourselves; but really it was you who made fools of us.

VIOLET: It was no business of yours, Jack, in any case.

TANNER: No business of mine! Why, Ramsden as good as accused me of being the unknown gentleman.

[*Ramsden makes a frantic demonstration; but Violet's cool keen anger extinguishes it.*]

VIOLET: You! Oh, how infamous! how abominable! how

disgracefully you have all been talking about me! If my husband knew it he would never let me speak to any of you again. [*To Ramsden*] I think you might have spared me that, at least.

RAMSDEN: But I assure you I never — at least it is a monstrous perversion of something I said that —

MISS RAMSDEN: You neednt apologize, Roebuck. She brought it all on herself. It is for her to apologize for having deceived us.

VIOLET: I can make allowances for you Miss Ramsden: you cannot understand how I feel on this subject, though I should have expected rather better taste from people of greater experience. However, I quite feel that you have placed yourselves in a very painful position; and the most truly considerate thing for me to do is to go at once. Good morning.

[*She goes, leaving them staring.*]

MISS RAMSDEN: Well, I must say!

RAMSDEN [*plaintively*]: I dont think she is quite fair to us.

TANNER: You must cower before the wedding ring like the rest of us, Ramsden. The cup of our ignominy is full.

ACT TWO

On the carriage drive in the park of a country house near Richmond an open touring car has broken down. It stands in front of a clump of trees round which the drive sweeps to the house, which is partly visible through them: indeed Tanner, standing in the drive with his back to us, could get an unobstructed view of the west corner of the house on his left were he not far too much interested in a pair of supine legs in dungaree overalls which protrude from beneath the machine. He is watching them intently with bent back and hands supported on his knees. His leathern overcoat and peaked cap proclaim him one of the dismounted passengers.

THE LEGS: Aha! I got him.

TANNER: All right now?

THE LEGS: Aw rawt nah.

[Tanner stoops and takes the legs by the ankles, drawing their owner forth like a wheelbarrow, walking on his hands, with a hammer in his mouth. He is a young man in a neat suit of blue serge, clean shaven, dark eyed, square fingered, with short well brushed black hair and rather irregular sceptically turned eye-brows. When he is manipulating the car his movements are swift and sudden, yet attentive and deliberate. With Tanner and Tanner's friends his manner is not in the least deferential, but cool and reticent, keeping them quite effectually at a distance whilst giving them no excuse for complaining of him. Nevertheless he has a vigilant eye on them always, and that, too, rather cynically, like a man who knows the world well from its seamy side. He speaks slowly and with a touch of sarcasm; and as he does not at all affect the gentleman in his speech, it may be inferred that his smart appearance is a mark of respect to himself and his own class, not to that which employs him.

He now gets into the car to stow away his tools and divest himself of his overalls. Tanner takes off his leathern overcoat and pitches it into the car with a sigh of relief, glad to be

85

rid of it. The chauffeur, noting this, tosses his head contemptuously, and surveys his employer sardonically.]

THE CHAUFFEUR: Had enough of it, eh?

TANNER: I may as well walk to the house and stretch my legs and calm my nerves a little. [*Looking at his watch*] I suppose you know that we have come from Hyde Park Corner to Richmond in twenty-one minutes.

THE CHAUFFEUR: I'd ha done it under fifteen if I'd had a clear road all the way.

TANNER: Why do you do it? Is it for love of sport or for the fun of terrifying your unfortunate employer?

THE CHAUFFEUR: What are you afraid of?

TANNER: The police, and breaking my neck.

THE CHAUFFEUR: Well, if you like easy going, you can take a bus, you know. It's cheaper. You pay me to save your time and give you the value of what you paid for the car. [*He sits down calmly.*]

TANNER: I am the slave of that car and of you too. I dream of the accursed thing at night.

THE CHAUFFEUR: Youll get over that all right. If youre going up to the house, may I ask how long youre goin to stay? Because if you mean to put in the whole morning in there talkin to the ladies, I'll put the car in the garage and make myself agreeable with a view to lunching here. If not, I'll keep the car on the go about here till you come.

TANNER: Better wait here. We shant be long. Theres a young American gentleman, a Mr Malone, who is driving Mr Robinson down in his new American steam car.

THE CHAUFFEUR [*springing up and coming hastily out of the car to Tanner*]: American steam car! Wot! racin us dahn from London!

TANNER: Perhaps theyre here already.

THE CHAUFFEUR: If I'd known it! [*With deep reproach*] Why didnt you tell me, Mr Tanner?

TANNER: Because Ive been told that this car is capable of 84 miles an hour; and I already know what you are capable of when there is a rival car on the road. No, Henry: there are things it is not good for you to know; and this was one of them. However, cheer up: we are going to have a day after your own heart. The American is to take Mr Robinson and his sister and Miss White-field. We are to take Miss Rhoda.

THE CHAUFFEUR [*consoled, and musing on another matter*]: Thats Miss Whitefield's sister, isnt it?

TANNER: Yes.

THE CHAUFFEUR: And Miss Whitefield herself is goin in the other car? Not with you?

TANNER: Why the devil should she come with me? Mr Robinson will be in the other car. [*The Chauffeur looks at Tanner with cool incredulity, and turns to the car, whistling a popular air softly to himself. Tanner, a little annoyed, is about to pursue the subject, when he hears the footsteps of Octavius on the gravel. Octavius is coming from the house, dressed for motoring, but without his overcoat.*] Weve lost the race, thank Heaven: heres Mr Robinson. Well, Tavy, is the steam car a success?

OCTAVIUS: I think so. We came from Hyde Park Corner here in seventeen minutes. [*The Chauffeur, furious, kicks the car with a groan of vexation.*] How long were you?

TANNER: Oh, about three quarters of an hour or so.

THE CHAUFFEUR [*remonstrating*]: Now, now, Mr Tanner, come now! We could ha done it easy under fifteen.

TANNER: By the way, let me introduce you. Mr Octavius Robinson: Mr Enry Straker.

STRAKER: Pleased to meet you, sir. Mr Tanner is gittin at you with is Enry Straker, you know. You call it Henery. But I dont mind, bless you!

TANNER: You think it's simply bad taste in me to chaff him, Tavy. But youre wrong. This man takes more trouble to drop his aitches than ever his father did to pick them up. It's a mark of caste to him. I have never met anybody more swollen with the pride of class than Enry is.

STRAKER: Easy, easy! A little moderation, Mr Tanner.

TANNER: A little moderation, Tavy, you observe. Y o u

would tell me to draw it mild. But this chap has been educated. Whats more, he knows that we havnt. What was that Board School of yours, Straker?

STRAKER: Sherbrooke Road.

TANNER: Sherbrooke Road! Would any of us say Rugby! Harrow! Eton! in that tone of intellectual snobbery? Sherbrooke Road is a place where boys learn something: Eton is a boy farm where we are sent because we are nuisances at home, and because in after life, whenever a Duke is mentioned, we can claim him as an old schoolfellow.

STRAKER: You dont know nothing about it, Mr Tanner. It's not the Board School that does it: it's the Polytechnic.

TANNER: His university, Octavius. Not Oxford, Cambridge, Durham, Dublin, or Glasgow. Not even those Noncomformist holes in Wales. No, Tavy. Regent Street! Chelsea! the Borough! – I dont know half their confounded names: these are his universities, not mere shops for selling class limitations like ours. You despise Oxford, Enry, dont you?

STRAKER: No, I dont. Very nice sort of place, Oxford, I should think, for people that like that sort of place. They teach you to be a gentleman there. In the Polytechnic they teach you to be an engineer or such like. See?

TANNER: Sarcasm, Tavy, sarcasm! Oh, if you could only see into Enry's soul, the depth of his contempt for a gentleman, the arrogance of his pride in being an engineer, would appal you. He positively likes the car to break down because it brings out my gentlemanly helplessness and his workmanlike skill and resource.

STRAKER: Never you mind him, Mr Robinson. He likes to talk. We know him, dont we?

OCTAVIUS [*earnestly*]: But theres a great truth at the bottom of what he says. I believe most intensely in the dignity of labor.

STRAKER [*unimpressed*]: Thats because you never done any, Mr Robinson. My business is to do away with labor.

Youll get more out of me and a machine than you will out of twenty laborers, and not so much to drink either.

TANNER: For Heaven's sake, Tavy, dont start him on political economy. He knows all about it; and we dont. Youre only a poetic Socialist, Tavy: he's a scientific one.

STRAKER [unperturbed]: Yes. Well, this conversation is very improvin; but Ive got to look after the car; and you two want to talk about your ladies. I know. [He pretends to busy himself about the car, but presently saunters off to indulge in a cigaret.]

TANNER: Thats a very momentous social phenomenon.

OCTAVIUS: What is?

TANNER: Straker is. Here have we literary and cultured persons been for years setting up a cry of the New Woman whenever some unusually old fashioned female came along, and never noticing the advent of the New Man. Straker's the New Man.

OCTAVIUS: I see nothing new about him, except your way of chaffing him. But I dont want to talk about him just now. I want to speak to you about Ann.

TANNER: Straker knew even that. He learnt it at the Polytechnic, probably. Well, what about Ann? Have you proposed to her?

OCTAVIUS [self-reproachfully]: I was brute enough to do so last night.

TANNER: Brute enough! What do you mean?

OCTAVIUS [dithyrambically]: Jack: we men are all coarse: we never understand how exquisite a woman's sensibilities are. How could I have done such a thing!

TANNER: Done what, you maudlin idiot?

OCTAVIUS: Yes, I am an idiot. Jack: if you had heard her voice! If you had seen her tears! I have lain awake all night thinking of them. If she had reproached me, I could have borne it better.

TANNER: Tears! thats dangerous. What did she say?

OCTAVIUS: She asked me how she could think of anything now but her dear father. She stifled a sob – [he breaks down].

TANNER [*patting him on the back*]: Bear it like a man, Tavy, even if you feel it like an ass. It's the old game: she's not tired of playing with you yet.

OCTAVIUS [*impatiently*]: Oh, dont be a fool, Jack. Do you suppose this eternal shallow cynicism of yours has any real bearing on a nature like hers?

TANNER: Hm! Did she say anything else?

OCTAVIUS: Yes; and that is why I expose myself and her to your ridicule by telling you what passed.

TANNER [*remorsefully*]: No, dear Tavy, not ridicule, on my honor! However, no matter. Go on.

OCTAVIUS: Her sense of duty is so devout, so perfect, so —

TANNER: Yes: I know. Go on.

OCTAVIUS: You see, under this new arrangement, you and Ramsden are her guardians; and she considers that all her duty to her father is now transferred to you. She said she thought I ought to have spoken to you both in the first instance. Of course she is right; but somehow it seems rather absurd that I am to come to you and formally ask to be received as a suitor for your ward's hand.

TANNER: I am glad that love has not totally extinguished your sense of humor, Tavy.

OCTAVIUS: That answer wont satisfy her.

TANNER: My official answer is, obviously, Bless you, my children: may you be happy!

OCTAVIUS: I wish you would stop playing the fool about this. If it is not serious to you, it is to me, and to her.

TANNER: You know very well that she is as free to choose as you are.

OCTAVIUS: She does not think so.

TANNER: Oh, doesnt she! just! However, say what you want me to do?

OCTAVIUS: I want you to tell her sincerely and earnestly what you think about me. I want you to tell her that you can trust her to me — that is, if you feel you can.

TANNER: I have no doubt that I can trust her to you. What worries me is the idea of trusting you to her. Have you read Maeterlinck's book about the bee?

OCTAVIUS [*keeping his temper with difficulty*]: I am not discussing literature at present.

TANNER. Be just a little patient with me. *I* am not discussing literature: the book about the bee is natural history. It's an awful lesson to mankind. You think that you are Ann's suitor; that you are the pursuer and she the pursued; that it is your part to woo, to persuade, to prevail, to overcome. Fool: it is you who are the pursued, the marked down quarry, the destined prey. You need not sit looking longingly at the bait through the wires of the trap: the door is open, and will remain so until it shuts behind you for ever.

OCTAVIUS: I wish I could believe that, vilely as you put it.

TANNER: Why, man, what other work has she in life but to get a husband? It is a woman's business to get married as soon as possible, and a man's to keep unmarried as long as he can. You have your poems and your tragedies to work at: Ann has nothing.

OCTAVIUS: I cannot write without inspiration. And nobody can give me that except Ann.

TANNER: Well, hadnt you better get it from her at a safe distance? Petrarch didnt see half as much of Laura, nor Dante of Beatrice, as you see of Ann now; and yet they wrote first-rate poetry – at least so I'm told. They never exposed their idolatry to the test of domestic familiarity; and it lasted them to their graves. Marry Ann; and at the end of a week youll find no more inspiration in her than in a plate of muffins.

OCTAVIUS: You think I shall tire of her!

TANNER: Not at all: you dont get tired of muffins. But you dont find inspiration in them; and you wont in her when she ceases to be a poet's dream and becomes a solid eleven stone wife. Youll be forced to dream about somebody else; and then there will be a row.

OCTAVIUS: This sort of talk is no use, Jack. You dont understand. You have never been in love.

TANNER: I! I have never been out of it. Why, I am in love even with Ann. But I am neither the slave of love nor its dupe. Go to the bee, thou poet: consider her ways and be wise. By Heaven, Tavy, if women could do without our work, and we ate their children's bread instead of making it, they would kill us as the spider kills her mate or as the bees kill the drone. And they would be right if we were good for nothing but love.

OCTAVIUS: Ah, if we were only good enough for Love! There is nothing like Love: there is nothing else but Love: without it the world would be a dream of sordid horror.

TANNER: And this – this is the man who asks me to give him the hand of my ward! Tavy: I believe we were changed in our cradles, and that you are the real descendant of Don Juan.

OCTAVIUS: I beg you not to say anything like that to Ann.

TANNER: Dont be afraid. She has marked you for her own; and nothing will stop her now. You are doomed. [*Straker comes back with a newspaper.*] Here comes the New Man, demoralizing himself with a halfpenny paper as usual.

STRAKER: Now would you believe it, Mr Robinson, when we're out motoring we take in two papers: the Times for him, the Leader or the Echo for me. And do you think I ever see my paper? Not much. He grabs the Leader and leaves me to stodge myself with his Times.

OCTAVIUS: Are there no winners in the Times?

TANNER: Enry dont old with bettin, Tavy. Motor records are his weakness. Whats the latest?

STRAKER: Paris to Biskra at forty miles an hour average. not countin the Mediterranean.

TANNER: How many killed?

STRAKER: Two silly sheep. What does it matter? Sheep dont cost such a lot: they were glad to ave the price without the trouble o sellin em to the butcher. All the same, d'y'see, therell be a clamor agin it presently; and then the French Government'll stop it; and our chance'll be gone, see? Thats what makes me fairly mad: Mr Tanner wont do a good run while he can.

TANNER: Tavy: do you remember my uncle James?

OCTAVIUS: Yes, Why?

TANNER: Uncle James had a first rate cook: he couldnt digest anything except what she cooked. Well, the poor man was shy and hated society. But his cook was proud of her skill, and wanted to serve up dinners to princes and ambassadors. To prevent her from leaving him, that poor old man had to give a big dinner twice a month, and suffer agonies of awkwardness. Now here am I; and here is this chap Enry Straker, the New Man. I loathe travelling; but I rather like Enry. He cares for nothing but tearing along in a leather coat and goggles, with two inches of dust all over him, at sixty miles an hour and the risk of his life and mine. Except, of course, when he is lying on his back in the mud under the machine trying to find out where it has given way. Well, if I dont give him a thousand mile run at least once a fortnight I shall lose him. He will give me the sack and go to some American millionaire; and I shall have to put up with a nice respectful groom-gardener-amateur, who will touch his hat and know his place. I am Enry's slave, just as Uncle James was his cook's slave.

STRAKER [*exasperated*]: Garn! I wish I had a car that would go as fast as you can talk, Mr Tanner. What I say is that you lose money by a motor car unless you keep it workin. Might as well ave a pram and a nussmaid to wheel you in it as that car and me if you dont git the last inch out of us both.

TANNER [*soothingly*]: All right, Henry, all right. We'll go out for half an hour presently.

STRAKER [*in disgust*]: Arf an ahr! [*He returns to his machine; seats himself in it; and turns up a fresh page of his paper in search of more news.*]

OCTAVIUS: Oh, that reminds me. I have a note for you from Rhoda. [*He gives Tanner a note.*]

TANNER [*opening it*]: I rather think Rhoda is heading for a row with Ann. As a rule there is only one person an English girl hates more than she hates her eldest sister; and thats her mother. But Rhoda positively prefers her mother to Ann. She – [*indignantly*] Oh, I say!

OCTAVIUS: Whats the matter?

TANNER: Rhoda was to have come with me for a ride in the motor car. She says Ann has forbidden her to go out with me.

[*Straker suddenly begins whistling his favourite air with remarkable deliberation. Surprised by this burst of larklike melody, and jarred by a sardonic note in its cheerfulness, they turn and look inquiringly at him. But he is busy with his paper; and nothing comes of their movement.*]

OCTAVIUS [*recovering himself*]: Does she give any reason?

TANNER: Reason! An insult is not a reason. Ann forbids her to be alone with me on any occasion. Says I am not a fit person for a young girl to be with. What do you think of your paragon now?

OCTAVIUS: You must remember that she has a very heavy responsibility now that her father is dead. Mrs Whitefield is too weak to control Rhoda.

TANNER [*staring at him*]: In short, you agree with Ann.

OCTAVIUS: No; but I think I understand her. You must admit that your views are hardly suited for the formation of a young girl's mind and character.

TANNER: I admit nothing of the sort. I admit that the formation of a young lady's mind and character usually consists in telling her lies; but I object to the particular lie that I am in the habit of abusing the confidence of girls.

OCTAVIUS: Ann doesnt say that, Jack.

TANNER: What else does she mean?

STRAKER [*catching sight of Ann coming from the house*]: Miss Whitefield, gentlemen. [*He dismounts and strolls away down the avenue with the air of a man who knows he is no longer wanted.*]

ANN [*coming between Octavius and Tanner*]: Good morning, Jack. I have come to tell you that poor Rhoda has got one of her headaches and cannot go out with you today in the car. It is a cruel disappointment to her, poor child!

TANNER: What do you say now, Tavy?

OCTAVIUS: Surely you cannot misunderstand, Jack, Ann is shewing you the kindest consideration, even at the cost of deceiving you.

ANN: What do you mean?

TANNER: Would you like to cure Rhoda's headache, Ann?

ANN: Of course.

TANNER: Then tell her what you said just now; and add that you arrived about two minutes after I had received her letter and read it.

ANN: Rhoda has written to you!

TANNER: With full particulars.

OCTAVIUS: Never mind him, Ann. You were right – quite right. Ann was only doing her duty, Jack; and you know it. Doing it in the kindest way, too.

ANN [going to Octavius]: How kind you are, Tavy! How helpful! How well you understand!

[Octavius beams.]

TANNER: Ay: tighten the coils. You love her, Tavy, dont you?

OCTAVIUS: She knows I do.

ANN: Hush. For shame, Tavy!

TANNER: Oh, I give you leave. I am your guardian; and I commit you to Tavy's care for the next hour. I am off for a turn in the car.

ANN: No, Jack. I must speak to you about Rhoda. Ricky: will you go back to the house and entertain your American friend. He's rather on Mamma's hands so early in the morning. She wants to finish her housekeeping.

OCTAVIUS: I fly, dearest Ann [he kisses her hand].

ANN [tenderly]: Ricky Ticky Tavy!

[He looks at her with an eloquent blush, and runs off.]

TANNER [bluntly]: Now look here, Ann. This time youve landed yourself; and if Tavy were not in love with you past all salvation he'd have found out what an incorrigible liar you are.

ANN: You misunderstand, Jack. I didnt dare tell Tavy the truth.

TANNER: No: your daring is generally in the opposite

direction. What the devil do you mean by telling Rhoda that I am too vicious to associate with her? How can I ever have any human or decent relations with her again, now that you have poisoned her mind in that abominable way?

ANN: I know you are incapable of behaving badly –

TANNER: Then why did you lie to her?

ANN: I had to.

TANNER: Had to!

ANN: Mother made me.

TANNER [*his eye flashing*]: Ha! I might have known it. The mother! Always the mother!

ANN: It was that dreadful book of yours. You know how timid mother is. All timid women are conventional: we must be conventional, Jack, or we are so cruelly, so vilely misunderstood. Even you, who are a man, cannot say what you think without being misunderstood and vilified – yes: I admit it: I have had to vilify you. Do you want to have poor Rhoda misunderstood and vilified in the same way? Would it be right for mother to let her expose herself to such treatment before she is old enough to judge for herself?

TANNER: In short, the way to avoid misunderstanding is for everybody to lie and slander and insinuate and pretend as hard as they can. That is what obeying your mother comes to.

ANN: I love my mother, Jack.

TANNER [*working himself up into a sociological rage*]: Is that any reason why you are not to call your soul your own? Oh, I protest against this vile abjection of youth to age! Look at fashionable society as you know it. What does it pretend to be? An exquisite dance of nymphs. What is it? A horrible procession of wretched girls, each in the claws of a cynical, cunning, avaricious, disillusioned, ignorantly experienced, foul-minded old woman whom she calls mother, and whose duty it is to corrupt her mind and sell her to the highest bidder. Why do these unhappy slaves marry anybody, however old and vile, sooner than not marry at all? Because marriage is their only means of escape from these decrepit fiends who hide their selfish ambitions, their jealous hatreds of the young rivals who have supplanted them, under the mask of maternal duty and family affection. Such things are abominable: the voice of nature proclaims for the daughter a father's care and for the son a mother's. The law for father and son and mother and daughter is not the law of love: it is the law of revolution, of emancipation, of final supersession of the old and worn-out by the young and capable. I tell you, the first duty of manhood and womanhood is a Declaration of Independence: the man who pleads his father's authority is no man: the woman who pleads her mother's authority is unfit to bear citizens to a free people.

ANN [*watching him with quiet curiosity*]: I suppose you will go in seriously for politics some day, Jack.

TANNER [*heavily let down*]: Eh? What? Wh – ? [*Collecting his scattered wits*] What has that got to do with what I have been saying?

ANN: You talk so well.

TANNER: Talk! Talk! It means nothing to you but talk. Well, go back to your mother, and help her to poison Rhoda's imagination as she has poisoned yours. It is the tame elephants who enjoy capturing the wild ones.

ANN: I am getting on. Yesterday I was a boa constrictor: today I am an elephant.

TANNER: Yes. So pack your trunk and begone: I have no more to say to you.

ANN: You are so utterly unreasonable and impracticable. What can I do?

TANNER: Do! Break your chains. Go your way according to your own conscience and not according to your mother's. Get your mind clean and vigorous; and learn to enjoy a fast ride in a motor car instead of seeing nothing in it but an excuse for a detestable intrigue. Come with me to Marseilles and across to Algiers and to Biskra, at sixty miles an hour. Come right down to the Cape if you like. That will be a Declaration of Independence with a vengeance. You can write a book about it afterwards. That will finish your mother and make a woman of you.

ANN [*thoughtfully*]: I dont think there would be any harm in that, Jack. You are my guardian: you stand in my father's place, by his own wish. Nobody could say a word against our travelling together. It would be delightful: thank you a thousand times, Jack. I'll come.

TANNER [*aghast*]: Youll come!!!

ANN: Of course.

TANNER: But – [*he stops, utterly appalled; then resumes feebly*] No: look here, Ann: if theres no harm in it theres no point in doing it.

ANN: How absurd you are! You dont want to compromise me, do you?

TANNER: Yes: thats the whole sense of my proposal.

ANN: You are talking the greatest nonsense; and you know it. You would never do anything to hurt me.

TANNER: Well, if you dont want to be compromised, dont come.

ANN [*with simple earnestness*]: Yes, I will come, Jack, since you wish it. You are my guardian; and I think we ought to see more of one another and come to know one another better. [*Gratefully*] It's very thoughtful and very kind of you, Jack, to offer me this lovely holiday, especially after what I said about Rhoda. You really are good – much better than you think. When do we start?

TANNER: But –

[*The conversation is interrupted by the arrival of Mrs White-field from the house. She is accompanied by the American gentleman, and followed by Ramsden and Octavius.*

Hector Malone is an Eastern American; but he is not at all ashamed of his nationality. This makes English people of fashion think well of him, as of a young fellow who is manly enough to confess to an obvious disadvantage without any attempt to conceal or extenuate it. They feel that he ought not to be made to suffer for what is clearly not his fault, and make a

*point of being specially kind to him. His chivalrous manners
to women, and his elevated moral sentiments, being both
gratuitous and unusual, strike them as perhaps a little unfortunate; and though they find his vein of easy humor rather
amusing when it has ceased to puzzle them (as it does at
first), they have had to make him understand that he really must
not tell anecdotes unless they are strictly personal and scandalous, and also that oratory is an accomplishment which
belongs to a cruder stage of civilization than that in which his
migration has landed him. On these points Hector is not quite
convinced: he still thinks that the British are apt to make
merits of their stupidities, and to represent their various in-
capacities as points of good breeding. English life seems to
him to suffer from a lack of edifying rhetoric (which he calls
moral tone); English behaviour to shew a want of respect for
womanhood; English pronunciation to fail very vulgarly in
tackling such words as world, girl, bird, etc.; English society
to be plain spoken to an extent which stretches occasionally
to intolerable coarseness; and English intercourse to need enlivening by games and stories and other pastimes; so he does
not feel called upon to acquire these defects after taking great
pains to cultivate himself in a first rate manner before ven-
turing across the Atlantic. To this culture he finds English people
either totally indifferent, as they very commonly are to all
culture, or else politely evasive, the truth being that Hector's
culture is nothing but a state of saturation with our literary
exports of thirty years ago, reimported by him to be unpacked
at a moment's notice and hurled at the head of English literature, science, and art, at every conversational opportunity.
The dismay set up by these sallies encourages him in his belief
that he is helping to educate England. When he finds people
chattering harmlessly about Anatole France and Nietzsche, he
devastates them with Matthew Arnold, the Autocrat of the
Breakfast Table, and even Macaulay; and as he is devoutly
religious at bottom, he first leads the unwary, by humorous
irreverence, to leave popular theology out of account in discussing
moral questions with him, and then scatters them in confusion by demanding whether the carrying out of his ideals*

*of conduct was not the manifest object of God Almighty in
creating honest men and pure women. The engaging fresh-
ness of his personality and the dumbfoundering staleness of
his culture make it extremely difficult to decide whether he is
worth knowing; for whilst his company is undeniably pleasant
and enlivening, there is intellectually nothing new to be got
out of him, especially as he despises politics, and is careful not
to talk commercial shop, in which department he is probably
much in advance of his English capitalist friends. He gets
on best with romantic Christians of the amoristic sect: hence
the friendship which has sprung up between him and Octavius.
In appearance Hector is a neatly built young man of twenty-
four, with a short, smartly trimmed black beard, clear, well
shaped eyes, and an ingratiating vivacity of expression. He is,
from the fashionable point of view, faultlessly dressed. As he
comes along the drive from the house with Mrs Whitefield
he is sedulously making himself agreeable and entertaining,
and thereby placing on her slender wit a burden it is unable to
bear. An Englishman would let her alone, accepting boredom
and indifference as their common lot; and the poor lady wants
to be either let alone or let prattle about the things that
interest her.*

    *Ramsden strolls over to inspect the motor car. Octavius
joins Hector.]*

ANN [*pouncing on her mother joyously*]: Oh, mamma, what
do you think! Jack is going to take me to Nice in his
motor car. Isnt it lovely? I am the happiest person in
London.

TANNER [*desperately*]: Mrs Whitefield objects. I am sure
she objects. Doesn't she, Ramsden?

RAMSDEN: I should think it very likely indeed.

ANN: You dont object, do you, mother?

MRS WHITEFIELD: *I* object! Why should I? I think it
will do you good, Ann. [*Trotting over to Tanner*] I meant
to ask you to take Rhoda out for a run occasionally: she
is too much in the house; but it will do when you come
back.

TANNER: Abyss beneath abyss of perfidy!

ANN [*hastily, to distract attention from this outburst*]: Oh, I forgot: you have not met Mr Malone. Mr Tanner, my guardian: Mr Hector Malone.

HECTOR: Pleased to meet you, Mr Tanner. I should like to suggest an extension of the travelling party to Nice, if I may.

ANN: Oh, we're all coming. Thats understood, isnt it?

HECTOR: I also am the mawdest possessor of a motor car. If Miss Rawbnsn will allow me the privilege of taking her, my car is at her service.

OCTAVIUS: Violet!

[*General constraint.*]

ANN [*subduedly*]: Come, mother: we must leave them to talk over the arrangements. I must see to my travelling kit.

[*Mrs Whitefield looks bewildered; but Ann draws her discreetly away; and they disappear round the corner towards the house.*]

HECTOR: I think I may go so far as to say that I can depend on Miss Rawbnsn's consent.

[*Continued embarrassment.*]

OCTAVIUS: I'm afraid we must leave Violet behind. There are circumstances which make it impossible for her to come on such an expedition.

HECTOR [*amused and not at all convinced*]: Too American, eh? Must the young lady have a chaperone?

OCTAVIUS: It's not that, Malone – at least not altogether.

HECTOR: Indeed! May I ask what other objection applies?

TANNER [*impatiently*]: Oh, tell him, tell him. We shall never be able to keep the secret unless everybody knows what it is. Mr Malone: if you go to Nice with Violet, you go with another man's wife. She is married.

HECTOR [*thunderstruck*]: You dont tell me so!

TANNER: We do. In confidence.

RAMSDEN [*with an air of importance, lest Malone should suspect a misalliance*]: Her marriage has not yet been made known: she desires that it shall not be mentioned for the present.

HECTOR: I shall respect the lady's wishes. Would it be

indiscreet to ask who her husband is, in case I should have an opportunity of cawnsulting him about this trip?

TANNER: We dont know who he is.

HECTOR [*retiring into his shell in a very marked manner*]: In that case, I have no more to say.

[*They become more embarrassed than ever.*]

OCTAVIUS: You must think this very strange.

HECTOR: A little singular. Pardn mee for saying so.

RAMSDEN [*half apologetic, half huffy*]: The young lady was married secretly; and her husband has forbidden her, it seems, to declare his name. It is only right to tell you, since you are interested in Miss – er – in Violet.

OCTAVIUS [*sympathetically*]: I hope this is not a disappointment to you.

HECTOR [*softened, coming out of his shell again*]: Well: it is a blow. I can hardly understand how a man can leave his wife in such a position. Surely it's not customary. It's not manly. It's not considerate.

OCTAVIUS: We feel that, as you may imagine, pretty deeply.

RAMSDEN [*testily*]: It is some young fool who has not enough experience to know what mystifications of this kind lead to.

HECTOR [*with strong symptoms of moral repugnance*]: I hope so. A man need be very young and pretty foolish too to be excused for such conduct. You take a very lenient view, Mr Ramsden. Too lenient to my mind. Surely marriage should ennoble a man.

TANNER [*sardonically*]: Ha!

HECTOR: Am I to gather from that cachinnation that you dont agree with me, Mr Tanner?

TANNER [*drily*]: Get married and try. You may find it delightful for a while: you certainly wont find it ennobling. The greatest common measure of a man and a woman is not necessarily greater than the man's single measure.

HECTOR: Well, we think in America that a woman's morl number is higher than a man's, and that the purer nature of a woman lifts a man right out of himself, and makes him better than he was.

OCTAVIUS [*with conviction*]: So it does.

TANNER: No wonder American women prefer to live in Europe! It's more comfortable than standing all their lives on an altar to be worshipped. Anyhow, Violet's husband has not been ennobled. So whats to be done?

HECTOR [*shaking his head*]: I cant dismiss that man's cawnduct as lightly as you do, Mr Tanner. However, I'll say no more. Whoever he is, he's Miss Rawbnsn's husband; and I should be glad for her sake to think better of him.

OCTAVIUS [*touched; for he divines a secret sorrow*]: I'm very sorry, Malone. Very sorry.

HECTOR [*gratefully*]: Youre a good fellow, Rawbnsn. Thank you.

TANNER: Talk about something else. Violet's coming from the house.

HECTOR: I should esteem it a very great favor, gentlemen, if you would take the opportunity to let me have a few words with the lady alone. I shall have to cry off this trip; and it's rather a dullicate –

RAMSDEN [*glad to escape*]: Say no more. Come, Tanner. Come, Tavy. [*He strolls away into the park with Octavius and Tanner, past the motor car.*]

[*Violet comes down the avenue to Hector.*]

VIOLET: Are they looking?

HECTOR: No.

[*She kisses him.*]

VIOLET: Have you been telling lies for my sake?

HECTOR: Lying! Lying hardly describes it. I overdo it. I get carried away in an ecstasy of mendacity. Violet: I wish youd let me own up.

VIOLET [*instantly becoming serious and resolute*]: No, no, Hector: you promised me not to.

HECTOR: I'll keep my prawmis until you release me from it. But I feel mean, lying to those men, and denying my wife. Just dastardly.

VIOLET: I wish your father were not so unreasonable.

HECTOR: He's not unreasonable. He's right from his point of view. He has a prejudice against the English middle class.

VIOLET: It's too ridiculous. You know how I dislike saying such things to you, Hector; but if I were to – oh, well, no matter.

HECTOR: I know. If you were to marry the son of an English manufacturer of awffice furniture, your friends would consider it a misalliance. And here's my silly old dad, who is the biggest awffice furniture man in the world, would shew me the door for marrying the most perfect lady in England merely because she has no handle to her name. Of course it's just absurd. But I tell you, Violet, I dont like deceiving him. I feel as if I was stealing his money. Why wont you let me own up?

VIOLET: We cant afford it. You can be as romantic as you please about love, Hector; but you mustnt be romantic about money.

HECTOR [*divided between his uxoriousness and his habitual elevation of moral sentiment*]: Thats very English. [*Appealing to her impulsively*] Violet: dad's bound to find us out someday.

VIOLET: Oh yes, later on of course. But dont lets go over this every time we meet, dear. You promised –

HECTOR: All right, all right, I –

VIOLET [*not to be silenced*]: It is I and not you who suffer by this concealment; and as to facing a struggle and poverty and all that sort of thing I simply will not do it. It's too silly.

HECTOR: You shall not. I'll sort of borrow the money from my dad until I get on my own feet; and then I can own up and pay up at the same time.

VIOLET [*alarmed and indignant*]: Do you mean to work? Do you want to spoil our marriage?

HECTOR: Well, I dont mean to let marriage spoil my character. Your friend Mr Tanner has got the laugh on me a bit already about that; and –

VIOLET: The beast! I hate Jack Tanner.

HECTOR [*magnanimously*]: Oh, hee's all right: he only needs

the love of a good woman to ennoble him. Besides, he's
proposed a motoring trip to Nice; and I'm going to take you.

VIOLET: How jolly!

HECTOR: Yes; but how are we going to manage? You see,
theyve warned me off going with you, so to speak. Theyve
told me in cawnfidnce that youre married. Thats just the
most overwhelming cawnfidnce Ive ever been honored
with.

[*Tanner returns with Straker, who goes to his car.*]

TANNER: Your car is a great success, Mr Malone. Your
engineer is showing it off to Mr Ramsden.

HECTOR [*eagerly – forgetting himself*]: Lets come, Vi.

VIOLET [*coldly, warning him with her eyes*]: I beg your pardon,
Mr Malone: I did not quite catch –

HECTOR [*recollecting himself*]: I ask to be allowed the pleasure
of shewing you my little American steam car, Miss
Rawbnsn.

VIOLET: I shall be very pleased. [*They go off together down the
avenue.*]

TANNER: About this trip, Straker.

STRAKER [*preoccupied with the car*]: Yes?

TANNER: Miss Whitefield is supposed to be coming with me.

STRAKER: So I gather.

TANNER: Mr Robinson is to be one of the party.

STRAKER: Yes.

TANNER: Well, if you can manage so as to be a good deal
occupied with me, and leave Mr Robinson a good deal
occupied with Miss Whitefield, he will be deeply grateful
to you.

STRAKER [*looking round at him*]: Evidently.

TANNER: 'Evidently'! Your grandfather would have
simply winked.

STRAKER: My grandfather would have touched his at.

TANNER: And I would have given your good nice respectful
grandfather a sovereign.

STRAKER: Five shillins, more likely. [*He leaves the car and
approaches Tanner.*] What about the lady's views?

TANNER: She is just as willing to be left to Mr Robinson

as Mr Robinson is to be left to her. [*Straker looks at his principal with cool scepticism; then turns to the car whistling his favorite air.*] Stop that aggravating noise. What do you mean by it? [*Straker calmly resumes the melody and finishes it. Tanner politely hears it out before he again addresses Straker, this time with elaborate seriousness.*] Enry: I have ever been a warm advocate of the spread of music among the masses; but I object to your obliging the company whenever Miss Whitefield's name is mentioned. You did it this morning, too.

STRAKER [*obstinately*]: It's not a bit o use. Mr Robinson may as well give it up first as last.

TANNER: Why?

STRAKER: Garn! You know why. Course it's not my business; but you neednt start kiddin me about it.

TANNER: I am not kidding. I dont know why.

STRAKER [*cheerfully sulky*]: Oh, very well. All right. It aint my business.

TANNER [*impressively*]: I trust, Enry, that, as between employer and engineer, I shall always know how to keep my proper distance, and not intrude my private affairs on you. Even our business arrangements are subject to the approval of your Trade Union. But dont abuse your advantages. Let me remind you that Voltaire said that what was too silly to be said could be sung.

STRAKER: It wasnt Voltaire: it was Bow Mar Shay.

TANNER: I stand corrected: Beaumarchais of course. Now you seem to think that what is too delicate to be said can be whistled. Unfortunately your whistling, though melodious, is unintelligible. Come! theres nobody listening: neither my genteel relatives nor the secretary of your confounded Union. As man to man, Enry, why do you think that my friend has no chance with Miss Whitefield?

STRAKER: Cause she's arter summun else.

TANNER: Bosh! who else?

STRAKER: You.

TANNER: Me!!!

STRAKER: Mean to tell me you didn't know? Oh, come, Mr Tanner!

TANNER [*in fierce earnest*]: Are you playing the fool, or do you mean it?

STRAKER [*with a flash of temper*]: I'm not playin no fool. [*More coolly*] Why, it's as plain as the nose on your face. If you aint spotted that, you dont know much about these sort of things. [*Serene again*] Ex-cuse me, you know, Mr Tanner; but you asked me as man to man; and I told you as man to man.

TANNER [*wildly appealing to the heavens*]: Then I – *I* am the bee, the spider, the marked down victim, the destined prey.

STRAKER: I dunno about the bee and the spider. But the marked down victim, thats what you are and no mistake; and a jolly good job for you, too, I should say.

TANNER [*momentously*]: Henry Straker: the golden moment of your life has arrived.

STRAKER: What d'y' mean?

TANNER: That record to Biskra.

STRAKER [*eagerly*]: Yes?

TANNER: Break it.

STRAKER [*rising to the height of his destiny*]: D'y'mean it?

TANNER: I do.

STRAKER: When?

TANNER: Now. Is that machine ready to start?

STRAKER [*quailing*]: But you cant –

TANNER [*cutting him short by getting into the car*]: Off we go. First to the bank for money; then to my rooms for my kit; then to your rooms for your kit; then break the record from London to Dover or Folkestone; then across the Channel and away like mad to Marseilles, Gibraltar, Genoa, any port from which we can sail to a Mahometan country where men are protected from women.

STRAKER: Garn! youre kiddin.

TANNER [*resolutely*]: Stay behind then. If you wont come I'll do it alone. [*He starts the motor.*]

STRAKER [*running after him*]: Here! Mister! arf a mo! steady on! [*He scrambles in as the car plunges forward.*]

ACT THREE

Evening in the Sierra Nevada. Rolling slopes of brown with olive trees instead of apple trees in the cultivated patches, and occasional prickly pears instead of gorse and bracken in the wilds. Higher up, tall stone peaks and precipices, all handsome and distinguished. No wild nature here: rather a most aristocratic mountain landscape made by a fastidious artist-creator. No vulgar profusion of vegetation: even a touch of aridity in the frequent patches of stones: Spanish magnificence and Spanish economy everywhere.

Not very far north of a spot at which the high road over one of the passes crosses a tunnel on the railway from Malaga to Granada, is one of the mountain amphitheatres of the Sierra. Looking at it from the wide end of the horse-shoe, one sees, a little to the right, in the face of the cliff, a romantic cave which is really an abandoned quarry, and towards the left a little hill, commanding a view of the road, which skirts the amphitheatre on the left, maintaining its higher level on embankments and an occasional stone arch. On the hill, watching the road, is a man who is either a Spaniard or a Scotchman. Probably a Spaniard, since he wears the dress of a Spanish goatherd and seems at home in the Sierra Nevada, but very like a Scotchman for all that. In the hollow, on the slope leading to the quarry-cave, are about a dozen men who, as they recline at their ease round a heap of smouldering white ashes of dead leaf and brushwood, have an air of being conscious of themselves as picturesque scoundrels honoring the Sierra by using it as an effective pictorial background. As a matter of artistic fact they are not picturesque; and the mountains tolerate them as lions tolerate lice. An English policeman or Poor Law Guardian would recognize them as a selected band of tramps and ablebodied paupers.

This description of them is not wholly contemptuous. Whoever has intelligently observed the tramp, or visited the ablebodied ward of a workhouse, will admit that our social failures are not all drunkards and weaklings. Some of them are men who do not fit the class they were born into. Precisely the same qualities that make the

*educated gentleman an artist may make an uneducated manual
laborer an ablebodied pauper. There are men who fall helplessly into
the workhouse because they are good for nothing; but there are also
men who are there because they are strongminded enough to disregard
the social convention (obviously not a disinterested one on the part of
the ratepayer) which bids a man live by heavy and badly paid drudgery
when he has the alternative of walking into the workhouse, announcing himself as a destitute person, and legally compelling the
Guardians to feed, clothe, and house him better than he could feed,
clothe, and house himself without great exertion. When a man who is
born a poet refuses a stool in a stockbroker's office, and starves in a
garret, sponging on a poor landlady or on his friends and relatives
sooner than work against his grain; or when a lady, because she is a
lady, will face any extremity of parasitic dependence rather than take
a situation as cook or parlormaid, we make large allowances for
them. To such allowances the ablebodied pauper, and his nomadic
variant the tramp, are equally entitled.*

*Further, the imaginative man, if his life is to be tolerable to him,
must have leisure to tell himself stories, and a position which lends
itself to imaginative decoration. The ranks of unskilled labor offer no
such positions. We misuse our laborers horribly; and when a man
refuses to be misused, we have no right to say that he is refusing
honest work. Let us be frank in this matter before we go on with our
play; so that we may enjoy it without hypocrisy. If we were reasoning,
far-sighted people, four fifths of us would go straight to the Guardians
for relief, and knock the whole social system to pieces with most
beneficial reconstructive results. The reason we do not do this is
because we work like bees or ants, by instinct or habit, not reasoning
about the matter at all. Therefore when a man comes along who can
and does reason, and who, applying the Kantian test to his conduct,
can truly say to us, If everybody did as I do, the world would be
compelled to reform itself industrially, and abolish slavery and
squalor, which exist only because everybody does as you do, let us
honor that man and seriously consider the advisability of following
his example. Such a man is the ablebodied, ableminded pauper. Were
he a gentleman doing his best to get a pension or a sinecure instead of
sweeping a crossing, nobody would blame him for deciding that so*

long as the alternative lies between living mainly at the expense of the community and allowing the community to live mainly at his, it would be folly to accept what is to him personally the greater of the two evils.

We may therefore contemplate the tramps of the Sierra without prejudice, admitting cheerfully that our objects — briefly, to be gentlemen of fortune — are much the same as theirs, and the difference in our position and methods merely accidental. One or two of them, perhaps, it would be wiser to kill without malice in a friendly and frank manner; for there are bipeds, just as there are quadrupeds, who are too dangerous to be left unchained and unmuzzled; and these cannot fairly expect to have other men's lives wasted in the work of watching them. But as society has not the courage to kill them, and, when it catches them, simply wreaks on them some superstitious expiatory rites of torture and degradation, and then lets them loose with heightened qualifications for mischief, it is just as well that they are at large in the Sierra, and in the hands of a chief who looks as if he might possibly, on provocation, order them to be shot.

This chief, seated in the centre of the group on a squared block of stone from the quarry, is a tall strong man, with a striking cockatoo nose, glossy black hair, pointed beard, upturned moustache, and a Mephistophelean affectation which is fairly imposing, perhaps because the scenery admits of a larger swagger than Piccadilly, perhaps because of a certain sentimentality in the man which gives him that touch of grace which alone can excuse deliberate picturesqueness. His eyes and mouth are by no means rascally; he has a fine voice and a ready wit; and whether he is really the strongest man in the party or not, he looks it. He is certainly the best fed, the best dressed, and the best trained. The fact that he speaks English is not unexpected, in spite of the Spanish landscape; for with the exception of one man who might be guessed as a bullfighter ruined by drink, and one unmistakeable Frenchman, they are all cockney or American; therefore, in a land of cloaks and sombreros, they mostly wear seedy overcoats, woollen mufflers, hard hemispherical hats, and dirty brown gloves. Only a very few dress after their leader, whose broad sombrero with a cock's feather in the band, and voluminous cloak descending to his high boots, are as un-English as possible. None of them are armed;

and the ungloved ones keep their hands in their pockets because it is their national belief that it must be dangerously cold in the open air with the night coming on. (It is as warm an evening as any reasonable man could desire.)

Except the bullfighting inebriate there is only one person in the company who looks more than say, thirty-three. He is a small man with reddish whiskers, weak eyes, and the anxious look of a small tradesman in difficulties. He wears the only tall hat visible: it shines in the sunset with the sticky glow of some sixpenny patent hat reviver, often applied and constantly tending to produce a worse state of the original surface than the ruin it was applied to remedy. He has a collar and cuffs of celluloid; and his brown Chesterfield overcoat, with velvet collar, is still presentable. He is pre-eminently the respectable man of the party, and is certainly over forty, possibly over fifty. He is the corner man on the leader's right, opposite three men in scarlet ties on his left. One of these three is the Frenchman. Of the remaining two, who are both English, one is argumentative, solemn, and obstinate; the other rowdy and mischievous.

The chief, with a magnificent fling of the end of his cloak across his left shoulder, rises to address them. The applause which greets him shews that he is a favorite orator.

THE CHIEF: Friends and fellow brigands. I have a proposal to make to this meeting. We have now spent three evenings in discussing the question Have Anarchists or Social-Democrats the most personal courage? We have gone into the principles of Anarchism and Social-Democracy at great length. The cause of Anarchy has been ably represented by our one Anarchist, who doesnt know what Anarchism means [*laughter*] –

THE ANARCHIST [*rising*]: A point of order, Mendoza –

MENDOZA [*forcibly*]: No, by thunder: your last point of order took half an hour. Besides, Anarchists dont believe in order.

THE ANARCHIST [*mild, polite but persistent: he is, in fact, the respectable looking elderly man in the celluloid collar and cuffs*]: That is a vulgar error. I can prove –

MENDOZA: Order, order.

THE OTHERS [*shouting*]: Order, order. Sit down. Chair! Shut up.

[*The Anarchist is suppressed.*]

MENDOZA: On the other hand we have three Social-Democrats among us. They are not on speaking terms; and they have put before us three distinct and incompatible views of Social-Democracy.

THE THREE MEN IN SCARLET TIES: 1. Mr Chairman, I protest. A personal explanation. 2. It's a lie. I never said so. Be fair, Mendoza. 3. Je demande la parole. C'est absolument faux. C'est faux! faux!! faux!!! Assas-s-s-sin!!!!!!

MENDOZA: Order, order.

THE OTHERS: Order, order, order! Chair!

[*The Social-Democrats are suppressed.*]

MENDOZA: Now, we tolerate all opinions here. But after all, comrades, the vast majority of us are neither Anarchists nor Socialists, but gentlemen and Christians.

THE MAJORITY [*shouting assent*]: Hear, hear! So we are. Right.

THE ROWDY SOCIAL-DEMOCRAT [*smarting under suppression*]: You ain't no Christian. Youre a Sheeny, you are.

MENDOZA [*with crushing magnanimity*]: My friend: *I* am an exception to all rules. It is true that I have the honor to be a Jew; and when the Zionists need a leader to reassemble our race on its historic soil of Palestine, Mendoza will not be the last to volunteer [*sympathetic applause* – Hear, Hear, &c.]. But I am not a slave to any superstition. I have swallowed all the formulas, even that of Socialism; though, in a sense, once a Socialist, always a Socialist.

THE SOCIAL-DEMOCRATS: Hear, hear!

MENDOZA: But I am well aware that the ordinary man – even the ordinary brigand, who can scarcely be called an ordinary man [Hear, hear!] – is not a philosopher. Common sense is good enough for him; and in our business affairs common sense is good enough for me. Well, what is our business here in the Sierra Nevada, chosen by the Moors as the fairest spot in Spain? Is it to discuss abstruse questions of political economy? No: it is to hold up motor cars and secure a more equitable distribution of wealth.

THE SULKY SOCIAL-DEMOCRAT: All made by labor, mind you.

MENDOZA [*urbanely*]: Undoubtedly. All made by labor, and on its way to be squandered by wealthy vagabonds in the dens of vice that disfigure the sunny shores of the Mediterranean. We intercept that wealth. We restore it to circulation among the class that produced it and that chiefly needs it: the working class. We do this at the risk of our lives and liberties, by the exercise of the virtues of courage, endurance, foresight, and abstinence – especially abstinence. I myself have eaten nothing but prickly pears and broiled rabbit for three days.

THE SULKY SOCIAL-DEMOCRAT [*stubbornly*]: No more aint we.

MENDOZA [*indignantly*]: Have I taken more than my share?

THE SULKY SOCIAL-DEMOCRAT [*unmoved*]: Why should you?

THE ANARCHIST: Why should he not? To each according to his needs: from each according to his means.

THE FRENCHMAN [*shaking his fist at the Anarchist*]: Fumiste!

MENDOZA [*diplomatically*]: I agree with both of you.

THE GENUINELY ENGLISH BRIGANDS: Hear, hear! Bravo Mendoza!

MENDOZA: What I say is, let us treat one another as gentlemen, and strive to excel in personal courage only when we take the field.

THE ROWDY SOCIAL-DEMOCRAT [*derisively*]: Shikespear. [*A whistle comes from the goatherd on the hill. He springs up and points excitedly forward along the road to the north.*]

THE GOATHERD: Automobile! Automobile! [*He rushes down the hill and joins the rest, who all scramble to their feet.*]

MENDOZA [*in ringing tones*]: To arms! Who has the gun?

THE SULKY SOCIAL-DEMOCRAT [*handing a rifle to Mendoza*]: Here.

MENDOZA: Have the nails been strewn in the road?

THE ROWDY SOCIAL-DEMOCRAT: Two ahnces of em.

MENDOZA: Good! [*To the Frenchman*] With me, Duval. If the nails fail, puncture their tires with a bullet. [*He gives the rifle to Duval, who follows him up the hill. Mendoza produces an opera glass. The others hurry across to the road and disappear to the north.*]

MENDOZA [*on the hill, using his glass*]: Two only, a capitalist and his chauffeur. They look English.

DUVAL: Angliche! Aoh yess. Cochons! [*Handling the rifle*] Faut tirer, n'est-ce-pas?

MENDOZA: No: the nails have gone home. Their tire is down: they stop.

DUVAL [*shouting to the others*]: Fondez sur eux, nom de Dieu!

MENDOZA [*rebuking his excitement*]: Du calme, Duval: keep your hair on. They take it quietly. Let us descend and receive them.

[*Mendoza descends, passing behind the fire and coming forward, whilst Tanner and Straker, in their motoring goggles, leather coats, and caps, are led in from the road by the brigands.*]

TANNER: Is this the gentleman you describe as your boss? Does he speak English?

THE ROWDY SOCIAL-DEMOCRAT: Course e daz. Y' downt suppowz we Hinglishmen luts ahrselves be bossed by a bloomin Spenniard, do you?

MENDOZA [*with dignity*]: Allow me to introduce myself: Mendoza, President of the League of the Sierra! [*Posing loftily*] I am a brigand: I live by robbing the rich.

TANNER [*promptly*]: I am a gentleman: I live by robbing the poor. Shake hands.

THE ENGLISH SOCIAL-DEMOCRATS: Hear, hear!

[*General laughter and good humor. Tanner and Mendoza shake hands. The Brigands drop into their former places.*]

STRAKER: Ere! where do I come in?

TANNER [*introducing*]: My friend and chauffeur.

THE SULKY SOCIAL-DEMOCRAT [*suspiciously*]: Well, which is he? friend or show-foor? It makes all the difference, you know.

MENDOZA [*explaining*]: We should expect ransom for a

friend. A professional chauffeur is free of the mountains. He even takes a trifling percentage of his principal's ransom if he will honor us by accepting it.

STRAKER: I see. Just to encourage me to come this way again. Well, I'll think about it.

DUVAL [*impulsively rushing across to Straker*]: Mon frère! [*He embraces him rapturously and kisses him on both cheeks.*]

TRAKER [*disgusted*]: Ere, git aht: dont be silly. Who are you, pray?

DUVAL: Duval: Social-Democrat.

STRAKER: Oh, youre a Social-Democrat, are you?

THE ANARCHIST: He means that he has sold out to the parliamentary humbugs and the bourgeoisie. Compromise! that is his faith.

DUVAL [*furiously*]: I understand what he say. He say Bourgeois. He say Compromise. Jamais de la vie! Misérable menteur –

STRAKER: See here, Captain Mendoza, ah mach o this sort o thing do you put up with here? Are we avin a pleasure trip in the mountains, or are we at a Socialist meetin?

THE MAJORITY: Hear, hear! Shut up. Chuck it. Sit down, &c. &c. [*The Social-Democrats and the Anarchist are hustled into the background. Straker, after superintending this proceeding with satisfaction, places himself on Mendoza's left, Tanner being on his right.*]

MENDOZA: Can we offer you anything? Broiled rabbit and prickly pears –

TANNER: Thank you: we have dined.

MENDOZA [*to his followers*]: Gentlemen: business is over for the day. Go as you please until morning.

[*The Brigands disperse into groups lazily. Some go into the cave. Others sit down or lie down to sleep in the open. A few produce a pack of cards and move off towards the road; for it is now starlight, and they know that motor cars have lamps which can be turned to account for lighting a card party.*]

STRAKER [*calling after them*]: Dont none of you go fooling with that car, d'ye hear?

MENDOZA: No fear, Monsieur le Chauffeur. The first one we captured cured us of that.

STRAKER [*interested*]: What did it do?

MENDOZA: It carried three brave comrades of ours, who did not know how to stop it, into Granada, and capsized them opposite the police station. Since then we never touch one without sending for the chauffeur. Shall we chat at our ease?

TANNER: By all means.

[*Tanner, Mendoza, and Straker sit down on the turf by the fire. Mendoza delicately waives his presidential dignity, of which the right to sit on the squared stone block is the appanage, by sitting on the ground like his guests, and using the stone only as a support for his back.*]

MENDOZA: It is the custom in Spain always to put off business until tomorrow. In fact, you have arrived out of office hours. However, if you would prefer to settle the question of ransom at once, I am at your service.

TANNER: Tomorrow will do for me. I am rich enough to pay anything in reason.

MENDOZA [*respectfully, much struck by this admission*]: You are a remarkable man, sir. Our guests usually describe themselves as miserably poor.

TANNER: Pooh! Miserably poor people dont own motor cars.

MENDOZA: Precisely what we say to them.

TANNER: Treat us well: we shall not prove ungrateful.

STRAKER: No prickly pears and broiled rabbits, you know. Dont tell me you cant do us a bit better than that if you like.

MENDOZA: Wine, kids, milk, cheese, and bread can be procured for ready money.

STRAKER [*graciously*]: Now youre talkin.

TANNER: Are you all Socialists here, may I ask?

MENDOZA [*repudiating this humiliating misconception*]: Oh no, no, no: nothing of the kind, I assure you. We naturally have modern views as to the injustice of the existing distribution of wealth: otherwise we should lose our self-respect.

But nothing that you could take exception to, except two or three faddists.

TANNER: I had no intention of suggesting anything discreditable. In fact, I am a bit of a Socialist myself.

STRAKER [*drily*]: Most rich men are, I notice.

MENDOZA: Quite so. It has reached us, I admit. It is in the air of the century.

STRAKER: Socialism must be lookin up a bit if your chaps are taking to it.

MENDOZA: That is true, sir. A movement which is confined to philosophers and honest men can never exercise any real political influence: there are too few of them. Until a movement shews itself capable of spreading among brigands, it can never hope for a political majority.

TANNER: But are your brigands any less honest than ordinary citizens?

MENDOZA: Sir: I will be frank with you. Brigandage is abnormal. Abnormal professions attract two classes: those who are not good enough for ordinary bourgeois life and those who are too good for it. We are dregs and scum, sir: the dregs very filthy, the scum very superior.

STRAKER: Take care! some o the dregs'll hear you.

MENDOZA: It does not matter: each brigand thinks himself scum, and likes to hear the others called dregs.

TANNER: Come! you are a wit. [*Mendoza inclines his head, flattered.*] May one ask you a blunt question?

MENDOZA: As blunt as you please.

TANNER: How does it pay a man of your talent to shepherd such a flock as this on broiled rabbit and prickly pears? I have seen men less gifted, and I'll swear less honest, supping at the Savoy on foie gras and champagne.

MENDOZA: Pooh! they have all had their turn at the broiled rabbit, just as I shall have my turn at the Savoy. Indeed, I have had a turn there already – as waiter.

TANNER: A waiter! You astonish me!

MENDOZA [*reflectively*]: Yes: I, Mendoza of the Sierra, was a waiter. Hence, perhaps, my cosmopolitanism. [*With sudden intensity*] Shall I tell you the story of my life?

STRAKER [*apprehensively*]: If it aint too long, old chap —

TANNER [*interrupting him*]: Tsh-sh: you are a Philistine, Henry: you have no romance in you. [*To Mendoza*] You interest me extremely, President. Never mind Henry: he can go to sleep.

MENDOZA: The woman I loved —

STRAKER: Oh, this is a love story, is it? Right you are. Go on: I was only afraid you were going to talk about yourself.

MENDOZA: Myself! I have thrown myself away for her sake: that is why I am here. No matter: I count the world well lost for her. She had, I pledge you my word, the most magnificent head of hair I ever saw. She had humor; she had intellect; she could cook to perfection; and her highly strung temperament made her uncertain, incalculable, variable, capricious, cruel, in a word, enchanting.

STRAKER: A six shillin novel sort o woman, all but the cookin. Er name was Lady Gladys Plantagenet, wasnt it?

MENDOZA: No, sir: she was not an earl's daughter. Photography, reproduced by the half-tone process, has made me familiar with the appearance of the daughters of the English peerage; and I can honestly say that I would have sold the lot, faces, dowries, clothes, titles, and all, for a smile from this woman. Yet she was a woman of the people, a worker: otherwise — let me reciprocate your bluntness — I should have scorned her.

TANNER: Very properly. And did she respond to your love?

MENDOZA: Should I be here if she did? She objected to marry a Jew.

TANNER: On religious grounds?

MENDOZA: No: she was a freethinker. She said that every Jew considers in his heart that English people are dirty in their habits.

TANNER [*surprised*]: Dirty!

MENDOZA: It shewed her extraordinary knowledge of the world; for it is undoubtedly true. Our elaborate sanitary code makes us unduly contemptuous of the Gentile.

TANNER: Did you ever hear that, Henry?

STRAKER: Ive heard my sister say so. She was cook in a Jewish family once.

MENDOZA: I could not deny it; neither could I eradicate the impression it made on her mind. I could have got round any other objection; but no woman can stand a suspicion of indelicacy as to her person. My entreaties were in vain: she always retorted that she wasnt good enough for me, and recommended me to marry an accursed barmaid named Rebecca Lazarus, whom I loathed. I talked of suicide: she offered me a packet of beetle poison to do it with. I hinted at murder: she went into hysterics; and as I am a living man I went to America so that she might sleep without dreaming that I was stealing upstairs to cut her throat. In America I went out west and fell in with a man who was wanted by the police for holding up trains. It was he who had the idea of holding up motor cars in the South of Europe: a welcome idea to a desperate and disappointed man. He gave me some valuable introductions to capitalists of the right sort. I formed a syndicate; and the present enterprise is the result. I became leader, as the Jew always becomes leader, by his brains and imagination. But with all my pride of race I would give everything I possess to be an Englishman. I am like a boy: I cut her name on the trees and her initials on the sod. When I am alone I lie down and tear my wretched hair and cry Louisa –

STRAKER [*startled*]: Louisa!

MENDOZA: It is her name – Louisa – Louisa Straker –

TANNER: Straker!

STRAKER [*scrambling up on his knees most indignantly*]: Look here: Louisa Straker is my sister, see? Wot do you mean by gassing about her like this? Wotshe got to do with you?

MENDOZA: A dramatic coincidence! You are Enry, her favorite brother!

STRAKER: Oo are you callin Enry? What call have you to take a liberty with my name or with hers? For two pins I'd punch your fat edd, so I would.

MENDOZA [*with grandiose calm*]: If I let you do it, will you promise to brag of it afterwards to her? She will be reminded of her Mendoza: that is all I desire.

TANNER: This is genuine devotion, Henry. You should respect it.

STRAKER [*fiercely*]: Funk, more likely.

MENDOZA [*springing to his feet*]: Funk! Young man: I come of a famous family of fighters; and as your sister well knows, you would have as much chance against me as a perambulator against your motor car.

STRAKER [*secretly daunted, but rising from his knees with an air of reckless pugnacity*]: I aint afraid of you. With your Louisa! Louisa! Miss Straker is good enough for you, I should think.

MENDOZA: I wish you could persuade her to think so.

STRAKER [*exasperated*]: Here –

TANNER [*rising quickly and interposing*]: Oh come, Henry: even if you could fight the President you cant fight the whole League of the Sierra. Sit down again and be friendly. A cat may look at a king; and even a President of brigands may look at your sister. All this family pride is really very old fashioned.

STRAKER [*subdued, but grumbling*]: Let him look at her. But wot does he mean by making out that she ever looked at im? [*Reluctantly resuming his couch on the turf*] Ear him talk, one ud think she was keepin company with him. [*He turns his back on them and composes himself to sleep.*]

MENDOZA [*to Tanner, becoming more confidential as he finds himself virtually alone with a sympathetic listener in the still starlight of the mountains; for all the rest are asleep by this time*]: It was just so with her, sir. Her intellect reached forward into the twentieth century: her social prejudices and family affections reached back into the dark ages. Ah, sir, how the words of Shakespear seem to fit every crisis in our emotions!

> I loved Louisa: 40,000 brothers
> Could not with all their quantity of love
> Make up my sum.

And so on. I forget the rest. Call it madness if you will – infatuation. I am an able man, a strong man: in ten years I should have owned a first-class hotel. I met her; and – you see! – I am a brigand, an outcast. Even Shakespear cannot do justice to what I feel for Louisa. Let me read you some lines that I have written about her myself. However slight their literary merit may be, they express what I feel better than any casual words can. [*He produces a packet of hotel bills scrawled with manuscript, and kneels at the fire to decipher them, poking it with a stick to make it glow.*]

TANNER [*slapping him rudely on the shoulder*]: Put them in the fire, President.

MENDOZA [*startled*]: Eh?

TANNER: You are sacrificing your career to a monomania.

MENDOZA: I know it.

TANNER: No you dont. No man would commit such a crime against himself if he really knew what he was doing. How can you look round at these august hills, look up at this divine sky, taste this finely tempered air, and then talk like a literary hack on a second floor in Bloomsbury?

MENDOZA [*shaking his head*]: The Sierra is no better than Bloomsbury when once the novelty has worn off. Besides, these mountains make you dream of women – of women with magnificent hair.

TANNER: Of Louisa, in short. They will not make me dream of women, my friend: I am heartwhole.

MENDOZA: Do not boast until morning, sir. This is a strange country for dreams.

TANNER: Well, we shall see. Goodnight. [*He lies down and composes himself to sleep.*]

[*Mendoza, with a sigh, follows his example; and for a few moments there is peace in the Sierra. Then Mendoza sits up suddenly and says pleadingly to Tanner –*]

MENDOZA: Just allow me to read a few lines before you go to sleep. I should really like your opinion of them.

TANNER [*drowsily*]: Go on. I am listening.

MENDOZA: I saw thee first in Whitsun week
                    Louisa, Louisa –

TANNER [*rousing himself*]: My dear President, Louisa is a very pretty name; but it really doesnt rhyme well to Whitsun week.

MENDOZA: Of course not. Louisa is not the rhyme, but the refrain.

TANNER [*subsiding*]: Ah, the refrain. I beg your pardon. Go on.

MENDOZA: Perhaps you do not care for that one: I think you will like this better. [*He recites, in rich soft tones, and in slow time.*]

> Louisa, I love thee.
> I love thee, Louisa.
> Louisa, Louisa, Louisa, I love thee.
> One name and one phrase make my music, Louisa.
> Louisa, Louisa, Louisa, I love thee.
>
> Mendoza thy lover,
> Thy lover, Mendoza,
> Mendoza adoringly lives for Louisa.
> Theres nothing but that in the world for Mendoza.
> Louisa, Louisa, Mendoza adores thee.

[*Affected*] There is no merit in producing beautiful lines upon such a name. Louisa is an exquisite name, is it not?

TANNER [*all but asleep, responds with a faint groan.*]

MENDOZA: O wert thou, Louisa,
> The wife of Mendoza,
> Mendoza's Louisa, Louisa Mendoza,
> How blest were the life of Louisa's Mendoza!
> How painless his longing of love for Louisa!

That is real poetry – from the heart – from the heart of hearts. Dont you think it will move her?

[*No answer.*]

[*Resignedly*] Asleep, as usual. Doggerel to all the world: heavenly music to me! Idiot that I am to wear my heart on my sleeve! [*He composes himself to sleep, murmuring*]

Louisa, I love thee; I love thee, Louisa; Louisa, Louisa, Louisa, I –

[Straker snores; rolls over on his side; and relapses into sleep. Stillness settles on the Sierra; and the darkness deepens. The fire has again buried itself in white ash and ceased to glow. The peaks shew unfathomably dark against the starry firmament; but now the stars dim and vanish; and the sky seems to steal away out of the universe. Instead of the Sierra there is nothing: omnipresent nothing. No sky, no peaks, no light, no sound, no time nor space, utter void. Then somewhere the beginning of a pallor, and with it a faint throbbing buzz as a ghostly violoncello palpitating on the same note endlessly. A couple of ghostly violins presently take advantage of this bass

and therewith the pallor reveals a man in the void, an incorporeal but visible man, seated, absurdly enough, on nothing. For a moment he raises his head as the music passes him by. Then, with a heavy sigh, he droops in utter dejection; and the violins, discouraged, retrace their melody in despair and at last give it up, extinguished by wailings from uncanny wind instruments, thus:

It is all very odd. One recognizes the Mozartian strain; and on this hint, and by the aid of certain sparkles of violet light in the pallor, the man's costume explains itself as that of a Spanish nobleman of the XV-XVI century. Don Juan, of course; but where? why? how? Besides, in the brief lifting

of his face, now hidden by his hat brim, there was a curious suggestion of Tanner. A more critical, fastidious, handsome face, paler and colder, without Tanner's impetuous credulity and enthusiasm, and without a touch of his modern pluto-cratic vulgarity, but still a resemblance, even an identity. The name too: Don Juan Tenorio, John Tanner. Where on earth — or elsewhere — have we got to from the XX century and the Sierra?

Another pallor in the void, this time not violet, but a dis-agreeable smoky yellow. With it, the whisper of a ghostly clarionet turning this tune into infinite sadness:

The yellowish pallor moves: there is an old crone wandering in the void, bent and toothless; draped, as well as one can guess, in the coarse brown frock of some religious order. She wanders and wanders in her slow hopeless way, much as a wasp flies in its rapid busy way, until she blunders against the thing she seeks: companionship. With a sob of relief the poor old creature clutches at the presence of the man and addresses him in her dry unlovely voice, which can still express pride and resolution as well as suffering.]

THE OLD WOMAN: Excuse me; but I am so lonely; and this place is so awful.

DON JUAN: A new comer?

THE OLD WOMAN: Yes: I suppose I died this morning. I confessed; I had extreme unction; I was in bed with my family about me and my eyes fixed on the cross. Then it grew dark; and when the light came back it was this light by which I walk seeing nothing. I have wandered for hours in horrible loneliness.

DON JUAN [*sighing*]: Ah! you have not yet lost the sense of time. One soon does, in eternity.

THE OLD WOMAN: Where are we?

DON JUAN: In Hell.

THE OLD WOMAN [*proudly*]: Hell! I in Hell! How dare you?

DON JUAN [*unimpressed*]: Why not, Señora?

THE OLD WOMAN: You do not know to whom you are speaking. I am a lady, and a faithful daughter of the Church.

DON JUAN: I do not doubt it.

THE OLD WOMAN: But how then can I be in Hell? Purgatory, perhaps: I have not been perfect: who has? But Hell! oh, you are lying.

DON JUAN: Hell, Señora, I assure you; Hell at its best: that is, its most solitary – though perhaps you would prefer company.

THE OLD WOMAN: But I have sincerely repented; I have confessed –

DON JUAN: How much?

THE OLD WOMAN: More sins than I really committed. I loved confession.

DON JUAN: Ah, that is perhaps as bad as confessing too little. At all events, Señora, whether by oversight or intention, you are certainly damned, like myself; and there is nothing for it now but to make the best of it.

THE OLD WOMAN [*indignantly*]: Oh! and I might have been so much wickeder! All my good deeds wasted! It is unjust.

DON JUAN: No: you were fully and clearly warned. For your bad deeds, vicarious atonement, mercy without justice. For your good deeds, justice without mercy. We have many good people here.

THE OLD WOMAN: Were you a good man?

DON JUAN: I was a murderer.

THE OLD WOMAN: A murderer! Oh, how dare they send me to herd with murderers! I was not as bad as that: I was a good woman. There is some mistake: where can I have it set right?

DON JUAN: I do not know whether mistakes can be corrected here. Probably they will not admit a mistake even if they have made one.

THE OLD WOMAN: But whom can I ask?

DON JUAN: I should ask the Devil, Señora: he understands the ways of this place, which is more than I ever could.

THE OLD WOMAN: The Devil! *I* speak to the Devil!

DON JUAN: In Hell, Señora, the Devil is the leader of the best society.

THE OLD WOMAN: I tell you, wretch, I know I am not in Hell.

DON JUAN: How do you know?

THE OLD WOMAN: Because I feel no pain.

DON JUAN: Oh, then there is no mistake: you are intentionally damned.

THE OLD WOMAN: Why do you say that?

DON JUAN: Because Hell, Señora, is a place for the wicked. The wicked are quite comfortable in it: it was made for them. You tell me you feel no pain. I conclude you are one of those for whom Hell exists.

THE OLD WOMAN: Do you feel no pain?

DON JUAN: I am not one of the wicked, Señora; therefore it bores me, bores me beyond description, beyond belief.

THE OLD WOMAN: Not one of the wicked! You said you were a murderer.

DON JUAN: Only a duel. I ran my sword through an old man who was trying to run his through me.

THE OLD WOMAN: If you were a gentleman, that was not a murder.

DON JUAN: The old man called it murder, because he was, he said, defending his daughter's honor. By this he meant that because I foolishly fell in love with her and told her so, she screamed; and he tried to assassinate me after calling me insulting names.

THE OLD WOMAN: You were like all men. Libertines and murderers, all, all, all!

DON JUAN: And yet we meet here, dear lady.

THE OLD WOMAN: Listen to me. My father was slain by just such a wretch as you, in just such a duel, for just such a cause. I screamed: it was my duty. My father drew on my assailant: his honor demanded it. He fell: that was the reward of honor. I am here: in Hell, you tell me: that is the reward of duty. Is there justice in Heaven?

DON JUAN: No; but there is justice in Hell: Heaven is far above such idle human personalities. You will be welcome in Hell, Señora. Hell is the home of honor, duty, justice, and the rest of the seven deadly virtues. All the wickedness on earth is done in their name: where else but in Hell should they have their reward? Have I not told you that the truly damned are those who are happy in Hell?

THE OLD WOMAN: And are you happy here?

DON JUAN [*springing to his feet*]: No; and that is the enigma on which I ponder in darkness. Why am I here? I, who repudiated all duty, trampled honor underfoot, and laughed at justice!

THE OLD WOMAN: Oh, what do I care why you are here? Why am *I* here? I, who sacrificed all my inclinations to womanly virtue and propriety!

DON JUAN: Patience, lady: you will be perfectly happy and at home here. As saith the poet, 'Hell is a city much like Seville.'

THE OLD WOMAN: Happy! here! where I am nothing! where I am nobody!

DON JUAN: Not at all: you are a lady; and wherever ladies are is Hell. Do not be surprised or terrified: you will find everything here that a lady can desire, including devils who will serve you from sheer love of servitude, and magnify your importance for the sake of dignifying their service – the best of servants.

THE OLD WOMAN: My servants will be devils!

DON JUAN: Have you ever had servants who were not devils?

THE OLD WOMAN: Never: they were devils, perfect devils, all of them. But that is only a manner of speaking. I thought you meant that my servants here would be real devils.

DON JUAN: No more real devils than you will be a real

lady. Nothing is real here. That is the horror of damnation.

THE OLD WOMAN: Oh, this is all madness. This is worse than fire and the worm.

DON JUAN: For you, perhaps, there are consolations. For instance: how old were you when you changed from time to eternity?

THE OLD WOMAN: Do not ask me how old I was — as if I were a thing of the past. I am 77.

DON JUAN: A ripe age, Señora. But in Hell old age is not tolerated. It is too real. Here we worship Love and Beauty. Our souls being entirely damned, we cultivate our hearts. As a lady of 77, you would not have a single acquaintance in Hell.

THE OLD WOMAN: How can I help my age, man?

DON JUAN: You forget that you have left your age behind you in the realm of time. You are no more 77 than you are 7 or 17 or 27.

THE OLD WOMAN: Nonsense!

DON JUAN: Consider, Señora: was not this true even when you lived on earth? When you were 70, were you really older underneath your wrinkles and your grey hairs than when you were 30?

THE OLD WOMAN: No, younger: at 30 I was a fool. But of what use is it to feel younger and look older?

DON JUAN: You see, Señora, the look was only an illusion. Your wrinkles lied, just as the plump smooth skin of many a stupid girl of 17, with heavy spirits and decrepit ideas, lies about her age! Well, here we have no bodies: we see each other as bodies only because we learnt to think about one another under that aspect when we were alive; and we still think in that way, knowing no other. But we can appear to one another at what age we choose. You have but to will any of your old looks back, and back they will come.

THE OLD WOMAN: It cannot be true.

DON JUAN: Try.

THE OLD WOMAN: Seventeen!

DON JUAN: Stop. Before you decide, I had better tell you that these things are a matter of fashion. Occasionally we have a rage for 17; but it does not last long. Just at present the fashionable age is 40 – or say 37; but there are signs of a change. If you were at all good-looking at 27, I should suggest your trying that, and setting a new fashion.

THE OLD WOMAN: I do not believe a word you are saying. However, 27 be it. [*Whisk! the old woman becomes a young one, magnificently attired, and so handsome that in the radiance into which her dull yellow halo has suddenly lightened one might almost mistake her for Ann Whitefield.*]

DON JUAN: Doña Ana de Ulloa!

ANA: What? You know me!

DON JUAN: And you forget me!

ANA: I cannot see your face. [*He raises his hat.*] Don Juan Tenorio! Monster! You slew my father! even here you pursue me.

DON JUAN: I protest I do not pursue you. Allow me to withdraw [*going*].

ANA [*seizing his arm*]: You shall not leave me alone in this dreadful place.

DON JUAN: Provided my staying be not interpreted as pursuit.

ANA [*releasing him*]: You may well wonder how I can endure your presence. My dear, dear father!

DON JUAN: Would you like to see him?

ANA: My father here!!!

DON JUAN: No: he is in Heaven.

ANA: I knew it. My noble father! He is looking down on us now. What must he feel to see his daughter in this place, and in conversation with his murderer!

DON JUAN: By the way, if we should meet him –

ANA: How can we meet him? He is in Heaven.

DON JUAN: He condescends to look in upon us here from time to time. Heaven bores him. So let me warn you that if you meet him he will be mortally offended if you speak of me as his murderer! He maintains that he was a much better swordsman than I, and that if his foot had not slipped he would have killed me. No doubt he is right: I was not a good fencer. I never dispute the point; so we are excellent friends.

ANA: It is no dishonor to a soldier to be proud of his skill in arms.

DON JUAN: You would rather not meet him, probably.

ANA: How dare you say that?

DON JUAN: Oh, that is the usual feeling here. You may remember that on earth – though of course we never confessed it – the death of anyone we knew, even those we liked best, was always mingled with a certain satisfaction at being finally done with them.

ANA: Monster! Never, never.

DON JUAN [*placidly*]: I see you recognize the feeling. Yes: a funeral was always a festivity in black, especially the funeral of a relative. At all events, family ties are rarely kept up here. Your father is quite accustomed to this: he will not expect any devotion from you.

ANA: Wretch: I wore mourning for him all my life.

DON JUAN: Yes: it became you. But a life of mourning is one thing: an eternity of it quite another. Besides, here you are as dead as he. Can anything be more ridiculous than one dead person mourning for another? Do not look shocked, my dear Ana; and do not be alarmed: there is plenty of humbug in Hell (indeed there is hardly anything else); but the humbug of death and age and change is dropped because here we are all dead and all eternal. You will pick up our ways soon.

ANA: And will all the men call me their dear Ana?

DON JUAN: No. That was a slip of the tongue. I beg your pardon.

ANA [*almost tenderly*]: Juan: did you really love me when you behaved so disgracefully to me?

DON JUAN [*impatiently*]: Oh, I beg you not to begin talking about love. Here they talk of nothing else but love: its beauty, its holiness, its spirituality, its devil knows what! – excuse me; but it does so bore me. They dont know what theyre talking about: I do. They think they have achieved the perfection of love because they have no bodies. Sheer imaginative debauchery! Faugh!

ANA: Has even death failed to refine your soul, Juan? Has the terrible judgment of which my father's statue was the minister taught you no reverence?

DON JUAN: How is that very flattering statue, by the way? Does it still come to supper with naughty people and cast them into this bottomless pit?

ANA: It has been a great expense to me. The boys in the monastery school would not let it alone: the mischievous ones broke it; and the studious ones wrote their names on it. Three new noses in two years, and fingers without end. I had to leave it to its fate at last; and now I fear it is shockingly mutilated. My poor father!

DON JUAN: Hush! Listen! [*Two great chords rolling on syncopated waves of sound break forth. D minor and its dominant: a sound of dreadful joy to all musicians.*] Ha! Mozart's statue music. It is your father. You had better disappear until I prepare him. [*She vanishes.*]

[*From the void comes a living statue of white marble, designed to represent a majestic old man. But he waives his majesty with infinite grace; walks with a feather-like step; and makes every wrinkle in his war worn visage brim over with holiday joyousness. To his sculptor he owes a perfectly trained figure, which he carries erect and trim; and the ends of his moustache curl up, elastic as watchsprings, giving him an air which, but for its Spanish dignity, would be called jaunty. He is on the pleasantest terms with Don Juan. His voice, save for a much more distinguished intonation, is so like the voice of Roebuck Ramsden that it calls attention to the fact that they are not unlike one another in spite of their very different fashions of shaving.*]

DON JUAN: Ah, here you are, my friend. Why dont you learn to sing the splendid music Mozart has written for you?

THE STATUE: Unluckily he has written it for a bass voice. Mine is a counter tenor. Well: have you repented yet?

DON JUAN: I have too much consideration for you to repent, Don Gonzalo. If I did, you would have no excuse for coming from Heaven to argue with me.

THE STATUE: True. Remain obdurate, my boy. I wish I had killed you, as I should have done but for an accident. Then I should have come here: and you would have had a statue and a reputation for piety to live up to. Any news?

DON JUAN: Yes: your daughter is dead.

THE STATUE [*puzzled*]: My daughter? [*Recollecting*] Oh! the one you were taken with. Let me see: what was her name?

DON JUAN: Ana.

THE STATUE: To be sure: Ana. A goodlooking girl, if I recollect aright. Have you warned Whatshisname? her husband.

DON JUAN: My friend Ottavio? No: I have not seen him since Ana arrived.

[*Ana comes indignantly to light.*]

ANA: What does this mean? Ottavio here and your friend! And you, father, have forgotten my name. You are indeed turned to stone.

THE STATUE: My dear: I am so much more admired in marble than I ever was in my own person that I have retained the shape the sculptor gave me. He was one of the first men of his day: you must acknowledge that.

ANA: Father! Vanity! personal vanity! from you!

THE STATUE: Ah, you outlived that weakness, my daughter: you must be nearly 80 by this time. I was cut off (by an accident) in my 64th year, and am considerably your junior in consequence. Besides, my child, in this place, what our libertine friend here would call the farce of parental wisdom is dropped. Regard me, I beg, as a fellow creature, not as a father.

ANA: You speak as this villain speaks.

THE STATUE: Juan is a sound thinker, Ana. A bad fencer, but a sound thinker.

ANA [*horror creeping upon her*]: I begin to understand. These are devils, mocking me. I had better pray.

THE STATUE [*consoling her*]: No, no, no, my child: do not pray. If you do, you will throw away the main advantage of this place. Written over the gate here are the words 'Leave every hope behind, ye who enter.' Only think what a relief that is! For what is hope? A form of moral responsibility. Here there is no hope, and consequently no duty, no work, nothing to be gained by praying, nothing to be lost by doing what you like. Hell, in short, is a place where you have nothing to do but amuse yourself. [*Don Juan sighs deeply.*] You sigh, friend Juan; but if you dwelt in Heaven, as I do, you would realize your advantages.

DON JUAN: You are in good spirits today, Commander. You are positively brilliant. What is the matter?

THE STATUE: I have come to a momentous decision, my boy. But first, where is our friend the Devil? I must consult him in the matter. And Ana would like to make his acquaintance, no doubt.

ANA: You are preparing some torment for me.

DON JUAN: All that is superstition, Ana. Reassure yourself. Remember: the devil is not so black as he is painted.

THE STATUE: Let us give him a call.

[*At the wave of the statue's hand the great chords roll out again; but this time Mozart's music gets grotesquely adulterated with Gounod's. A scarlet halo begins to glow; and into it the Devil rises, very Mephistophelean, and not at all unlike Mendoza, though not so interesting. He looks older; is getting prematurely bald; and, in spite of an effusion of goodnature and friendliness, is peevish and sensitive when his advances are not reciprocated. He does not inspire much confidence in his powers of hard work or endurance, and is, on the whole, a disagreeably self-indulgent looking person: but he is clever and plausible, though perceptibly less well bred than the two other men, and enormously less vital than the woman.*]

THE DEVIL [*heartily*]: Have I the pleasure of again receiving a visit from the illustrious Commander of Calatrava? [*Coldly*] Don Juan, your servant. [*Politely*] And a strange lady? My respects, Señora.

ANA: Are you –

THE DEVIL [*bowing*]: Lucifer, at your service.

ANA: I shall go mad.

THE DEVIL [*gallantly*]: Ah, Señora, do not be anxious. You come to us from earth, full of the prejudices and terrors of that priest-ridden place. You have heard me ill spoken of; and yet, believe me, I have hosts of friends there.

ANA: Yes: you reign in their hearts.

THE DEVIL [*shaking his head*]: You flatter me, Señora; but you are mistaken. It is true that the world cannot get on without me; but it never gives me credit for that: in its heart it mistrusts and hates me. Its sympathies are all with misery, with poverty, with starvation of the body, and of the heart. I call on it to sympathize with joy, with love, with happiness, with beauty –

DON JUAN [*nauseated*]: Excuse me: I am going. You know I cannot stand this.

THE DEVIL [*angrily*]: Yes: I know that you are no friend of mine.

THE STATUE: What harm is he doing you, Juan? It seems to me that he was talking excellent sense when you interrupted him.

THE DEVIL [*warmly patting the statue's hand*]: Thank you, my friend: thank you. You have always understood me: he has always disparaged and avoided me.

DON JUAN: I have treated you with perfect courtesy.

THE DEVIL: Courtesy! What is courtesy? I care nothing for mere courtesy. Give me warmth of heart, true sincerity, the bond of sympathy with love and joy –

DON JUAN: You are making me ill.

THE DEVIL: There! [*Appealing to the statue*] You hear, sir! Oh, by what irony of fate was this cold selfish egotist sent to my kingdom, and you taken to the icy mansions of the sky!

THE STATUE: I cant complain. I was a hypocrite; and it served me right to be sent to Heaven.

THE DEVIL: Why, sir, do you not join us, and leave a

sphere for which your temperament is too sympathetic, your heart too warm, your capacity for enjoyment too generous?

THE STATUE: I have this day resolved to do so. In future, excellent Son of the Morning, I am yours. I have left Heaven for ever.

THE DEVIL [*again touching the marble hand*]: Ah, what an honor! What a triumph for our cause! Thank you, thank you. And now, my friend – I may call you so at last – could you not persuade him to take the place you have left vacant above?

THE STATUE [*shaking his head*]: I cannot conscientiously recommend anybody with whom I am on friendly terms to deliberately make himself dull and uncomfortable.

THE DEVIL: Of course not; but are you sure he would be uncomfortable? Of course you know best: you brought him here originally; and we had the greatest hopes of him. His sentiments were in the best taste of our best people. You remember how he sang? [*He begins to sing in a nasal operatic baritone, tremulous from an eternity of misuse in the French manner*]

> Vivan le femmine!
> Viva il buon vino!

THE STATUE [*taking up the tune an octave higher in his counter tenor*]:

> Sostegno e gloria
> D'umanità.

THE DEVIL: Precisely. Well, he never sings for us now.

DON JUAN: Do you complain of that? Hell is full of musical amateurs: music is the brandy of the damned. May not one lost soul be permitted to abstain?

THE DEVIL: You dare blaspheme against the sublimest of the arts!

DON JUAN [*with cold disgust*]: You talk like a hysterical woman fawning on a fiddler.

THE DEVIL: I am not angry. I merely pity you. You

have no soul; and you are unconscious of all that you lose. Now you, Señor Commander, are a born musician. How well you sing! Mozart would be delighted if he were still here; but he moped and went to Heaven. Curious how these clever men, whom you would have supposed born to be popular here, have turned out social failures, like Don Juan!

DON JUAN: I am really very sorry to be a social failure.

THE DEVIL: Not that we dont admire your intellect, you know. We do. But I look at the matter from your own point of view. You dont get on with us. The place doesnt suit you. The truth is, you have – I wont say no heart; for we know that beneath all your affected cynicism you have a warm one –

DON JUAN [*shrinking*]: Dont, please dont.

THE DEVIL [*nettled*]: Well, youve no capacity for enjoyment. Will that satisfy you?

DON JUAN: It is a somewhat less insufferable form of cant than the other. But if youll allow me, I'll take refuge, as usual, in solitude.

THE DEVIL: Why not take refuge in Heaven? Thats the proper place for you. [*To Ana*] Come, Señora! could you not persuade him for his own good to try change of air?

ANA: But can he go to Heaven if he wants to?

THE DEVIL: Whats to prevent him?

ANA: Can anybody – can *I* go to Heaven, if I want to?

THE DEVIL [*rather contemptuously*]: Certainly, if your taste lies that way.

ANA: But why doesnt everybody go to Heaven, then?

THE STATUE [*chuckling*]: *I* can tell you that, my dear. It's because Heaven is the most angelically dull place in all creation: thats why.

THE DEVIL: His excellency the Commander puts it with military bluntness; but the strain of living in Heaven is intolerable. There is a notion that I was turned out of it; but as a matter of fact nothing could have induced me to stay there. I simply left it and organized this place.

THE STATUE: I dont wonder at it. Nobody could stand an eternity of Heaven.

THE DEVIL: Oh, it suits some people. Let us be just, Commander: it is a question of temperament. I dont admire the heavenly temperament: I dont understand it: I dont know that I particularly want to understand it; but it takes all sorts to make a universe. There is no accounting for tastes: there are people who like it. I think Don Juan would like it.

DON JUAN: But – pardon my frankness – could you really go back there if you desired to; or are the grapes sour?

THE DEVIL: Back there! I often go back there. Have you never read the book of Job? Have you any canonical authority for assuming that there is any barrier between our circle and the other one?

ANA: But surely there is a great gulf fixed.

THE DEVIL: Dear lady: a parable must not be taken literally. The gulf is the difference between the angelic and the diabolic temperament. What more impassable gulf could you have? Think of what you have seen on earth. There is no physical gulf between the philosopher's class room and the bull ring; but the bull fighters do not come to the class room for all that. Have you ever been in the country where I have the largest following? England. There they have great racecourses, and also concert rooms where they play the classical compositions of his Excellency's friend Mozart. Those who go to the racecourses can stay away from them and go to the classical concerts instead if they like: there is no law against it; for Englishmen never will be slaves: they are free to do whatever the Government and public opinion allow them to do. And the classical concert is admitted to be a higher, more cultivated, poetic, intellectual, ennobling place than the racecourse. But do the lovers of racing desert their sport and flock to the concert room? Not they. They would suffer there all the weariness the Commander has suffered in Heaven. There is the great gulf of the parable between the two places. A mere physical gulf they could bridge; or at least I could bridge it for them (the earth is full of Devil's Bridges); but the gulf of dislike is impassable and eternal. And that is the only gulf that separates my friends here from those who are invidiously called the blest.

ANA: I shall go to Heaven at once.

THE STATUE: My child: one word of warning first. Let me complete my friend Lucifer's similitude of the classical concert. At every one of these concerts in England you will find rows of weary people who are there, not because they really like classical music, but because they think they ought to like it. Well, there is the same thing in Heaven. A number of people sit there in glory, not because they are happy, but because they think they owe it to their position to be in Heaven. They are almost all English.

THE DEVIL: Yes: the Southerners give it up and join me just as you have done. But the English really do not seem to know when they are thoroughly miserable. An Englishman thinks he is moral when he is only uncomfortable.

THE STATUE: In short, my daughter, if you go to Heaven without being naturally qualified for it, you will not enjoy yourself there.

ANA: And who dares say that I am not naturally qualified for it? The most distinguished princes of the Church have never questioned it. I owe it to myself to leave this place at once.

THE DEVIL [offended]: As you please, Señora. I should have expected better taste from you.

ANA: Father: I shall expect you to come with me. You cannot stay here. What will people say?

THE STATUE: People! Why, the best people are here – princes of the Church and all. So few go to Heaven, and so many come here, that the blest, once called a heavenly host, are a continually dwindling minority. The saints, the fathers, the elect of long ago are the cranks, the faddists, the outsiders of today.

THE DEVIL: It is true. From the beginning of my career I knew that I should win in the long run by sheer weight of public opinion, in spite of the long campaign of misrepresentation and calumny against me. At bottom the universe is a constitutional one; and with such a majority as mine I cannot be kept permanently out of office.

DON JUAN: I think, Ana, you had better stay here.

ANA [*jealously*]: You do not want me to go with you.

DON JUAN: Surely you do not want to enter Heaven in the company of a reprobate like me.

ANA: All souls are equally precious. You repent, do you not?

DON JUAN: My dear Ana, you are silly. Do you suppose Heaven is like earth, where people persuade themselves that what is done can be undone by repentance; that what is spoken can be unspoken by withdrawing it; that what is true can be annihilated by a general agreement to give it the lie? No: Heaven is the home of the masters of reality: that is why I am going thither.

ANA: Thank you: I am going to Heaven for happiness. I have had quite enough of reality on earth.

DON JUAN: Then you must stay here; for Hell is the home of the unreal and of the seekers for happiness. It is the only refuge from Heaven, which is, as I tell you, the home of the masters of reality, and from earth, which is the home of the slaves of reality. The earth is a nursery in which men and women play at being heroes and heroines, saints and sinners; but they are dragged down from their fool's paradise by their bodies: hunger and cold and thirst, age and decay and disease, death above all, make them slaves of reality: thrice a day meals must be eaten and digested: thrice a century a new generation must be engendered: ages of faith, of romance, and of science are all driven at last to have but one prayer. 'Make me a healthy animal.' But here you escape this tyranny of the flesh; for here you are not an animal at all: you are a ghost, an appearance, an illusion, a convention, deathless, ageless: in a word, bodiless. There are no social questions here, no political questions, no religious questions, best of all, perhaps, no sanitary questions. Here you call your appearance beauty, your emotions love, your sentiments heroism, your aspirations virtue, just as you did on earth; but here there are no hard facts to contradict you, no ironic contrast of your needs with your pretensions, no human comedy, nothing but a perpetual romance, a universal melodrama. As our German friend put it in his poem, 'the poetically nonsensical here is good sense; and the Eternal Feminine draws us ever upward and on' – without us getting a step farther. And yet you want to leave this paradise!

ANA: But if Hell be so beautiful as this, how glorious must Heaven be!

[*The Devil, the Statue, and Don Juan all begin to speak at once in violent protest; then stop, abashed.*]

DON JUAN: I beg your pardon.

THE DEVIL: Not at all. I interrupted you.

THE STATUE: You were going to say something.

DON JUAN: After you, gentlemen.

THE DEVIL [*to Don Juan*]: You have been so eloquent on the advantages of my dominions that I leave you to do equal justice to the drawbacks of the alternative establishment.

DON JUAN: In Heaven, as I picture it, dear lady, you live and work instead of playing and pretending. You face things as they are; you escape nothing but glamor; and your steadfastness and your peril are your glory. If the play still goes on here and on earth, and all the world is a stage, Heaven is at least behind the scenes. But Heaven cannot be described by metaphor. Thither I shall go presently, because there I hope to escape at last from lies and from the tedious, vulgar pursuit of happiness, to spend my eons in contemplation –

THE STATUE: Ugh!

DON JUAN: Señor Commander: I do not blame your disgust: a picture gallery is a dull place for a blind man. But even as you enjoy the contemplation of such romantic mirages as beauty and pleasure; so would I enjoy the contemplation of that which interests me above all things: namely, Life: the force that ever strives to attain greater power of contemplating itself. What made this brain of mine, do you think? Not the need to move my limbs; for a rat with half my brains moves as well as I. Not merely the need to do, but the need to know what I do, lest in my blind efforts to live I should be slaying myself.

THE STATUE: You would have slain yourself in your blind efforts to fence but for my foot slipping, my friend.

DON JUAN: Audacious ribald: your laughter will finish in hideous boredom before morning.

THE STATUE: Ha ha! Do you remember how I frightened you when I said something like that to you from my pedestal in Seville? It sounds rather flat without my trombones.

DON JUAN: They tell me it generally sounds flat with them, Commander.

ANA: Oh, do not interrupt with these frivolities, father. Is there nothing in Heaven but contemplation, Juan?

DON JUAN: In the Heaven I seek, no other joy! But there is the work of helping Life in its struggle upward. Think of how it wastes and scatters itself, how it raises up obstacles to itself and destroys itself in its ignorance and blindness. It needs a brain, this irresistible force, lest in its ignorance it should resist itself. What a piece of work is man! says the poet. Yes; but what a blunderer! Here is the highest miracle of organization yet attained by life, the most intensely alive thing that exists, the most conscious of all the organisms; and yet, how wretched are his brains! Stupidity made sordid and cruel by the realities learnt from toil and poverty: Imagination resolved to starve sooner than face these realities, piling up illusions to hide them, and calling itself cleverness, genius! And each accusing the other of its own defect: Stupidity accusing Imagination of folly, and Imagination accusing Stupidity of ignorance: whereas, alas! Stupidity has all the knowledge, and Imagination all the intelligence.

THE DEVIL: And a pretty kettle of fish they make of it between them. Did I not say, when I was arranging that affair of Faust's, that all Man's reason has done for him is to make him beastlier than any beast. One splendid body is worth the brains of a hundred dyspeptic, flatulent philosophers.

DON JUAN: You forget that brainless magnificence of body has been tried. Things immeasurably greater than man in every respect but brain have existed and perished. The megatherium, the ichthyosaurus have paced the earth with seven-league steps and hidden the day with cloud vast wings. Where are they now? Fossils in museums, and so few and imperfect at that, that a knuckle bone or a tooth of one of them is prized beyond the lives of a thousand soldiers. These things lived and wanted to live: but for lack of brains they did not know how to carry out their purpose, and so destroyed themselves.

THE DEVIL: And is Man any the less destroying himself for all this boasted brain of his? Have you walked up and down upon the earth lately? I have; and I have examined Man's wonderful inventions. And I tell you that in the arts of life man invents nothing; but in the arts of death he outdoes Nature herself, and produces by chemistry and machinery all the slaughter of plague, pestilence, and famine. The peasant I tempt today eats and drinks what was eaten and drunk by the peasants of ten thousand years ago; and the house he lives in has not altered as much in a thousand centuries as the fashion of a lady's bonnet in a score of weeks. But when he goes out to slay, he carries a marvel of mechanism that lets loose at the touch of his finger all the hidden molecular energies, and leaves the javelin, the arrow, the blowpipe of his fathers far behind. In the arts of peace Man is a bungler. I have seen his cotton factories and the like, with machinery that a greedy dog could have invented if it had wanted money instead of food. I know his clumsy typewriters and bungling locomotives and tedious bicycles: they are toys compared to the Maxim gun, the submarine torpedo boat. There is nothing in Man's industrial machinery but his greed and sloth: his heart is in his weapons. This marvellous force of Life of which you boast is a force of Death: Man measures his strength by his destructiveness. What is his religion? An excuse for hating me. What is his law? An excuse for hanging you. What is his morality? Gentility! an excuse for consuming without producing. What is his art? An excuse for gloating over pictures of slaughter. What are his politics? Either the worship of a despot because a despot can kill, or parliamentary cock-fighting. I spent an evening lately in a certain celebrated legislature, and heard the pot lecturing the kettle for its blackness, and ministers answering questions. When I left I chalked up on the door the old nursery saying 'Ask no questions and you will be told no lies.' I bought a sixpenny family magazine, and found it full of pictures of young men shooting and stabbing one another. I saw a man die: he was a London bricklayer's laborer with seven children. He left seventeen pounds club money; and his wife spent it all on his funeral and went into the workhouse with the children next day. She would not have spent sevenpence on her children's schooling: the law had to force her to let them be taught gratuitously; but on death she spent all she had. Their imagination glows, their energies rise up at the idea of death, these people: they love it; and the more horrible it is the more they enjoy it. Hell is a place far above their comprehension: they derive their notion of it from two of the greatest fools that ever lived, an Italian and an Englishman. The Italian described it as a place of mud, frost, filth, fire, and venomous serpents: all torture. This ass, when he was not lying about me, was maundering about some woman whom he saw once in the street. The Englishman described me as being expelled from Heaven by cannons and gunpowder; and to this day every Briton believes that the whole of his silly story is in the Bible. What else he says I do not know; for it is all in a long poem which neither I nor anyone else ever succeeded in wading through. It is the same in everything. The highest form of literature is the tragedy, a play in which everybody is murdered at the end. In the old chronicles you read of earthquakes and pestilences, and are told that these shewed the power and majesty of God and the littleness of Man. Nowadays the chronicles describe battles. In a battle two bodies of men shoot at one another with bullets and explosive shells until one body runs away, when the others chase the fugitives on horseback and cut them to pieces as they fly. And this, the chronicle concludes, shews the greatness and majesty of empires, and the littleness of the vanquished. Over such battles the people run about the streets yelling with delight, and egg their Governments on to spend hundreds of millions of money in the slaughter, whilst the strongest Ministers dare not spend an extra penny in the pound against the poverty and pestilence through which they themselves daily walk. I could give you a thousand instances; but they all come to the same thing: the power that governs the earth is not the power of Life but of Death; and the inner need that has nerved Life to the effort of organizing itself into the human being is not the need for higher life but for a more efficient engine of destruction. The plague, the famine, the earthquake, the tempest were too spasmodic in their action ; the tiger and crocodile were too easily satiated and not cruel enough: something more constantly, more ruthlessly, more ingeniously destructive was needed; and that something was Man, the inventor of the rack, the stake, the gallows, the electric chair; of sword and gun and poison gas: above all, of justice, duty, patriotism, and all the other isms by which even those who are clever enough to be humanely disposed are persuaded to become the most destructive of all the destroyers.

DON JUAN: Pshaw! all this is old. Your weak side, my diabolic friend, is that you have always been a gull: you take Man at his own valuation. Nothing would flatter him more than your opinion of him. He loves to think of himself as bold and bad. He is neither one nor the other: he is only a coward. Call him tyrant, murderer, pirate, bully; and he will adore you, and swagger about with the consciousness of having the blood of the old sea kings in his veins. Call him liar and thief; and he will only take an action against you for libel. But call him coward; and he will go mad with rage: he will face death to outface that stinging truth. Man gives every reason for his conduct save one, every excuse for his crimes save one, every plea for his safety save one: and that one is his cowardice. Yet all his civilization is founded on his cowardice, on his abject tameness, which he calls his respectability. There are limits to what a mule or an ass will stand; but Man will suffer himself to be degraded until his vileness becomes so loathsome to his oppressors that they themselves are forced to reform it.

THE DEVIL: Precisely. And these are the creatures in whom you discover what you call a Life Force!

DON JUAN: Yes; for now comes the most surprising part of the whole business.

THE STATUE: What's that?

DON JUAN: Why, that you can make any of these cowards brave by simply putting an idea into his head.

THE STATUE: Stuff! As an old soldier I admit the cowardice: it's as universal as sea sickness, and matters just as little. But that about putting an idea into a man's head is stuff and nonsense. In a battle all you need to make you fight is a little hot blood and the knowledge that it's more dangerous to lose than to win.

DON JUAN: That is perhaps why battles are so useless. But men never really overcome fear until they imagine they are fighting to further a universal purpose – fighting for an idea, as they call it. Why was the Crusader braver than the pirate? Because he fought, not for himself, but for the Cross. What force was it that met him with a valor as reckless as his own? The force of men who fought, not for themselves, but for Islam. They took Spain from us, though we were fighting for our very hearths and homes; but when we, too, fought for that mighty idea, a Catholic Church, we swept them back to Africa.

THE DEVIL [*ironically*]: What! you a Catholic, Señor Don Juan! A devotee! My congratulations.

THE STATUE [*seriously*]: Come, come! as a soldier, I can listen to nothing against the Church.

DON JUAN: Have no fear, Commander: this idea of a Catholic Church will survive Islam, will survive the Cross, will survive even that vulgar pageant of incompetent schoolboyish gladiators which you call the Army.

THE STATUE: Juan: you will force me to call you to account for this.

DON JUAN: Useless: I cannot fence. Every idea for which Man will die will be a Catholic idea. When the Spaniard learns at last that he is no better than the Saracen, and his prophet no better than Mahomet, he will arise, more Catholic than ever, and die on a barricade across the filthy slum he starves in, for universal liberty and equality.

THE STATUE: Bosh!

DON JUAN: What you call bosh is the only thing men dare die for. Later on, Liberty will not be Catholic enough: men will die for human perfection, to which they will sacrifice all their liberty gladly.

THE DEVIL: Ay: they will never be at a loss for an excuse for killing one another.

DON JUAN: What of that? It is not death that matters, but the fear of death. It is not killing and dying that degrades us, but base living, and accepting the wages and profits of degradation. Better ten dead men than one live slave or his master. Men shall yet rise up, father against son and brother against brother, and kill one another for the great Catholic idea of abolishing slavery.

THE DEVIL: Yes, when the Liberty and Equality of which you prate shall have made free white Christians cheaper in the labor market than black heathen slaves sold by auction at the block.

DON JUAN: Never fear! the white laborer shall have his

146

turn too. But I am not now defending the illusory forms the great ideas take. I am giving you examples of the fact that this creature Man, who in his own selfish affairs is a coward to the backbone, will fight for an idea like a hero. He may be abject as a citizen; but he is dangerous as a fanatic. He can only be enslaved whilst he is spiritually weak enough to listen to reason. I tell you, gentlemen, if you can shew a man a piece of what he now calls God's work to do, and what he will later on call by many new names, you can make him entirely reckless of the consequences to himself personally.

ANA: Yes: he shirks all his responsibilities, and leaves his wife to grapple with them.

THE STATUE: Well said, daughter. Do not let him talk you out of your common sense.

THE DEVIL: Alas! Señor Commander, now that we have got on to the subject of Woman, he will talk more than ever. However, I confess it is for me the one supremely interesting subject.

DON JUAN: To a woman, Señora, man's duties and responsibilities begin and end with the task of getting bread for her children. To her, Man is only a means to the end of getting children and rearing them.

ANA: Is that your idea of a woman's mind? I call it cynical and disgusting animalism.

DON JUAN: Pardon me, Ana: I said nothing about a woman's whole mind. I spoke of her view of Man as a separate sex. It is no more cynical than her view of herself as above all things a Mother. Sexually, Woman is Nature's contrivance for perpetuating its highest achievement. Sexually, Man is Woman's contrivance for fulfilling Nature's behest in the most economical way. She knows by instinct that far back in the evolutional process she invented him, differentiated him, created him in order to produce something better than the single-sexed process can produce. Whilst he fulfils the purpose for which she made him, he is welcome to his dreams, his follies, his ideals, his heroisms, provided that the keystone of them all is the worship of woman, of motherhood, of the family, of the hearth. But how rash and dangerous it was to invent a separate creature whose sole function was her own impregnation! For mark what has happened. First Man has multiplied on her hands until there are as many men as women; she that she has been unable to employ for her purposes more than a fraction of the immense energy she has left at his disposal by saving him the exhausting labor of gestation. This superfluous energy has gone to his brain and to his muscle. He has become too strong to be controlled by her bodily, and too imaginative and mentally vigorous to be content with mere self-reproduction. He has created civilization without consulting her, taking her domestic labor for granted as the foundation of it.

ANA: That is true, at all events.

THE DEVIL: Yes; and this civilization! what is it, after all?

DON JUAN: After all, an excellent peg to hang your cynical commonplaces on; but before all, it is an attempt on Man's part to make himself something more than the mere instrument of Woman's purpose. So far, the result of Life's continual effort not only to maintain itself, but to achieve higher and higher organization and completer self-consciousness, is only, at best, a doubtful campaign between its forces and those of Death and Degeneration. The battles in this campaign are mere blunders, mostly won, like actual military battles, in spite of the commanders.

THE STATUE: That is a dig at me. No matter: go on, go on.

DON JUAN: It is a dig at a much higher power than you, Commander. Still, you must have noticed in your profession that even a stupid general can win battles when the enemy's general is a little stupider.

THE STATUE [very seriously]: Most true, Juan, most true. Some donkeys have amazing luck.

DON JUAN: Well, the Life Force is stupid; but it is not so stupid as the forces of Death and Degeneration. Besides, these are in its pay all the time. And so Life wins, after a fashion. What mere copiousness of fecundity can supply and mere greed preserve, we possess. The survival of whatever form of civilization can produce the best rifle and the best fed riflemen is assured.

THE DEVIL: Exactly! the survival, not of the most effective means of Life but of the most effective means of Death. You always come back to my point, in spite of your wrigglings and evasions and sophistries, not to mention the intolerable length of your speeches.

DON JUAN: Oh, come! who began making long speeches? However, if I overtax your intellect, you can leave us and seek the society of love and beauty and the rest of your favorite boredoms.

THE DEVIL [*much offended*]: This is not fair, Don Juan, and not civil. I am also on the intellectual plane. Nobody can appreciate it more than I do. I am arguing fairly with you, and, I think, successfully refuting you. Let us go on for another hour if you like.

DON JUAN: Good: let us.

THE STATUE: Not that I see any prospect of your coming to any point in particular, Juan. Still, since in this place, instead of merely killing time we have to kill eternity, go ahead by all means.

DON JUAN [*somewhat impatiently*]: My point, you marble-headed old masterpiece, is only a step ahead of you. Are we agreed that Life is a force which has made innumerable experiments in organizing itself; that the mammoth and the man, the mouse and the megatherium, the flies and the fleas and the Fathers of the Church, are all more or less successful attempts to build up that raw force into higher and higher individuals, the ideal individual being omnipotent, omniscient, infallible, and withal completely, unilludedly self-conscious: in short, a god?

THE DEVIL: I agree, for the sake of argument.

THE STATUE: I agree, for the sake of avoiding argument.

ANA: I most emphatically disagree as regards the Fathers of the Church; and I must beg you not to drag them into the argument.

DON JUAN: I did so purely for the sake of alliteration, Ana;

and I shall make no further allusion to them. And now, since we are, with that exception, agreed so far, will you not agree with me further that Life has not measured the success of its attempts at godhead by the beauty or bodily perfection of the result, since in both these respects the birds, as our friend Aristophanes long ago pointed out, are so extraordinarily superior, with their power of flight and their lovely plumage, and, may I add, the touching poetry of their loves and nestings, that it is inconceivable that Life, having once produced them, should, if love and beauty were her object, start off on another line and labor at the clumsy elephant and the hideous ape, whose grandchildren we are?

ANA: Aristophanes was a heathen; and you, Juan, I am afraid, are very little better.

THE DEVIL: You conclude, then, that Life was driving at clumsiness and ugliness?

DON JUAN: No, perverse devil that you are, a thousand times no. Life was driving at brains – at its darling object: an organ by which it can attain not only self-consciousness but self-understanding.

THE STATUE: This is metaphysics, Juan. Why the devil should – [to the Devil] I beg your pardon.

THE DEVIL: Pray dont mention it. I have always regarded the use of my name to secure additional emphasis as a high compliment to me. It is quite at your service, Commander.

THE STATUE: Thank you: thats very good of you. Even in Heaven, I never quite got out of my old military habits of speech. What I was going to ask Juan was why Life should bother itself about getting a brain. Why should it want to understand itself? Why not be content to enjoy itself?

DON JUAN: Without a brain, Commander, you would enjoy yourself without knowing it, and so lose all the fun.

THE STATUE: True, most true. But I am quite content with brain enough to know that I'm enjoying myself. I dont want to understand why. In fact, I'd rather not. My experience is that one's pleasures dont bear thinking about.

DON JUAN: That is why intellect is so unpopular. But to Life, the force behind the Man, intellect is a necessity, because without it he blunders into death. Just as Life, after ages of struggle, evolved that wonderful bodily organ the eye, so that the living organism could see where it was going and what was coming to help or threaten it, and thus avoid a thousand dangers that formerly slew it, so it is evolving today a mind's eye that shall see, not the physical world, but the purpose of Life, and thereby enable the individual to work for that purpose instead of thwarting and baffling it by setting up shortsighted personal aims as at present. Even as it is, only one sort of man has ever been happy, has ever been universally respected among all the conflicts of interests and illusions.

THE STATUE: You mean the military man.

DON JUAN: Commander: I do not mean the military man. When the military man approaches, the world locks up its spoons and packs off its womankind. No: I sing, not arms and the hero, but the philosophic man: he who seeks in contemplation to discover the inner will of the world, in invention to discover the means of fulfilling that will, and in action to do that will by the so-discovered means. Of all other sorts of men I declare myself tired. They are tedious failures. When I was on earth, professors of all sorts prowled round me feeling for an unhealthy spot in me on which they could fasten. The doctors of medicine bade me consider what I must do to save my body, and offered me quack cures for imaginary diseases. I replied that I was not a hypochondriac; so they call me Ignoramus and went their way. The doctors of divinity bade me consider what I must do to save my soul; but I was not a spiritual hypochondriac any more than a bodily one, and would not trouble myself about that either; so they called me Atheist and went their way. After them came the politician, who said there was only one purpose in nature, and that was to get him into parliament. I told him I did not care whether he got into parliament or not; so he called me Mugwump and went his way. Then came the romantic man, the Artist, with his love songs and his paintings and his poems; and with him I had great delight for many years, and some profit; for I cultivated my senses for his sake; and his songs taught me to hear better, his paintings to see better, and his poems to feel more deeply. But he led me at last into the worship of Woman.

ANA: Juan!

DON JUAN: Yes: I came to believe that in her voice was all the music of the song, in her face all the beauty of the painting, and in her soul all the emotion of the poem.

ANA: And you were disappointed, I suppose. Well, was it her fault that you attributed all these perfections to her?

DON JUAN: Yes, partly. For with a wonderful instinctive cunning, she kept silent and allowed me to glorify her: to mistake my own visions, thoughts, and feelings for hers. Now my friend the romantic man was often too poor or too timid to approach those women who were beautiful or refined enough to seem to realize his ideal; and so he went to his grave believing in his dream. But I was more favored by nature and circumstance. I was of noble birth and rich; and when my person did not please, my conversation flattered, though I generally found myself fortunate in both.

THE STATUE: Coxcomb!

DON JUAN: Yes; but even my coxcombry pleased. Well, I found that when I had touched a woman's imagination, she would allow me to persuade myself that she loved me; but when my suit was granted she never said 'I am happy; my love is satisfied': she always said, first, 'At last, the barriers are down,' and second, 'When will you come again?'

ANA: That is exactly what men say.

DON JUAN: I protest I never said it. But all women say it. Well, these two speeches always alarmed me; for the first meant that the lady's impulse had been solely to throw down my fortifications and gain my citadel; and the second openly announced that henceforth she regarded me as her property, and counted my time as already wholly at her disposal.

THE DEVIL: That is where your want of heart came in.

THE STATUE [*shaking his head*]: You shouldnt repeat what a woman says, Juan.

ANA [*severely*]: It should be sacred to you.

THE STATUE: Still, they certainly do say it. I never minded the barriers; but there was always a slight shock about the other, unless one was very hard hit indeed.

DON JUAN: Then the lady, who had been happy and idle enough before, became anxious, preoccupied with me, always intriguing, conspiring, pursuing, watching, waiting, bent wholly on making sure of her prey: I being the prey, you understand. Now this was not what I had bargained for. It may have been very proper and very natural; but it was not music, painting, poetry, and joy incarnated in a beautiful woman. I ran away from it. I ran away from it very often: in fact I became famous for running away from it.

ANA: Infamous, you mean.

DON JUAN: I did not run away from you. Do you blame me for running away from the others?

ANA: Nonsense, man. You are talking to a woman of 77 now. If you had had the chance, you would have run away from me too – if I had let you. You would not have found it so easy with me as with some of the others. If men will not be faithful to their home and their duties, they must be made to be. I daresay you all want to marry lovely incarnations of music and painting and poetry. Well, you cant have them, because they dont exist. If flesh and blood is not good enough for you, you must go without: thats all. Women have to put up with flesh-and-blood husbands – and little enough of that too, sometimes; and you will have to put up with flesh-and-blood wives. [*The Devil looks dubious. The Statue makes a wry face.*] I see you dont like that, any of you; but it's true, for all that; so if you dont like it, you can lump it.

DON JUAN: My dear lady, you have put my whole case

against romance into a few sentences. That is just why I turned my back on the romantic man with the artist nature, as he called his infatuation. I thanked him for teaching me to use my eyes and ears; but I told him that his beauty worshipping and happiness hunting and woman idealizing was not worth a dump as a philosophy of life; so he called me Philistine and went his way.

ANA: It seems that Woman taught you something, too, with all her defects.

DON JUAN: She did more: she interpreted all the other teaching for me. Ah, my friends, when the barriers were down for the first time, what an astounding illumination! I had been prepared for infatuation, for intoxication, for all the illusions of love's young dream; and lo! never was my perception clearer, nor my criticism more ruthless. The most jealous rival of my mistress never saw every blemish in her more keenly than I. I was not duped: I took her without chloroform.

ANA: But you did take her.

DON JUAN: That was the revelation. Up to that moment I had never lost the sense of being my own master; never consciously taken a single step until my reason had examined and approved it. I had come to believe that I was a purely rational creature: a thinker! I said, with the foolish philosopher, 'I think; therefore I am.' It was Woman who taught me to say 'I am; therefore I think.' And also 'I would think more; therefore I must be more.'

THE STATUE: This is extremely abstract and metaphysical, Juan. If you would stick to the concrete, and put your discoveries in the form of entertaining anecdotes about your adventures with women, your conversation would be easier to follow.

DON JUAN: Bah! what need I add? Do you not understand that when I stood face to face with Woman, every fibre in my clear critical brain warned me to spare her and save myself. My morals said No. My conscience said No. My chivalry and pity for her said No. My prudent regard for myself said No. My ear, practised on a thousand songs and symphonies; my eye, exercised on a thousand paintings; tore her voice, her features, her color to shreds. I caught all those tell-tale resemblances to her father and mother by which I knew what she would be like in thirty years' time. I noted the gleam of gold from a dead tooth in the laughing mouth: I made curious observations of the strange odors of the chemistry of the nerves. The visions of my romantic reveries, in which I had trod the plains of Heaven with a deathless, ageless creature of coral and ivory, deserted me in that supreme hour. I remembered them and desperately strove to recover their illusion; but they now seemed the emptiest of inventions: my judgment was not to be corrupted: my brain still said No on every issue. And whilst I was in the act of framing my excuse to the lady, Life seized me and threw me into her arms as a sailor throws a scrap of fish into the mouth of a seabird.

THE STATUE: You might as well have gone without thinking such a lot about it, Juan. You are like all the clever men: you have more brains than is good for you.

THE DEVIL: And were you not the happier for the experience, Señor Don Juan?

DON JUAN: The happier, no: the wiser, yes. That moment introduced me for the first time to myself, and, through myself, to the world. I saw then how useless it is to attempt to impose conditions on the irresistible force of Life; to preach prudence, careful selection, virtue, honor, chastity –

ANA: Don Juan: a word against chastity is an insult to me.

DON JUAN: I say nothing against your chastity, Señora, since it took the form of a husband and twelve children. What more could you have done had you been the most abandoned of women?

ANA: I could have had twelve husbands and no children: thats what I could have done, Juan. And let me tell you that that would have made all the difference to the earth which I replenished.

THE STATUE: Bravo Ana! Juan, you are floored, quelled, annihilated.

DON JUAN: No: for though that difference is the true essential difference – Doña Ana has, I admit, gone straight to the real point – yet it is not a difference of love or chastity, or even constancy; for twelve children by twelve different husbands would have replenished the earth perhaps more effectively. Suppose my friend Ottavio had died when you were thirty, you would never have remained a widow: you were too beautiful. Suppose the successor of Ottavio had died when you were forty, you would still have been irresistible; and a woman who marries twice marries three times if she becomes free to do so. Twelve lawful children borne by one highly respectable lady to three different fathers is not impossible nor condemned by public opinion. That such a lady may be more law abiding than the poor girl whom we used to spurn into the gutter for bearing one unlawful infant is no doubt true; but dare you say she is less self-indulgent?

ANA: She is more virtuous: that is enough for me.

DON JUAN: In that case, what is virtue but the Trade Unionism of the married? Let us face the facts, dear Ana. The Life Force respects marriage only because marriage is a contrivance of its own to secure the greatest number of children and the closest care of them. For honor, chastity, and all the rest of your moral figments it cares not a rap. Marriage is the most licentious of human institutions –

ANA: Juan!

THE STATUE [protesting]: Really! –

DON JUAN [determinedly]: I say the most licentious of human institutions: that is the secret of its popularity. And a woman seeking a husband is the most unscrupulous of all the beasts of prey. The confusion of marriage with morality has done more to destroy the conscience of the human race than any other single error. Come, Ana! do not look shocked: you know better than any of us that marriage is a mantrap baited with simulated accomplishments and delusive idealizations. When your sainted mother, by dint of scoldings and punishments, forced you to learn how to play half a dozen pieces on the spinet – which she hated as much as you did – had she any other purpose than to delude your suitors into the belief that your husband would have in his home an angel who would fill it with melody, or at least play him to sleep after dinner? You married my friend Ottavio: well, did you ever open the spinet from the hour when the Church united him to you?

ANA: You are a fool, Juan. A young married woman has something else to do than sit at the spinet without any support for her back; so she gets out of the habit of playing.

DON JUAN: Not if she loves music. No: believe me, she only throws away the bait when the bird is in the net.

ANA [*bitterly*]: And men, I suppose, never throw off the mask when their bird is in the net. The husband never becomes negligent, selfish, brutal – oh, never!

DON JUAN: What do these recriminations prove, Ana? Only that the hero is as gross an imposture as the heroine.

ANA: It is all nonsense: most marriages are perfectly comfortable.

DON JUAN: 'Perfectly' is a strong expression, Ana. What you mean is that sensible people make the best of one another. Send me to the galleys and chain me to the felon whose number happens to be next before mine; and I must accept the inevitable and make the best of the companionship. Many such companionships, they tell me, are touchingly affectionate; and most are at least tolerably friendly. But that does not make a chain a desirable ornament nor the galleys an abode of bliss. Those who talk most about the blessings of marriage and the constancy of its vows are the very people who declare that if the chain were broken and the prisoners left free to choose, the whole social fabric would fly asunder. You cannot have the argument both ways. If the prisoner is happy, why lock him in? If he is not, why pretend that he is?

ANA: At all events, let me take an old woman's privilege again, and tell you flatly that marriage peoples the world and debauchery does not.

DON JUAN: How if a time come when this shall cease to be true? Do you not know that where there is a will there is a way? that whatever Man really wishes to do he will finally discover a means of doing? Well, you have done your best, you virtuous ladies, and others of your way of thinking, to bend Man's mind wholly towards honorable love as the highest good, and to understand by honorable love romance and beauty and happiness in the possession of beautiful, refined, delicate, affectionate women. You have taught women to value their own youth, health, shapeliness, and refinement above all things. Well, what place have squalling babies and household cares in this exquisite paradise of the senses and emotions? Is it not the inevitable end of it all that the human will shall say to the human brain: Invent me a means by which I can have love, beauty, romance, emotion, passion, without their wretched penalties, their expenses, their worries, their trials, their illnesses and agonies and risks of death, their retinue of servants and nurses and doctors and schoolmasters.

THE DEVIL: All this, Señor Don Juan, is realized here in my realm.

DON JUAN: Yes, at the cost of death. Man will not take it at that price: he demands the romantic delights of your Hell whilst he is still on earth. Well, the means will be found: the brain will not fail when the will is in earnest. The day is coming when great nations will find their numbers dwindling from census to census; when the six roomed villa will rise in price above the family mansion; when the viciously reckless poor and the stupidly pious rich will delay the extinction of the race only by degrading it; whilst the boldly prudent, the thriftily selfish and ambitious, the imaginative and poetic, the lovers of money and solid comfort, the worshippers of success, of art, and of love, will all oppose to the Force of Life the device of sterility.

THE STATUE: That is all very eloquent, my young friend; but if you had lived to Ana's age, or even to mine, you would have learned that the people who get rid of the fear of poverty and children and all the other family troubles, and devote themselves to having a good time of it, only leave their minds free for the fear of old age and ugliness and impotence and death. The childless laborer is more tormented by his wife's idleness and her constant demands for amusement and distraction than he could be by twenty children; and his wife is more wretched than he. I have had my share of vanity; for as a young man I was admired by women; and as a statue I am praised by art critics. But I confess that had I found nothing to do in the world but wallow in these delights I should have cut my throat. When I married Ana's mother – or perhaps, to be strictly correct, I should rather say when I at last gave in and allowed Ana's mother to marry me – I knew that I was planting thorns in my pillow, and that marriage for me, a swaggering young officer thitherto unvanquished, meant defeat and capture.

ANA [*scandalized*]: Father!

THE STATUE: I am sorry to shock you, my love; but since Juan has stripped every rag of decency from the discussion I may as well tell the frozen truth.

ANA: Hmf! I suppose I was one of the thorns.

THE STATUE: By no means: you were often a rose. You see, your mother had most of the trouble you gave.

DON JUAN: Then may I ask, Commander, why you have left Heaven to come here and wallow, as you express it, in sentimental beatitudes which you confess would once have driven you to cut your throat?

THE STATUE [*struck by this*]: Egad, thats true.

THE DEVIL [*alarmed*]: What! You are going back from your word! [*To Don Juan*] And all your philosophizing has been nothing but a mask for proselytizing! [*To the Statue*] Have you forgotten already the hideous dulness from which I am offering you a refuge here? [*To Don Juan*] And does your demonstration of the approaching sterilization and extinction of mankind lead to anything better than making the most of those pleasures of art and love which you yourself admit refined you, elevated you, developed you?

DON JUAN: I never demonstrated the extinction of mankind. Life cannot will its own extinction either in its blind amorphous state or in any of the forms into which it has organized itself. I had not finished when His Excellency interrupted me.

THE STATUE: I begin to doubt whether you ever will finish, my friend. You are extremely fond of hearing yourself talk.

DON JUAN: True; but since you have endured so much, you may as well endure to the end. Long before this sterilization which I described becomes more than a clearly foreseen possibility, the reaction will begin. The great central purpose of breeding the race: ay, breeding it to heights now deemed superhuman: that purpose which is now hidden in a mephitic cloud of love and romance and prudery and fastidiousness, will break through into clear sunlight as a purpose no longer to be confused with the gratification of personal fancies, the impossible realization of boys' and girls' dreams of bliss, or the need of older people for companionship or money. The plain-spoken marriage services of the vernacular Churches will no longer be abbreviated and half suppressed as indelicate. The sober decency, earnestness, and authority of their declaration of the real purpose of marriage will be honored and accepted, whilst their romantic vowings and pledging and until-death-do-us-partings and the like will be expunged as unbearable frivolities. Do my sex the justice to admit, Señora, that we have always recognized that the sex relation is not a personal or friendly relation at all.

ANA: Not a personal or friendly relation! What relation is more personal? more sacred? more holy?

DON JUAN: Sacred and holy, if you like, Ana, but not personally friendly. Your relation to God is sacred and holy: dare you call it personally friendly? In the sex relation the universal creative energy, of which the parties are both the helpless agents, overrides and sweeps away all personal consideration, and dispenses with all personal relations. The pair may be utter strangers to one another, speaking different languages, differing in race and color, in age and disposition, with no bond between them but a possibility of that fecundity for the sake of which the Life Force throws them into one another's arms at the exchange of a glance. Do we not recognize this by allowing marriages to be made by parents without consulting the woman? Have you not often expressed your disgust at the immorality of the English nation, in which women and men of noble birth become acquainted and court each other like peasants? And how much does even the peasant know of his bride or she of him before he engages himself? Why, you would not make a man your lawyer or your family doctor on so slight an acquaintance as you would fall in love with and marry him!

ANA: Yes, Juan, we know the libertine's philosophy. Always ignore the consequences to the woman.

DON JUAN: The consequences, yes: they justify her fierce grip of the man. But surely you do not call that attachment a sentimental one. As well call the policeman's attachment to his prisoner a love relation.

ANA: You see you have to confess that marriage is necessary, though, according to you, love is the slightest of all human relations.

DON JUAN: How do you know that it is not the greatest of all human relations? far too great to be a personal matter. Could your father have served his country if he had refused to kill any enemy of Spain unless he personally hated him? Can a woman serve her country if she refuses to marry any man she does not personally love? You know it is not so: the woman of noble birth marries as the man of noble birth fights, on political and family grounds, not on personal ones.

THE STATUE [*impressed*]: A very clever point that, Juan: I must think it over. You are really full of ideas. How did you come to think of this one?

DON JUAN: I learnt it by experience. When I was on earth, and made those proposals to ladies which, though universally condemned, have made me so interesting a hero of legend, I was not infrequently met in some such way as this. The lady would say that she would countenance my advances, provided they were honorable. On inquiring what that proviso meant, I found that it meant that I proposed to get possession of her property if she had any, or to undertake her support for life if she had not; that I desired her continual companionship, counsel, and conversation to the end of my days, and would take a most solemn oath to be always enraptured by them: above all, that I would turn my back on all other women for ever for her sake. I did not object to these conditions because they were exorbitant and inhuman: it was their extraordinary irrelevance that prostrated me. I invariably replied with perfect frankness that I had never dreamt of any of these things; that unless the lady's character and intellect were equal or superior to my own, her conversation must degrade and her counsel mislead me; that her constant companionship might, for all I knew, become intolerably tedious to me; that I could not answer for my feelings for a week in advance, much less to the end of my life; that to cut me off from all natural and unconstrained intercourse with half my fellowcreatures would narrow and warp me if I submitted to it, and, if not, would bring me under the curse of clandestinity; that, finally, my proposals to her were wholly unconnected with any of these matters, and were the outcome of a perfectly simple impulse of my manhood towards her womanhood.

ANA: You mean that it was an immoral impulse.

DON JUAN: Nature, my dear lady, is what you call immoral. I blush for it; but I cannot help it. Nature is a pandar, Time a wrecker, and Death a murderer. I have always preferred to stand up to those facts and build institutions on their recognition. You prefer to propitiate the three devils by proclaiming their chastity, their thrift, and their loving kindness; and to base your institutions on these flatteries. Is it any wonder that the institutions do not work smoothly?

THE STATUE: What used the ladies to say, Juan?

DON JUAN: Oh, come! Confidence for confidence. First tell me what you used to say to the ladies.

THE STATUE: I! Oh, I swore that I would be faithful to the death; that I should die if they refused me; that no woman could ever be to me what she was –

ANA: She! Who?

THE STATUE: Whoever it happened to be at the time, my dear. I had certain things I always said. One of them was that even when I was eighty, one white hair of the woman I loved would make me tremble more than the thickest gold tress from the most beautiful young head. Another was that I could not bear the thought of anyone else being the mother of my children.

DON JUAN [*revolted*]: You old rascal!

THE STATUE [*stoutly*]: Not a bit; for I really believed it with all my soul at the moment. I had a heart: not like you. And it was this sincerity that made me successful.

DON JUAN: Sincerity! To be fool enough to believe a ramping, stamping, thumping lie: that is what you call sincerity! To be so greedy for a woman that you deceive yourself in your eagerness to deceive her: sincerity, you call it!

THE STATUE: Oh, damn your sophistries! I was a man in love, not a lawyer. And the women loved me for it, bless them!

DON JUAN: They made you think so. What will you say when I tell you that though I played the lawyer so callously, they made me think so too? I also had my moments of infatuation in which I gushed nonsense and believed it. Sometimes the desire to give pleasure by saying beautiful things so rose in me on the flood of emotion that I said them recklessly. At other times I argued against myself with a devilish coldness that drew tears. But I found it just as hard to escape when I was cruel as when I was kind. When the lady's instinct was set on me, there was nothing for it but lifelong servitude or flight.

ANA: You dare boast, before me and my father, that every woman found you irresistible.

DON JUAN: Am I boasting? It seems to me that I cut the most pitiable of figures. Besides, I said 'when the lady's instinct was set on me'. It was not always so; and then, heavens! what transports of virtuous indignation! what overwhelming defiance to the dastardly seducer! what scenes of Imogen and Iachimo!

ANA: I made no scenes. I simply called my father.

DON JUAN: And he came, sword in hand, to vindicate outraged honor and morality by murdering me.

THE STATUE: Murdering! What do you mean? Did I kill you or did you kill me?

DON JUAN: Which of us was the better fencer?

THE STATUE: I was.

DON JUAN: Of course you were. And yet you, the hero of those scandalous adventures you have just been relating to us, you had the effrontery to pose as the avenger of outraged morality and condemn me to death! You would have slain me but for an accident.

THE STATUE: I was expected to, Juan. That is how things were arranged on earth. I was not a social reformer; and I always did what it was customary for a gentleman to do.

DON JUAN: That may account for your attacking me, but not for the revolting hypocrisy of your subsequent proceedings as a statue.

THE STATUE: That all came of my going to Heaven.

THE DEVIL: I still fail to see, Señor Don Juan, that these episodes in your earthly career and in that of the Señor Commander in any way discredit my view of life. Here, I repeat, you have all that you sought without anything that you shrank from.

DON JUAN: On the contrary, here I have everything that disappointed me without anything that I have not already tried and found wanting. I tell you that as long as I can conceive something better than myself I cannot be easy unless I am striving to bring it into existence or clearing the way for it. That is the law of my life. That is the working within me of Life's incessant aspiration to higher organization, wider, deeper, intenser self-consciousness, and clearer self-understanding. It was the supremacy of this purpose that reduced love for me to the mere pleasure of a moment, art for me to the mere schooling of my faculties, religion for me to a mere excuse for laziness, since it had set up a God who looked at the world and saw it was good, against the instinct in me that looked through my eyes at the world and saw that it could be improved. I tell you that in the pursuit of my own pleasure, my own health, my own fortune, I have never known happiness. It was not love for Woman that delivered me into her hands: it was fatigue, exhaustion. When I was a child, and bruised my head against a stone, I ran to the nearest woman and cried away my pain against her apron. When I grew up, and bruised my soul against the brutalities and stupidities with which I had to strive, I did again just what I had done as a child. I have enjoyed, too, my rests, my recuperations, my breathing times, my very prostrations after strife; but rather would I be dragged through all the circles of the foolish Italian's Inferno than through the pleasures of Europe. That is what has made this place of eternal pleasures so deadly to me. It is the absence of this instinct in you that makes you that strange monster called a Devil. It is the success with which you have diverted the attention of men from their real purpose, which in one degree or another is the same as mine, to yours, that has earned you the name of The Tempter. It is the fact that they are doing your will, or rather drifting with your want of will, instead of doing their own, that makes them the uncomfortable, false, restless, artificial, petulant, wretched creatures they are.

THE DEVIL [*mortified*]: Señor Don Juan: you are uncivil to my friends.

DON JUAN: Pooh! why should I be civil to them or to you? In this Palace of Lies a truth or two will not hurt you. Your friends are all the dullest dogs I know. They are not beautiful: they are only decorated. They are not clean: they are only shaved and starched. They are not dignified: they are only fashionably dressed. They are not educated: they are only college passmen. They are not religious: they are only pewrenters. They are not moral: they are only conventional. They are not virtuous: they are only cowardly. They are not even vicious: they are only 'frail.' They are not artistic: they are only lascivious. They are not prosperous: they are only rich. They are not loyal, they are only servile; not dutiful, only sheepish; not public spirited, only patriotic; not courageous, only quarrelsome; not determined, only obstinate; not masterful, only domineering; not self-controlled, only obtuse; not self-respecting, only vain; not kind, only sentimental; not social, only gregarious; not considerate, only polite; not intelligent, only opinionated; not progressive, only factious; not imaginative, only superstitious; not just, only vindictive; not generous, only propitiatory; not disciplined, only cowed; and not truthful at all: liars every one of them, to the very backbone of their souls.

THE STATUE: Your flow of words is simply amazing, Juan. How I wish I could have talked like that to my soldiers.

THE DEVIL: It is mere talk, though. It has all been said before; but what change has it ever made? What notice has the world ever taken of it?

DON JUAN: Yes, it is mere talk. But why is it mere talk? Because, my friend, beauty, purity, respectability, religion, morality, art, patriotism, bravery, and the rest are nothing but words which I or anyone else can turn inside out like a glove. Were they realities, you would have to plead guilty to my indictment; but fortunately for your self-respect, my diabolical friend, they are not realities. As you say, they are mere words, useful for duping barbarians into adopting civilization, or the civilized poor into submitting to be robbed and enslaved. That is the family secret of the governing caste; and if we who are of that caste aimed at more Life for the world instead of at more power and luxury for our miserable selves, that secret would make us great. Now, since I, being a nobleman, am in the secret too, think how tedious to me must be your unending cant about all these moralistic figments, and how squalidly disastrous your sacrifice of your lives to them! If you even believed in your moral game enough to play it fairly, it would be interesting to watch; but you dont: you cheat at every trick; and if your opponent outcheats you, you upset the table and try to murder him.

THE DEVIL: On earth there may be some truth in this, because the people are uneducated and cannot appreciate my religion of love and beauty; but here –

DON JUAN: Oh yes: I know. Here there is nothing but love and beauty. Ugh! it is like sitting for all eternity at the first act of a fashionable play, before the complications begin. Never in my worst moments of superstitious terror on earth did I dream that Hell was so horrible. I live, like a hairdresser, in the continual contemplation of beauty, toying with silken tresses. I breathe an atmosphere of sweetness, like a confectioner's shopboy. Commander: are there any beautiful women in Heaven?

THE STATUE: None. Absolutely none. All dowdies. Not two pennorth of jewellery among a dozen of them. They might be men of fifty.

DON JUAN: I am impatient to get there. Is the word beauty ever mentioned; and are there any artistic people?

THE STATUE: I give you my word they wont admire a fine statue even when it walks past them.

DON JUAN: I go.

THE DEVIL: Don Juan: shall I be frank with you?

DON JUAN: Were you not so before?

THE DEVIL: As far as I went, yes. But I will now go further, and confess to you that men get tired of everything, of Heaven no less than of Hell; and that all history is nothing but a record of the oscillations of the world between these two extremes. An epoch is but a swing of the pendulum; and each generation thinks the world is progressing because it is always moving. But when you are as old as I am; when you have a thousand times wearied of Heaven, like myself and the Commander, and a thousand times wearied of Hell, as you are wearied now, you will no longer imagine that every swing from Heaven to Hell is an emancipation, every swing from Hell to Heaven an evolution. Where you now see reform, progress, fulfilment of upward tendency, continual ascent by Man on the stepping stones of his dead selves to higher things, you will see nothing but an infinite comedy of illusion. You will discover the profound truth of the saying of my friend Koheleth, that there is nothing new under the sun. Vanitas vanitatum —

DON JUAN [*out of all patience*]: By Heaven, this is worse than your cant about love and beauty. Clever dolt that you are, is a man no better than a worm, or a dog than a wolf, because he gets tired of everything? Shall he give up eating because he destroys his appetite in the act of gratifying it? Is a field idle when it is fallow? Can the Commander expend his hellish energy here without accumulating heavenly energy for his next term of blessedness? Granted that the great Life Force has hit on the device of the clockmaker's pendulum, and uses the earth for its bob; that the history of each oscillation, which seems so novel to us the actors, is but the history of the last oscillation repeated; nay more, that in the unthinkable infinitude of time the sun throws off the earth and catches it again a thousand times as a circus rider throws up a ball, and that our agelong epochs are but the moments between the toss and the catch, has the colossal mechanism no purpose?

THE DEVIL: None, my friend. You think, because you have a purpose, Nature must have one. You might as well expect it to have fingers and toes because you have them.

DON JUAN: But I should not have them if they served no purpose. And I, my friend, am as much a part of Nature as my own finger is a part of me. If my finger is the organ by which I grasp the sword and the mandoline, my brain is the organ by which Nature strives to understand itself. My dog's brain serves only my dog's purposes; but my own brain labors at a knowledge which does nothing for me personally but make my body bitter to me and my decay and death a calamity. Were I not possessed with a purpose beyond my own I had better be a ploughman than a philosopher; for the ploughman lives as long as the philosopher, eats more, sleeps better, and rejoices in the wife of his bosom with less misgiving. This is because the philosopher is in the grip of the Life Force. This Life Force says to him 'I have done a thousand wonderful things unconsciously by merely willing to live and following the line of least resistance: now I want to know myself and my destination, and choose my path; so I have made a special brain – a philosopher's brain – to grasp this knowledge for me as the husbandman's hand grasps the plough for me. And this' says the Life Force to the philosopher 'must thou strive to do for me until thou diest, when I will make another brain and another philosopher to carry on the work.'

THE DEVIL: What is the use of knowing?

DON JUAN: Why, to be able to choose the line of greatest advantage instead of yielding in the direction of the least resistance. Does a ship sail to its destination no better than a log drifts nowhither? The philosopher is Nature's pilot. And there you have our difference: to be in Hell is to drift: to be in Heaven is to steer.

THE DEVIL: On the rocks, most likely.

DON JUAN: Pooh! which ship goes oftenest on the rocks or to the bottom? the drifting ship or the ship with a pilot on board?

THE DEVIL: Well, well, go your way, Señor Don Juan. I prefer to be my own master and not the tool of any blundering universal force. I know that beauty is good to look at; that music is good to hear; that love is good to feel; and that they are all good to think about and talk about. I know that to be well exercised in these sensations, emotions, and studies is to be a refined and cultivated being. Whatever they may say of me in churches on earth, I know that it is universally admitted in good society that the Prince of Darkness is a gentleman; and that is enough for me. As to your Life Force, which you think irresistible, it is the most resistible thing in the world for a person of any character. But if you are naturally vulgar and credulous, as all reformers are, it will thrust you first into religion, where you will sprinkle water on babies to save their souls from me; then it will drive you from religion into science, where you will snatch the babies from the water sprinkling and inoculate them with disease to save them from catching it accidentally; then you will take to politics, where you will become the catspaw of corrupt functionaries and the henchman of ambitious humbugs; and the end will be despair and decrepitude, broken nerve and shattered hopes, vain regrets for that worst and silliest of wastes and sacrifices, the waste and sacrifice of the power of enjoyment: in a word, the punishment of the fool who pursues the better before he has secured the good.

DON JUAN: But at least I shall not be bored. The service of the Life Force has that advantage, at all events. So fare you well, Señor Satan.

THE DEVIL [*amiably*]: Fare you well, Don Juan. I shall often think of our interesting chats about things in general. I wish you every happiness: Heaven, as I said before, suits some people. But if you should change your mind, do not forget that the gates are always open here to the repentant prodigal. If you feel at any time that warmth of heart, sincere unforced affection, innocent enjoyment, and warm, breathing, palpitating reality —

DON JUAN: Why not say flesh and blood at once, though we have left those two greasy commonplaces behind us?

THE DEVIL [*angrily*]: You throw my friendly farewell back in my teeth, then, Don Juan?

DON JUAN: By no means. But though there is much to be learnt from a cynical devil, I really cannot stand a sentimental one. Señor Commander: you know the way to the frontier of Hell and Heaven. Be good enough to direct me.

THE STATUE: Oh, the frontier is only the difference between two ways of looking at things. Any road will take you across it if you really want to get there.

DON JUAN: Good. [*Saluting Doña Ana*] Señora: your servant.

ANA: But I am going with you.

DON JUAN: I can find my own way to Heaven, Ana; not yours [*he vanishes*].

ANA: How annoying!

THE STATUE [*calling after him*]: Bon voyage, Juan! [*He wafts a final blast of his great rolling chords after him as a parting salute. A faint echo of the first ghostly melody comes back in acknowledgment.*] Ah! there he goes. [*Puffing a long breath out through his lips*] Whew! How he does talk! They'll never stand it in Heaven.

THE DEVIL [*gloomily*]: His going is a political defeat. I cannot keep these Life Worshippers: they all go. This is the greatest loss I have had since that Dutch painter went: a fellow who would paint a hag of 70 with as much enjoyment as a Venus of 20.

THE STATUE: I remember: he came to Heaven. Rembrandt.

THE DEVIL: Ay, Rembrandt. There is something unnatural about these fellows. Do not listen to their gospel, Señor Commander: it is dangerous. Beware of the pursuit of the Superhuman: it leads to an indiscriminate contempt for the Human. To a man, horses and dogs and cats are mere species, outside the moral world. Well, to the Superman, men and women are a mere species too, also outside the moral world. This Don Juan was kind to women and courteous to men as your daughter here was kind to her

171

pet cats and dogs; but such kindness is a denial of the exclusively human character of the soul.

THE STATUE: And who the deuce is the Superman?

THE DEVIL: Oh, the latest fashion among the Life Force fanatics. Did you not meet in Heaven, among the new arrivals, that German Polish madman? what was his name? Nietzsche?

THE STATUE: Never heard of him.

THE DEVIL: Well, he came here first, before he recovered his wits. I had some hopes of him; but he was a confirmed Life Force worshipper. It was he who raked up the Superman, who is as old as Prometheus; and the 20th century will run after this newest of the old crazes when it gets tired of the world, the flesh, and your humble servant.

THE STATUE: Superman is a good cry; and a good cry is half the battle. I should like to see this Nietzsche.

THE DEVIL: Unfortunately he met Wagner here, and had a quarrel with him.

THE STATUE: Quite right, too. Mozart for me!

THE DEVIL: Oh, it was not about music. Wagner once drifted into Life Force worship, and invented a Superman called Siegfried. But he came to his senses afterwards. So when they met here, Nietzsche denounced him as a renegade; and Wagner wrote a pamphlet to prove that Nietzsche was a Jew; and it ended in Nietzsche's going to heaven in a huff. And a good riddance too. And now, my friend, let us hasten to my palace and celebrate your arrival with a grand musical service.

THE STATUE: With pleasure: youre most kind.

THE DEVIL: This way, Commander. We go down the old trap [*he places himself on the grave trap*].

THE STATUE: Good. [*Reflectively*]: All the same, the Superman is a fine conception. There is something statuesque about it. [*He places himself on the grave trap beside The Devil. It begins to descend slowly. Red glow from the abyss.*] Ah, this reminds me of old times.

THE DEVIL: And me also.

ANA: Stop! [*The trap stops.*]

THE DEVIL: You, Señora, cannot come this way. You will have an apotheosis. But you will be at the palace before us.

ANA: That is not what I stopped you for. Tell me: where can I find the Superman?

THE DEVIL: He is not yet created, Señora.

THE STATUE: And never will be, probably. Let us proceed: the red fire will make me sneeze. [*They descend.*]

ANA: Not yet created! Then my work is not yet done. [*Crossing herself devoutly*] I believe in the Life to Come. [*Crying to the universe*] A father! a father for the Superman!

[*She vanishes into the void; and again there is nothing: all existence seems suspended infinitely. Then, vaguely, there is a live human voice crying somewhere. One sees, with a shock, a mountain peak shewing faintly against a lighter background. The sky has returned from afar; and we suddenly remember where we were. The cry becomes distinct and urgent: it says* Automobile, Automobile. *The complete reality comes back with a rush: in a moment it is full morning in the Sierra; and the brigands are scrambling to their feet and making for the road as the goatherd runs down from the hill, warning them of the approach of another motor. Tanner and Mendoza rise amazedly and stare at one another with scattered wits. Straker sits up to yawn for a moment before he gets on his feet, making it a point of honor not to shew any undue interest in the excitement of the bandits. Mendoza gives a quick look to see that his followers are attending to the alarm; then exchanges a private word with Tanner.*]

MENDOZA: Did you dream?

TANNER: Damnably. Did you?

MENDOZA: Yes. I forget what. You were in it.

TANNER: So were you. Amazing!

MENDOZA: I warned you. [*A shot is heard from the road.*] Dolts! they will play with that gun. [*The brigands come running back scared.*] Who fired that shot? [*To Duval*] Was it you?

DUVAL [*breathless*]: I have not shoot. Dey shoot first.

ANARCHIST: I told you to begin by abolishing the State. Now we are all lost.

THE ROWDY SOCIAL-DEMOCRAT [*stampeding across the amphitheatre*]: Ran, everybody.

MENDOZA [*collaring him; throwing him on his back; and drawing a knife*]: I stab the man who stirs. [*He blocks the way. The stampede is checked.*] What has happened?

THE SULKY SOCIAL-DEMOCRAT: A motor —

THE ANARCHIST: Three men —

DUVAL: Deux femmes —

MENDOZA: Three men and two women! Why have you not brought them here? Are you afraid of them?

THE ROWDY ONE [*getting up*]: Thyve a hescort. Ow, de-ooh luts ook it, Mendowza.

THE SULKY ONE: Two armored cars full o soldiers at the ed o the valley.

ANARCHIST: The shot was fired in the air. It was a signal. [*Straker whistles his favorite air, which falls on the ears of the brigands like a funeral march.*]

TANNER: It is not an escort, but an expedition to capture you. We were advised to wait for it; but I was in a hurry.

THE ROWDY ONE [*in an agony of apprehension*]: And Ow my good Lord, ere we are, wytin for em! Luts tike to the mahntns.

MENDOZA: Idiot, what do you know about the mountains? Are you a Spaniard? You would be given up by the first shepherd you met. Besides, we are already within range of their rifles.

THE ROWDY ONE: Bat —

MENDOZA: Silence. Leave this to me. [*To Tanner*] Comrade: you will not betray us.

STRAKER: Oo are you callin comrade?

MENDOZA: Last night the advantage was with me. The robber of the poor was at the mercy of the robber of the rich. You offered your hand: I took it.

TANNER: I bring no charge against you, comrade. We have spent a pleasant evening with you: that is all.

STRAKER: I gev my and to nobody, see?

MENDOZA [*turning on him impressively*]: Young man: if I am tried, I shall plead guilty, and explain what drove me from England, home, and duty. Do you wish to have the respectable name of Straker dragged through the mud of a Spanish criminal court? The police will search me. They will find Louisa's portrait. It will be published in the illustrated papers. You blench. It will be your doing, remember.

STRAKER [*with baffled rage*]: I dont care about the court. It's avin our name mixed up with yours that I object to, you blackmailin swine, you.

MENDOZA: Language unworthy of Louisa's brother! But no matter: you are muzzled: that is enough for us. [*He turns to face his own men, who back uneasily across the amphitheatre towards the cave to take refuge behind him as a fresh party, muffled for motoring, comes from the road in riotous spirits. Ann, who makes straight for Tanner, comes first; then Violet, helped over the rough ground by Hector holding her right hand and Ramsden her left. Mendoza goes to his presidential block and seats himself calmly with his rank and file grouped behind him, and his Staff consisting of Duval and the Anarchist on his right and the two Social-Democrats on his left, supporting him in flank.*]

ANN: It's Jack!

TANNER: Caught!

HECTOR: Why, certainly it is. I said it was you, Tanner. Weve just been stopped by a puncture: the road is full of nails.

VIOLET: What are you doing here with all these men?

ANN: Why did you leave us without a word of warning?

HECTOR: I wawnt that bunch of roses, Miss Whitefield. [*To Tanner*] When we found you were gone, Miss Whitefield bet me a bunch of roses my car would not overtake yours before you reached Monte Carlo.

TANNER: But this is not the road to Monte Carlo.

HECTOR: No matter. Miss Whitefield tracked you at every stopping place: she is a regular Sherlock Holmes.

TANNER: The Life Force! I am lost.

OCTAVIUS [*bounding gaily down from the road into the amphi-*

theatre, and coming between Tanner and Straker]: I am so glad you are safe, old chap. We were afraid you had been captured by brigands.

RAMSDEN [*who has been staring at Mendoza*]: I seem to remember the face of your friend here. [*Mendoza rises politely and advances with a smile between Ann and Ramsden.*]

HECTOR: Why, so do I.

OCTAVIUS: I know you perfectly well, sir; but I cant think where I have met you.

MENDOZA [*to Violet*]: Do you remember me, madam?

VIOLET: Oh, quite well; but I am so stupid about names.

MENDOZA: It was at the Savoy Hotel. [*To Hector*] You, sir, used to come with this lady [*Violet*] to lunch. [*To Octavius*] You, sir, often brought this lady [*Ann*] and her mother to dinner on your way to the Lyceum Theatre. [*To Ramsden*] You, sir, used to come to supper, with [*dropping his voice to a confidential but perfectly audible whisper*] several different ladies.

RAMSDEN [*angrily*]: Well, what is that to you, pray?

OCTAVIUS: Why, Violet, I thought you hardly knew one another before this trip, you and Malone!

VIOLET [*vexed*]: I suppose this person was the manager.

MENDOZA: The waiter, madam. I have a grateful recollection of you all. I gathered from the bountiful way in which you treated me that you all enjoyed your visits very much.

VIOLET: What impertinence! [*She turns her back on him, and goes up the hill with Hector.*]

RAMSDEN: That will do, my friend. You do not expect these ladies to treat you as an acquaintance, I suppose, because you have waited on them at table.

MENDOZA: Pardon me: it was you who claimed my acquaintance. The ladies followed your example. However, this display of the unfortunate manners of your class closes the incident. For the future, you will please address me with the respect due to a stranger and fellow traveller. [*He turns haughtily away and resumes his presidential seat.*]

TANNER: There! I have found one man on my journey

capable of reasonable conversation; and you all instinctively insult him. Even the New Man is as bad as any of you. Enry: you have behaved just like a miserable gentleman.

STRAKER: Gentleman! Not me.

RAMSDEN: Really, Tanner, this tone —

ANN: Dont mind him, Granny: you ought to know him by this time [*she takes his arm and coaxes him away to the hill to join Violet and Hector. Octavius follows her, doglike.*]

VIOLET [*calling from the hill*]: Here are the soldiers. They are getting out of their motors.

DUVAL [*panicstricken*]: Oh, nom de Dieu!

THE ANARCHIST: Fools: the State is about to crush you because you spared it at the prompting of the political hangers-on of the bourgeoisie.

THE SULKY SOCIAL-DEMOCRAT [*argumentative to the last*]: On the contrary, only by capturing the State machine —

THE ANARCHIST: It is going to capture you.

THE ROWDY SOCIAL-DEMOCRAT [*his anguish culminating*]: Ow, chack it. Wot are we ere for? Wot are we wytin for?

MENDOZA [*between his teeth*]: Go on. Talk politics, you idiots: nothing sounds more respectable. Keep it up, I tell you.

[*The soldiers line the road, commanding the amphitheatre with their rifles. The brigands, struggling with an overwhelming impulse to hide behind one another, look as unconcerned as they can. Mendoza rises superbly, with undaunted front. The officer in command steps down from the road into the amphitheatre; looks hard at the brigands; and then inquiringly at Tanner.*]

THE OFFICER: Who are these men, Señor Ingles?

TANNER: My escort.

[*Mendoza, with a Mephistophelean smile, bows profoundly. An irrepressible grin runs from face to face among the brigands. They touch their hats, except the Anarchist, who defies the State with folded arms.*]

ACT FOUR

The garden of a villa in Granada. Whoever wishes to know what it is like must go to Granada to see. One may prosaically specify a group of hills dotted with villas, the Alhambra on the top of one of the hills, and a considerable town in the valley, approached by dusty white roads in which the children, no matter what they are doing or thinking about, automatically whine for halfpence and reach out little clutching brown palms for them; but there is nothing in this description except the Alhambra, the begging, and the colour of the roads, that does not fit Surrey as well as Spain. The difference is that the Surrey hills are comparatively small and ugly, and should properly be called the Surrey Protuberances; but these Spanish hills are of mountain stock: the amenity which conceals their size does not compromise their dignity.

This particular garden is on a hill opposite the Alhambra; and the villa is as expensive and pretentious as a villa must be if it is to be let furnished by the week to opulent American and English visitors. If we stand on the lawn at the foot of the garden and look uphill, our horizon is the stone balustrade of a flagged platform on the edge of infinite space at the top of the hill. Between us and this platform is a flower garden with a circular basin and fountain in the centre, surrounded by geometrical flower beds, gravel paths, and clipped yew trees in the genteelest order. The garden is higher than our lawn; so we reach it by a few steps in the middle of its embankment. The platform is higher again than the garden, from which we mount a couple more steps to look over the balustrade at a fine view of the town up the valley and of the hills that stretch away beyond it to where, in the remotest distance, they become mountains. On our left is the villa, accessible by steps from the left hand corner of the garden. Returning from the platform through the garden and down again to the lawn (a movement which leaves the villa behind us on our right) we find evidence of literary interests on the part of the tenants in the fact that there is no tennis net nor set of croquet hoops, but, on our left, a little iron garden table with books on it, mostly yellow-backed, and a chair beside it. A chair on the right has also a couple of open books upon it. There are no newspapers, a circumstance which, with the absence of games, might lead an intelligent spectator to the most far reaching conclusions as to the sort of people who live in the villa. Such speculations are checked, however, on this delightfully fine afternoon, by the appearance at a little gate in a paling on our left, of Henry Straker in his professional costume. He opens the gate for an elderly gentleman, and follows him on to the lawn.

This elderly gentleman defies the Spanish sun in a black frock coat, tall silk hat, trousers in which narrow stripes of dark grey and lilac blend into a highly respectable color, and a black necktie tied into a bow over spotless linen. Probably therefore a man whose social position needs constant and scrupulous affirmation without regard to climate: one who would dress thus for the middle of the Sahara or the top of Mont Blanc. And since he has not the stamp of the class which accepts as its life-mission the advertizing and maintenance of first rate tailoring and millinery, he looks vulgar in his finery, though in a working dress of any kind he would look dignified enough. He is a bullet cheeked man with a red complexion, stubbly hair, smallish eyes, a hard mouth that folds down at the corners, and a dogged chin. The looseness of skin that comes with age has attacked his throat and the laps of his cheeks; but he is still hard as an apple above the mouth; so that the upper half of his face looks younger than the lower. He has the self-confidence of one who has made money, and something of the truculence of one who has made it in a brutalizing struggle, his civility having under it a perceptible menace that he has other methods in reserve if necessary. Withal, a man to be rather pitied when he is not to be feared; for there is something pathetic about him at times, as if the huge commercial machine which has worked him into his frock coat had allowed him very little of his own way and left his affections hungry and baffled. At the first word that falls from him it is clear that he is an Irishman whose native intonation has clung to him through many changes of place and rank. One can only guess that the original material of his speech was perhaps the surly Kerry brogue; but the degradation of speech that occurs in London, Glasgow, Dublin, and big cities generally has been at work on it so long that nobody but an arrant cockney would dream of calling it a brogue now; for its music is almost gone, though its surliness is still perceptible. Straker, being a very obvious cockney, inspires him with implacable contempt, as a stupid Englishman who cannot even speak his own language properly. Straker, on the other hand, regards the old gentleman's accent as a joke thoughtfully provided by Providence expressly for the amusement of the British race, and treats him normally with the indulgence due to an inferior and unlucky species, but occasionally with indignant alarm when the old gentleman shews signs of intending his Irish nonsense to be taken seriously.

STRAKER: I'll go tell the young lady. She said youd prefer to stay here [*he turns to go up through the garden to the villa*].

THE IRISHMAN [*who had been looking round him with lively curiosity*]: The young lady? Thats Miss Violet, eh?

STRAKER [*stopping on the steps with sudden suspicion*]: Well, you know, dont you?

THE IRISHMAN: Do I?

STRAKER [*his temper rising*]: Well, do you or dont you?

THE IRISHMAN: What business is that of yours?

[*Straker, now highly indignant, comes back from the steps and confronts the visitor.*]

STRAKER: I'll tell you what business it is of mine. Miss Robinson –

THE IRISHMAN [*interrupting*]: Oh, her name is Robinson, is it? Thank you.

STRAKER: Why, you dont know even her name?

THE IRISHMAN: Yes I do, now that youve told me.

STRAKER [*after a moment of stupefaction at the old man's readiness in repartee*]: Look here: what do you mean by gittin into my car and lettin me bring you here if youre not the person I took that note to?

THE IRISHMAN: Who else did you take it to, pray?

STRAKER: I took it to Mr Ector Malone, at Miss Robinson's request, see? Miss Robinson is not my principal: I took it to oblige her. I know Mr Malone; and he aint you, not by a long chalk. At the hotel they told me that your name is Ector Malone –

MALONE: Hector Malone.

STRAKER [*with calm superiority*]: Hector in your own country: thats what comes o livin in provincial places like

Ireland and America. Over here youre Ector: if you avnt noticed it before, you soon will.

[*The growing strain of the conversation is here relieved by Violet, who has sallied from the villa and through the garden to the steps, which she now descends, coming very opportunely between Malone and Straker.*]

VIOLET [*to Straker*]: Did you take my message?

STRAKER: Yes, miss. I took it to the hotel and sent it up, expecting to see young Mr Malone. Then out walks this gent, and says it's all right and he'll come with me. So as the hotel people said he was Mr Ector Malone, I fetched him. And now he goes back on what he said. But if he isnt the gentleman you meant, say the word: it's easy enough to fetch him back again.

MALONE: I should esteem it a great favor if I might have a short conversation with you, madam. I am Hector's father, as this bright Britisher would have guessed in the course of another hour or so.

STRAKER [*coolly defiant*]: No, not in another year or so. When weve ad you as long to polish up as weve ad im, perhaps youll begin to look a little bit up to is mark. At present you fall a long way short. Youve got too many aitches, for one thing. [*To Violet, amiably*] All right, Miss: you want to talk to him: I shant intrude. [*He nods affably to Malone and goes out through the little gate in the paling.*]

VIOLET [*very civilly*]: I am so sorry, Mr Malone, if that man has been rude to you. But what can we do? He is our chauffeur.

MALONE: Your hwat?

VIOLET: The driver of our automobile. He can drive a motor car at seventy miles an hour, and mend it when it breaks down. We are dependent on our motor cars; and our motor cars are dependent on him; so of course we are dependent on him.

MALONE: Ive noticed, madam, that every thousand dollars an Englishman gets seems to add one to the number of people he's dependent on. However, you neednt apologize for your man: I made him talk on purpose. By doing so I learnt that youre staying here in Grannida with a party of English, including my son Hector.

VIOLET [*conversationally*]: Yes. We intended to go to Nice; but we had to follow a rather eccentric member of our party who started first and came here. Wont you sit down? [*She clears the nearest chair of the two books on it.*]

MALONE [*impressed by this attention*]: Thank you. [*He sits down, examining her curiously as she goes to the iron table to put down the books. When she turns to him again, he says*] Miss Robinson, I believe?

VIOLET [*sitting down*]: Yes.

MALONE [*taking a letter from his pocket*]: Your note to Hector runs as follows [*Violet is unable to repress a start. He pauses quietly to take out and put on his spectacles, which have gold rims*]: 'Dearest: they have all gone to the Alhambra for the afternoon. I have shammed headache and have the garden all to myself. Jump into Jack's motor: Straker will rattle you here in a jiffy. Quick, quick, quick. Your loving Violet.' [*He looks at her; but by this time she has recovered herself, and meets his spectacles with perfect composure. He continues slowly*] Now I dont know on hwat terms young people associate in English society; but in America that note would be considered to imply a very considerable degree of affectionate intimacy between the parties.

VIOLET: Yes: I know your son very well, Mr Malone. Have you any objection?

MALONE [*somewhat taken aback*]: No, no objection exactly. Provided it is understood that my son is altogether dependent on me, and that I have to be consulted in any important step he may propose to take.

VIOLET: I am sure you would not be unreasonable with him, Mr Malone.

MALONE: I hope not, Miss Robinson; but at your age you might think many things unreasonable that dont seem so to me.

VIOLET [*with a little shrug*]: Oh, well, I suppose theres no use our playing at cross purposes, Mr Malone. Hector wants to marry me.

MALONE: I inferred from your note that he might. Well, Miss Robinson, he is his own master; but if he marries you he shall not have a rap from me. [*He takes off his spectacles and pockets them with the note.*]

VIOLET [*with some severity*]: That is not very complimentary to me, Mr Malone.

MALONE: I say nothing against you, Miss Robinson: I daresay you are an amiable and excellent young lady. But I have other views for Hector.

VIOLET: Hector may not have other views for himself, Mr Malone.

MALONE: Possibly not. Then he does without me: thats all. I daresay you are prepared for that. When a young lady writes to a young man to come to her quick, quick, quick, money seems nothing and love seems everything.

VIOLET [*sharply*]: I beg your pardon, Mr Malone: I do not think anything so foolish. Hector must have money.

MALONE [*staggered*]: Oh, very well, very well. No doubt he can work for it.

VIOLET: What is the use of having money if you have to work for it? [*She rises impatiently.*] Its all nonsense, Mr Malone: you must enable your son to keep up his position. It is his right.

MALONE [*grimly*]: I should not advise you to marry him on the strength of that right, Miss Robinson.

[*Violet, who has almost lost her temper, controls herself with an effort; unclenches her fingers; and resumes her seat with studied tranquillity and reasonableness.*]

VIOLET: What objection have you to me, pray? My social position is as good as Hector's, to say the least. He admits it.

MALONE [*shrewdly*]: You tell him so from time to time, eh? Hector's social position in England, Miss Robinson, is just what I choose to buy for him. I have made him a fair offer. Let him pick out the most historic house, castle, or abbey that England contains. The very day he tells me he wants it for a wife worthy of its traditions, I buy it for him, and give him the means of keeping it up.

VIOLET: What do you mean by a wife worthy of its traditions? Cannot any well bred woman keep such a house for him?

MALONE: No, she must be born to it.

VIOLET: Hector was not born to it, was he?

MALONE: His grandmother was a barefooted Irish girl that nursed me by a turf fire. Let him marry another such, and I will not stint her marriage portion. Let him raise himself socially with my money or raise somebody else: so long as there is a social profit somewhere, I'll regard my expenditure as justified. But there must be a profit for someone. A marriage with you would leave things just where they are.

VIOLET: Many of my relations would object very much to my marrying the grandson of a common woman, Mr Malone. That may be prejudice; but so is your desire to have him marry a title prejudice.

MALONE [rising, and approaching her with a scrutiny in which there is a good deal of reluctant respect]: You seem a pretty straightforward downright sort of a young woman.

VIOLET: I do not see why I should be made miserably poor because I cannot make profits for you. Why do you want to make Hector unhappy?

MALONE: He will get over it all right enough. Men thrive better on disappointments in love than on disappointments in money. I daresay you think that sordid; but I know what I'm talking about. Me father died of starvation in Ireland in the black 47. Maybe youve heard of it.

VIOLET: The Famine?

MALONE [with smouldering passion]: No, the starvation. When a country is full o food, and exporting it, there can be no famine. Me father was starved dead; and I was starved out to America in me mother's arms. English rule drove me and mine out of Ireland. Well, you can keep Ireland. Me and me like are coming back to buy England; and we'll buy the best of it. I want no middle class properties and no middle class women for Hector. Thats straightforward, isnt it, like yourself?

VIOLET [*icily pitying his sentimentality*]: Really, Mr Malone, I am astonished to hear a man of your age and good sense talking in that romantic way. Do you suppose English noblemen will sell their places to you for the asking?

MALONE: I have the refusal of two of the oldest family mansions in England. One historic owner cant afford to keep all the rooms dusted: the other cant afford the death duties. What do you say now?

VIOLET: Of course it is very scandalous; but surely you know that the Government will sooner or later put a stop to all these Socialist attacks on property.

MALONE [*grinning*]: D'y'think they'll be able to get that done before I buy the house – or rather the abbey? Theyre both abbeys.

VIOLET [*putting that aside rather impatiently*]: Oh, well, let us talk sense, Mr Malone. You must feel that we havnt been talking sense so far.

MALONE: I cant say I do. I mean all I say.

VIOLET: Then you dont know Hector as I do. He is romantic and faddy – he gets it from you, I fancy – and he wants a certain sort of wife to take care of him. Not a faddy sort of person, you know.

MALONE: Somebody like you, perhaps?

VIOLET [*quietly*]: Well, yes. But you cannot very well ask me to undertake this with absolutely no means of keeping up his position.

MALONE [*alarmed*]: Stop a bit, stop a bit. Where are we getting to? I'm not aware that I'm asking you to undertake anything.

VIOLET: Of course, Mr Malone, you can make it very difficult for me to speak to you if you choose to misunderstand me.

MALONE [*half bewildered*]: I dont wish to take any unfair advantage; but we seem to have got off the straight track somehow.

[*Straker, with the air of a man who has been making haste, opens the little gate, and admits Hector, who, snorting with indignation, comes upon the lawn, and is making for his father*]

*when Violet, greatly dismayed, springs up and intercepts him.
Straker does not wait; at least he does not remain visibly within
earshot.*]

VIOLET: Oh, how unlucky! Now please, Hector, say nothing. Go away until I have finished speaking to your
father.

HECTOR [*inexorably*]: No, Violet: I mean to have this thing
out, right away. [*He puts her aside; passes her by; and faces
his father, whose cheeks darken as his Irish blood begins to sim-
mer.*] Dad: youve not played this hand straight.

MALONE: Hwat d'y'mean?

HECTOR: Youve opened a letter addressed to me. Youve
impersonated me and stolen a march on this lady. Thats
disawnerable.

MALONE [*threateningly*]: Now you take care what youre saying, Hector. Take care, I tell you.

HECTOR: I have taken care. I am taking care. I'm
taking care of my honor and my position in English
society.

MALONE [*hotly*]: Your position has been got by my money:
do you know that?

HECTOR: Well, youve just spoiled it all by opening that
letter. A letter from an English lady, not addressed to you
– a cawnfidential letter! a dullicate letter! a private letter! opened by my father! Thats a sort of thing a man
cant struggle against in England. The sooner we go back
together the better. [*He appeals mutely to the heavens to
witness the shame and anguish of two outcasts.*]

VIOLET [*snubbing him with an instinctive dislike for scene making*]:
Dont be unreasonable, Hector. It was quite natural for
Mr Malone to open my letter: his name was on the
envelope.

MALONE: There! Youve no common sense, Hector. I
thank you, Miss Robinson.

HECTOR: I thank you too. It's very kind of you. My father
knows no better.

MALONE [*furiously clenching his fists*]: Hector-

HECTOR [*with undaunted moral force*]: Oh, it's no use hectoring me. A private letter's a private letter, dad: you cant get over that.

MALONE [*raising his voice*]: I wont be talked back to by you, d'y'hear?

VIOLET: Ssh! please, please. Here they all come.

[*Father and son, checked, glare mutely at one another, as Tanner comes in through the little gate with Ramsden, followed by Octavius and Ann.*]

VIOLET: Back already!

TANNER: The Alhambra is not open this afternoon.

VIOLET: What a sell!

[*Tanner passes on, and presently finds himself between Hector and a strange elder, both apparently on the verge of personal combat. He looks from one to the other for an explanation. They sulkily avoid his eye, and nurse their wrath in silence.*]

RAMSDEN: Is it wise for you to be out in the sunshine with such a headache, Violet?

TANNER: Have you recovered too, Malone?

VIOLET: Oh, I forgot. We have not all met before. Mr Malone: wont you introduce your father?

HECTOR [*with Roman firmness*]: No, I will not. He is no father of mine.

MALONE [*very angry*]: You disown your dad before your English friends, do you?

VIOLET: Oh, please dont make a scene.

[*Ann and Octavius, lingering near the gate, exchange an astonished glance, and discreetly withdraw up the steps to the garden, where they can enjoy the disturbance without intruding. On their way to the steps Ann sends a little grimace of mute sympathy to Violet, who is standing with her back to the little table, looking on in helpless annoyance as her husband soars to higher and higher moral eminences without the least regard to the old man's millions.*]

HECTOR: I'm very sorry, Miss Rawbnsn; but I'm contending for a principle. I am a son, and, I hope, a dutiful one; but before everything I'm a Mahn!!! And when dad treats my private letters as his own, and takes it on himself to say that I shant marry you if I am happy and fortunate enough to gain your consent, then I just snap my fingers and go my own way.

TANNER: Marry Violet!

RAMSDEN: Are you in your senses?

TANNER: Do you forget what we told you?

HECTOR [*recklessly*]: I dont care what you told me.

RAMSDEN [*scandalized*]: Tut tut, sir! Monstrous! [*he flings away towards the gate, his elbows quivering with indignation.*]

TANNER: Another madman! These men in love should be locked up. [*He gives Hector up as hopeless, and turns away towards the garden; but Malone, taking offence in a new direction, follows him and compels him, by the aggressiveness of his tone, to stop.*]

MALONE: I dont understand this. Is Hector not good enough for this lady, pray?

TANNER: My dear sir, the lady is married already. Hector knows it; and yet he persists in his infatuation. Take him home and lock him up.

MALONE [*bitterly*]: So this is the highborn social tone Ive spoilt be me ignorant uncultivated behavior! Makin love to a married woman! [*He comes angrily between Hector and Violet, and almost bawls into Hector's left ear*] Youve picked up that habit of the British aristocracy, have you?

HECTOR: Thats all right. Dont you trouble yourself about that. I'll answer for the morality of what I'm doing.

TANNER [*coming forward to Hector's right hand with flashing eyes*]: Well said, Malone! You also see that mere marriage laws are not morality! I agree with you; but unfortunately Violet does not.

MALONE: I take leave to doubt that, sir. [*Turning on Violet*] Let me tell you, Mrs Robinson, or whatever your right name is, you had no right to send that letter to my son when you were the wife of another man.

HECTOR [*outraged*]: This is the last straw. Dad: you have insulted my wife.

MALONE: Your wife!

TANNER: You the missing husband! Another moral impostor! [*He smites his brow, and collapses into Malone's chair.*]

MALONE: Youve married without my consent!

RAMSDEN: You have deliberately humbugged us, sir!

HECTOR: Here: I have had just about enough of being badgered. Violet and I are married: thats the long and the short of it. Now what have you got to say – any of you?

MALONE: I know what Ive got to say. She's married a beggar.

HECTOR: No: she's married a Worker [*his American pronunciation imparts an overwhelming intensity to this simple and unpopular word*]. I start to earn my own living this very afternoon.

MALONE [*sneering angrily*]: Yes: youre very plucky now, because you got your remittance from me yesterday or this morning, I reckon. Waitl it's spent. You wont be so full of cheek then.

HECTOR [*producing a letter from his pocketbook*]: Here it is [*thrusting it on his father*]. Now you just take your remittance and yourself out of my life. I'm done with remittances; and I'm done with you. I dont sell the privilege of insulting my wife for a thousand dollars.

MALONE [*deeply wounded and full of concern*]: Hector: you dont know what poverty is.

HECTOR [*fervidly*]: Well, I wawnt to know what it is. I wawnt'be a Mahn. Violet: you come along with me, to your own home: I'll see you through.

OCTAVIUS [*jumping down from the garden to the lawn and running to Hector's left hand*]: I hope youll shake hands with me before you go, Hector. I admire and respect you more than I can say. [*He is affected almost to tears as they shake hands.*]

VIOLET [*also almost in tears, but of vexation*]: Oh, dont be an idiot, Tavy. Hector's about as fit to become a workman as you are.

TANNER [*rising from his chair on the other side of Hector*]: Never fear: theres no question of his becoming a navvy, Mrs Malone. [*To Hector*] Theres really no difficulty about capital to start with. Treat me as a friend: draw on me.

OCTAVIUS [*impulsively*]: Or on me.

MALONE [*with fierce jealousy*]: Who wants your durty money? Who should he draw on but his own father? [*Tanner and Octavius recoil, Octavius rather hurt, Tanner consoled by the solution of the money difficulty. Violet looks up hopefully.*] Hector: dont be rash, my boy. I'm sorry for what I said: I never meant to insult Violet: I take it all back. She's just the wife you want: there!

HECTOR [*patting him on the shoulder*]: Well, thats all right, dad. Say no more: we're friends again. Only, I take no money from anybody.

MALONE [*pleading abjectly*]: Dont be hard on me, Hector. I'd rather you quarrelled and took the money than made friends and starved. You dont know what the world is: I do.

HECTOR: No, no, NO. Thats fixed: thats not going to change. [*He passes his father inexorably by, and goes to Violet.*] Come, Mrs Malone: youve got to move to the hotel with me, and take your proper place before the world.

VIOLET: But I must go in, dear, and tell Davis to pack. Wont you go on and make them give you a room overlooking the garden for me? I'll join you in half an hour.

HECTOR: Very well. Youll dine with us, Dad, wont you?

MALONE [*eager to conciliate him*]: Yes, yes.

HECTOR: See you all later. [*He waves his hand to Ann, who has now been joined by Tanner, Octavius, and Ramsden in the garden, and goes out through the little gate, leaving his father and Violet together on the lawn.*]

MALONE: Youll try to bring him to his senses, Violet: I know you will.

VIOLET: I had no idea he could be so headstrong. If he goes on like that, what can I do?

MALONE: Dont be discurridged: domestic pressure may be slow; but it's sure. Youll wear him down. Promise me you will.

VIOLET: I will do my best. Of course I think it's the greatest nonsense deliberately making us poor like that.

MALONE: Of course it is.

VIOLET [*after a moment's reflection*]: You had better give me the remittance. He will want it for his hotel bill. I'll see whether I can induce him to accept it. Not now, of course, but presently.

MALONE [*eagerly*]: Yes, yes, yes: thats just the thing. [*He hands her the thousand dollar bill, and adds cunningly*] Y'understand that this is only a bachelor allowance.

VIOLET [*coolly*]: Oh, quite. [*She takes it.*] Thank you. By the way, Mr Malone, those two houses you mentioned – the abbeys.

MALONE: Yes?

VIOLET: Dont take one of them until Ive seen it. One never knows what may be wrong with these places.

MALONE: I wont. I'll do nothing without consulting you, never fear.

VIOLET [*politely, but without a ray of gratitude*]: Thanks: that will be much the best way. [*She goes calmly back to the villa, escorted obsequiously by Malone to the upper end of the garden.*]

TANNER [*drawing Ramsden's attention to Malone's cringing attitude as he takes leave of Violet*]: And that poor devil is a billionaire! one of the master spirits of the age! Led in a string like a pug dog by the first girl who takes the trouble to despise him! I wonder will it ever come to that with me. [*He comes down to the lawn.*]

RAMSDEN [*following him*]: The sooner the better for you.

MALONE [*slapping his hands as he returns through the garden*]: That'll be a grand woman for Hector. I wouldnt exchange her for ten duchesses. [*He descends to the lawn and comes between Tanner and Ramsden.*]

RAMSDEN [*very civil to the billionaire*]: It's an unexpected pleasure to find you in this corner of the world, Mr Malone. Have you come to buy up the Alhambra?

MALONE: Well, I dont say I mightnt. I think I could do better with it than the Spanish government. But thats not what I came about. To tell you the truth, about a month ago I overheard a deal between two men over a bundle of shares. They differed about the price: they were young and greedy, and didnt know that if the shares were worth what was bid for them they must be worth what was asked, the margin being too small to be of any account, you see. To amuse meself, I cut in and bought the shares. Well, to this day I havnt found out what the business is. The office is in this town; and the name is Mendoza, Limited. Now whether Mendoza's a mine, or a steamboat line, or a bank, or a patent article –

TANNER: He's a man. I know him: his principles are thoroughly commercial. Let us take you round the town in our motor, Mr Malone, and call on him on the way.

MALONE: If youll be so kind, yes. And may I ask who –

TANNER: Mr Roebuck Ramsden, a very old friend of your daughter-in-law.

MALONE: Happy to meet you, Mr Ramsden.

RAMSDEN: Thank you. Mr Tanner is also one of our circle.

MALONE: Glad to know you also, Mr Tanner.

TANNER: Thanks. [*Malone and Ramsden go out very amicably through the little gate. Tanner calls to Octavius, who is wandering in the garden with Ann.*] Tavy! [*Tavy comes to the steps, Tanner whispers loudly to him*] Violet's father-in-law is a financier of brigands. [*Tanner hurries away to overtake Malone and Ramsden. Ann strolls to the steps with an idle impulse to torment Octavius.*]

ANN: Wont you go with them, Tavy?

OCTAVIUS [*tears suddenly flushing his eyes*]: You cut me to the heart, Ann, by wanting me to go [*he comes down on the lawn to hide his face from her. She follows him caressingly*].

ANN: Poor Ricky Ticky Tavy! Poor heart!

OCTAVIUS: It belongs to you, Ann. Forgive me: I must speak of it. I love you. You know I love you.

ANN: Whats the good, Tavy? You know that my mother is determined that I shall marry Jack.

OCTAVIUS [*amazed*]: Jack!

ANN: It seems absurd, doesnt it?

OCTAVIUS [*with growing resentment*]: Do you mean to say that Jack has been playing with me all this time? That he has

been urging me not to marry you because he intends to
marry you himself?

ANN [*alarmed*]: No, no: you mustnt lead him to believe that
I said that. I dont for a moment think that Jack knows his
own mind. But it's clear from my father's will that he
wished me to marry Jack. And my mother is set on it.

OCTAVIUS: But you are not bound to sacrifice yourself
always to the wishes of your parents.

ANN: My father loved me. My mother loves me. Surely
their wishes are a better guide than my own selfishness.

OCTAVIUS: Oh, I know how unselfish you are, Ann. But
believe me – though I know I am speaking in my own
interest – there is another side to this question. Is it fair
to Jack to marry him if you do not love him? Is it fair to
destroy my happiness as well as your own if you can bring
yourself to love me?

ANN [*looking at him with a faint impulse of pity*]: Tavy, my dear,
you are a nice creature – a good boy.

OCTAVIUS [*humiliated*]: Is that all?

ANN [*mischievously in spite of her pity*]: Thats a great deal, I
assure you. You would always worship the ground I trod
on, wouldnt you?

OCTAVIUS: I do. It sounds ridiculous; but it's no exaggera-
tion. I do; and I always shall.

ANN: Always is a long word, Tavy. You see, I shall have to
live up always to your idea of my divinity; and I dont
think I could do that if we were married. But if I marry
Jack, youll never be disillusioned – at least not until I
grow too old.

OCTAVIUS: I too shall grow old, Ann. And when I am
eighty, one white hair of the woman I love will make me
tremble more than the thickest gold tress from the most
beautiful young head.

ANN [*quite touched*]: Oh, thats poetry, Tavy, real poetry. It
gives me that strange sudden sense of an echo from a
former existence which always seems to me such a striking
proof that we have immortal souls.

OCTAVIUS: Do you believe that it is true?

ANN: Tavy: if it is to come true, you must lose me as well as love me.

OCTAVIUS: Oh! [*he hastily sits down at the little table and covers his face with his hands.*]

ANN [*with conviction*]: Tavy: I wouldnt for worlds destroy your illusions. I can neither take you nor let you go. I can see exactly what will suit you. You must be a sentimental old bachelor for my sake.

OCTAVIUS [*desperately*]: Ann: I'll kill myself.

ANN: Oh, no, you wont: that wouldnt be kind. You wont have a bad time. You will be very nice to women; and you will go a good deal to the opera. A broken heart is a very pleasant complaint for a man in London if he has a comfortable income.

OCTAVIUS [*considerably cooled, but believing that he is only recovering his self-control*]: I know you mean to be kind, Ann. Jack has persuaded you that cynicism is a good tonic for me. [*He rises with quiet dignity.*]

ANN [*studying him slyly*]: You see, I'm disillusionizing you already. Thats what I dread.

OCTAVIUS: You do not dread disillusionizing Jack.

ANN [*her face lighting up with mischievous ecstasy – whispering*]: I cant: he has no illusions about me. I shall surprise Jack the other way. Getting over an unfavorable impression is ever so much easier than living up to an ideal. Oh, I shall enrapture Jack sometimes!

OCTAVIUS [*resuming the calm phase of despair, and beginning to enjoy his broken heart and delicate attitude without knowing it*]: I dont doubt that. You will enrapture him always. And he – the fool! – thinks you would make him wretched.

ANN: Yes: thats the difficulty so far.

OCTAVIUS [*heroically*]: Shall *I* tell him that you love him?

ANN [*quickly*]: Oh no: he'd run away again.

OCTAVIUS [*shocked*]: Ann: would you marry an unwilling man?

ANN: What a queer creature you are, Tavy! Theres no such thing as a willing man when you really go for him. [*She laughs naughtily.*] I'm shocking you, I suppose. But you

know you are really getting a sort of satisfaction already
in being out of danger yourself.

OCTAVIUS [*startled*]: Satisfaction! [*Reproachfully*] You say
that to me!

ANN: Well, if it were really agony, would you ask for more
of it?

OCTAVIUS: Have I asked for more of it?

ANN: You have offered to tell Jack that I love him. Thats
self-sacrifice, I suppose; but there must be some satisfaction in it. Perhaps it's because youre a poet. You are
like the bird that presses its breast against the sharp thorn
to make itself sing.

OCTAVIUS: It's quite simple. I love you; and I want you to
be happy. You dont love me; so I cant make you happy
myself; but I can help another man to do it.

ANN: Yes: it seems quite simple. But I doubt if we ever
know why we do things. The only really simple thing is
to go straight for what you want and grab it. I suppose I
dont love you, Tavy; but sometimes I feel as if I should
like to make a man of you somehow. You are very foolish
about women.

OCTAVIUS [*almost coldly*]: I am content to be what I am in
that respect.

ANN: Then you must keep away from them, and only
dream about them. I wouldnt marry you for worlds, Tavy.

OCTAVIUS: I have no hope, Ann: I accept my ill luck. But
I dont think you quite know how much it hurts.

ANN: You are so softhearted! It's queer that you should be
so different from Violet. Violet's as hard as nails.

OCTAVIUS: Oh no. I am sure Violet is thoroughly womanly
at heart.

ANN [*with some impatience*]: Why do you say that? Is it un-
womanly to be thoughtful and businesslike and sensible?
Do you want Violet to be an idiot – or something worse,
like me?

OCTAVIUS: Something worse – like you! What do you
mean, Ann?

ANN: Oh well, I dont mean that, of course. But I have a

great respect for Violet. She gets her own way always.

OCTAVIUS [*sighing*]: So do you.

ANN: Yes; but somehow she gets it without coaxing — without having to make people sentimental about her.

OCTAVIUS [*with brotherly callousness*]: Nobody could get very sentimental about Violet, I think, pretty as she is.

ANN: Oh yes they could, if she made them.

OCTAVIUS: But surely no really nice woman would deliberately practise on men's instincts in that way.

ANN [*throwing up her hands*]: Oh, Tavy, Tavy, Ricky Ticky Tavy, heaven help the woman who marries you!

OCTAVIUS [*his passion reviving at the name*]: Oh why, why, why do you say that? Dont torment me. I dont understand.

ANN: Suppose she were to tell fibs and lay snares for men?

OCTAVIUS: Do you think *I* could marry such a woman — I, who have known and loved you?

ANN: Hm! Well, at all events, she wouldnt let you if she were wise. So thats settled. And now I cant talk any more. Say you forgive me, and that the subject is closed.

OCTAVIUS: I have nothing to forgive; and the subject is closed. And if the wound is open, at least you shall never see it bleed.

ANN: Poetic to the last, Tavy. Goodbye, dear. [*She pats his cheek; has an impulse to kiss him and then another impulse of distaste which prevents her; finally runs away through the garden and into the villa.*]

> Octavius again takes refuge at the table, bowing his head on his arms and sobbing softly. Mrs Whitefield, who has been pottering round the Granada shops, and has a net full of little parcels in her hand, comes in through the gate and sees him.

MRS WHITEFIELD [*running to him and lifting his head*]: Whats the matter, Tavy? Are you ill?

OCTAVIUS: No, nothing, nothing.

MRS WHITEFIELD [*still holding his head, anxiously*]: But youre crying. Is it about Violet's marriage?

OCTAVIUS: No, no. Who told you about Violet?

MRS WHITEFIELD [*restoring the head to its owner*]: I met

Roebuck and that awful old Irishman. Are you sure youre
not ill? Whats the matter?

OCTAVIUS [*affectionately*]: It's nothing. Only a man's broken
heart. Doesnt that sound ridiculous?

MRS WHITEFIELD: But what is it all about? Has Ann been
doing anything to you?

OCTAVIUS: It's not Ann's fault. And dont think for a
moment that I blame you.

MRS WHITEFIELD [*startled*]: For what?

OCTAVIUS [*pressing her hand consolingly*]: For nothing. I said
I didnt blame you.

MRS WHITEFIELD: But I havnt done anything. Whats the
matter?

OCTAVIUS [*smiling sadly*]: Cant you guess? I daresay you
are right to prefer Jack to me as a husband for Ann; but I
love Ann; and it hurts rather. [*He rises and moves away from
her towards the middle of the lawn.*]

MRS WHITEFIELD [*following him hastily*]: Does Ann say that
I want her to marry Jack?

OCTAVIUS: Yes: she has told me.

MRS WHITEFIELD [*thoughtfully*]: Then I'm very sorry for
you, Tavy. It's only her way of saying she wants to marry
Jack. Little she cares what *I* say or what *I* want!

OCTAVIUS: But she would not say it unless she believed it.
Surely you dont suspect Ann of – of deceit!!

MRS WHITEFIELD: Well, never mind, Tavy. I dont know
which is best for a young man: to know too little, like you,
or too much, like Jack.

[*Tanner returns.*]

TANNER: Well, Ive disposed of old Malone. Ive introduced
him to Mendoza, Limited; and left the two brigands together to talk it out. Hullo, Tavy! anything wrong?

OCTAVIUS: I must go wash my face, I see. [*To Mrs
Whitefield*] Tell him what you wish. [*To Tanner*] You may
take it from me, Jack, that Ann approves of it.

TANNER [*puzzled by his manner*]: Approves of what?

OCTAVIUS: Of what Mrs Whitefield wishes. [*He goes his way
with sad dignity to the villa.*]

TANNER [*to Mrs Whitefield*]: This is very mysterious. What is it you wish? It shall be done, whatever it is.

MRS WHITEFIELD [*with snivelling gratitude*]: Thank you, Jack. [*She sits down. Tanner brings the other chair from the table and sits close to her with his elbows on his knees, giving her his whole attention.*] I dont know why it is that other people's children are so nice to me, and that my own have so little consideration for me. It's no wonder I dont seem able to care for Ann and Rhoda as I do for you and Tavy and Violet. It's a very queer world. It used to be so straightforward and simple; and now nobody seems to think and feel as they ought. Nothing has been right since that speech that Professor Tyndall made at Belfast.

TANNER: Yes: life is more complicated than we used to think. But what am I to do for you?

MRS WHITEFIELD: Thats just what I want to tell you. Of course youll marry Ann whether I like it or not –

TANNER [*starting*]: It seems to me that I shall presently be married to Ann whether I like it myself or not.

MRS WHITEFIELD [*peacefully*]: Oh, very likely you will: you know what she is when she has set her mind on anything. But dont put it on me: thats all I ask. Tavy has just let out that she's been saying that I am making her marry you; and the poor boy is breaking his heart about it; for he is in love with her himself, though what he sees in her so wonderful, goodness knows: *I* dont. It's no use telling Tavy that Ann puts things into people's heads by telling them that I want them when the thought of them never crossed my mind. It only sets Tavy against me. But you know better than that. So if you marry her, dont put the blame on me.

TANNER [*emphatically*]: I havnt the slightest intention of marrying her.

MRS WHITEFIELD [*slyly*]: She'd suit you better than Tavy. She'd meet her match in you, Jack. I'd like to see her meet her match.

TANNER: No man is a match for a woman, except with a poker and a pair of hobnailed boots. Not always even then. Anyhow, *I* cant take the poker to her. I should be a mere slave.

MRS WHITEFIELD: No: she's afraid of you. At all events, you would tell her the truth about herself. She wouldnt be able to slip out of it as she does with me.

TANNER: Everybody would call me a brute if I told Ann the truth about herself in terms of her own moral code. To begin with, Ann says things that are not strictly true.

MRS WHITEFIELD: I'm glad somebody sees she is not an angel.

TANNER: In short – to put it as a husband would put it when exasperated to the point of speaking out – she is a liar. And since she has plunged Tavy head over ears in love with her without any intention of marrying him, she is a coquette, according to the standard definition of a coquette as a woman who rouses passions she has no intention of gratifying. And as she has now reduced you to the point of being willing to sacrifice me at the altar for the mere satisfaction of getting me to call her a liar to her face, I may conclude that she is a bully as well. She cant bully men as she bullies women; so she habitually and unscrupulously uses her personal fascination to make men give her whatever she wants. That makes her almost something for which I know no polite name.

MRS WHITEFIELD [*in mild expostulation*]: Well, you cant expect perfection, Jack.

TANNER: I dont. But what annoys me is that Ann does. I know perfectly well that all this about her being a liar and a bully and a coquette and so forth is a trumped-up moral indictment which might be brought against any-body. We all lie; we all bully as much as we dare; we all bid for admiration without the least intention of earning it; we all get as much rent as we can out of our powers of fascination. If Ann would admit this I shouldnt quarrel with her. But she wont. If she has children she'll take advantage of their telling lies to amuse herself by whack-ing them. If another woman makes eyes at me, she'll refuse to know a coquette. She will do just what she likes herself whilst insisting on everybody else doing what the conventional code prescribes. In short, I can stand everything except her confounded hypocrisy. Thats what beats me.

MRS WHITEFIELD [*carried away by the relief of hearing her own opinion so eloquently expressed*]: Oh, she is a hypocrite. She is: she is. Isnt she?

TANNER: Then why do you want to marry me to her?

MRS WHITEFIELD [*querulously*]: There now! put it on me, of course. I never thought of it until Tavy told me she said I did. But, you know, I'm very fond of Tavy: he's a sort of son to me; and I dont want him to be trampled on and made wretched.

TANNER: Whereas I dont matter, I suppose.

MRS WHITEFIELD: Oh, you are different, somehow: you are able to take care of yourself. Youd serve her out. And anyhow, she must marry somebody.

TANNER: Aha! there speaks the life instinct. You detest her; but you feel that you must get her married.

MRS WHITEFIELD [*rising, shocked*]: Do you mean that I detest my own daughter! Surely you dont believe me to be so wicked and unnatural as that, merely because I see her faults.

TANNER [*cynically*]: You love her, then?

MRS WHITEFIELD: Why, of course I do. What queer things you say, Jack! We cant help loving our own blood relations.

TANNER: Well, perhaps it saves unpleasantness to say so. But for my part, I suspect that the tables of consanguinity have a natural basis in a natural repugnance [*he rises*].

MRS WHITEFIELD: You shouldnt say things like that, Jack. I hope you wont tell Ann that I have been speaking to you. I only wanted to set myself right with you and Tavy. I couldnt sit mumchance and have everything put on me.

TANNER [*politely*]: Quite so.

MRS WHITEFIELD [*dissatisfied*]: And now Ive only made matters worse. Tavy's angry with me because I dont worship Ann. And when it's been put into my head that Ann ought to marry you, what can I say except that it would serve her right?

TANNER: Thank you.

MRS WHITEFIELD: Now dont be silly and twist what I say into something I dont mean. I ought to have fair play – [*Ann comes from the villa, followed presently by Violet, who is dressed for driving.*]

ANN [*coming to her mother's right hand with threatening suavity*]: Well, mamma darling, you seem to be having a delightful chat with Jack. We can hear you all over the place.

MRS WHITEFIELD [*appalled*]: Have you overheard –

TANNER: Never fear: Ann is only – well, we were discussing that habit of hers just now. She hasnt heard a word.

MRS WHITEFIELD [*stoutly*]: I dont care whether she has or not: I have a right to say what I please.

VIOLET [*arriving on the lawn and coming between Mrs Whitefield and Tanner*]: Ive come to say goodbye. I'm off for my honeymoon.

MRS WHITEFIELD [*crying*]: Oh, dont say that, Violet. And no wedding, no breakfast, no clothes, nor anything.

VIOLET [*petting her*]: It wont be for long.

MRS WHITEFIELD: Dont let him take you to America. Promise me that you wont.

VIOLET [*very decidedly*]: I should think not, indeed. Dont cry, dear: I'm only going to the hotel.

MRS WHITEFIELD: But going in that dress, with your luggage, makes one realize – [*She chokes, and then breaks out again*] How I wish you were my daughter, Violet!

VIOLET [*soothing her*]: There, there: so I am. Ann will be jealous.

MRS WHITEFIELD: Ann doesnt care a bit for me.

ANN: Fie, mother! Come, now: you mustnt cry any more: you know Violet doesnt like it [*Mrs Whitefield dries her eyes, and subsides*].

VIOLET: Goodbye, Jack.

TANNER: Goodbye, Violet.

VIOLET: The sooner you get married too, the better. You will be much less misunderstood.

TANNER [*restively*]: I quite expected to get married in the course of the afternoon. You all seem to have set your minds on it.

VIOLET: You might do worse. [*To Mrs Whitefield: putting her arm round her*] Let me take you to the hotel with me: the drive will do you good. Come in and get a wrap. [*She takes her towards the villa.*]

MRS WHITEFIELD [*as they go up through the garden*]: I dont know what I shall do when you are gone, with no one but Ann in the house; and she always occupied with the men! It's not to be expected that your husband will care to be bothered with an old woman like me. Oh, you neednt tell me: politeness is all very well; but I know what people think – [*She talks herself and Violet out of sight and hearing.*]

> Ann, alone with Tanner, watches him and waits. He makes an irresolute movement towards the gate; but some magnetism in her draws him to her, a broken man.

ANN: Violet is quite right. You ought to get married.

TANNER [*explosively*]: Ann: I will not marry you. Do you hear? I wont, wont, wont, wont, WONT marry you.

ANN [*placidly*]: Well, nobody axd you, sir she said, sir she said, sir she said. So thats settled.

TANNER: Yes, nobody has asked me; but everybody treats the thing as settled. It's in the air. When we meet, the others go away on absurd pretexts to leave us alone together. Ramsden no longer scowls at me: his eye beams, as if he were already giving you away to me in church. Tavy refers me to your mother and gives me his blessing. Straker openly treats you as his future employer: it was he who first told me of it.

ANN: Was that why you ran away?

TANNER: Yes, only to be stopped by a lovesick brigand and run down like a truant schoolboy.

ANN: Well, if you dont want to be married, you neednt be [*she turns away from him and sits down, much at her ease*].

TANNER [*following her*]: Does any man want to be hanged? Yet men let themselves be hanged without a struggle for life, though they could at least give the chaplain a black eye. We do the world's will, not our own. I have a frightful feeling that I shall let myself be married because it is the world's will that you should have a husband.

ANN: I daresay I shall, someday.

TANNER: But why me? me of all men! Marriage is to me apostasy, profanation of the sanctuary of my soul, violation of my manhood, sale of my birthright, shameful surrender, ignominious capitulation, acceptance of defeat. I shall decay like a thing that has served its purpose and is done with; I shall change from a man with a future to a man with a past; I shall see in the greasy eyes of all the other husbands their relief at the arrival of a new prisoner to share their ignominy. The young men will scorn me as one who has sold out: to the women I, who have always been an enigma and a possibility, shall be merely somebody else's property – and damaged goods at that: a secondhand man at best.

ANN: Well, your wife can put on a cap and make herself ugly to keep you in countenance, like my grandmother.

TANNER: So that she may make her triumph more insolent by publicly throwing away the bait the moment the trap snaps on the victim!

ANN: After all, though, what difference would it make? Beauty is all very well at first sight; but who ever looks at it when it has been in the house three days? I thought our pictures very lovely when papa bought them; but I havnt looked at them for years. You never bother about my looks: you are too well used to me. I might be the umbrella stand.

TANNER: You lie, you vampire: you lie.

ANN: Flatterer. Why are you trying to fascinate me, Jack, if you dont want to marry me?

TANNER: The Life Force. I am in the grip of the Life Force.

ANN: I dont understand in the least: it sounds like the Life Guards.

TANNER: Why dont you marry Tavy? He is willing. Can you not be satisfied unless your prey struggles?

ANN [*turning to him as if to let him into a secret*]: Tavy will never marry. Havnt you noticed that that sort of man never marries?

TANNER: What! a man who idolizes women! who sees nothing in nature but romantic scenery for love duets! Tavy, the chivalrous, the faithful, the tenderhearted and true! Tavy never marry! Why, he was born to be swept by the first pair of blue eyes he meets in the street.

ANN: Yes, I know. All the same, Jack, men like that always live in comfortable bachelor lodgings with broken hearts, and are adored by their landladies, and never get married. Men like you always get married.

TANNER [*smiting his brow*]: How frightfully, horribly true! It has been staring me in the face all my life; and I never saw it before.

ANN: Oh, it's the same with women. The poetic temperament's a very nice temperament, very amiable, very harmless and poetic, I daresay; but it's an old maid's temperament.

TANNER: Barren. The Life Force passes it by.

ANN: If thats what you mean by the Life Force, yes.

TANNER: You dont care for Tavy?

ANN [*looking round carefully to make sure that Tavy is not within earshot*]: No.

TANNER: And you do care for me?

ANN [*rising quietly and shaking her finger at him*]: Now, Jack! Behave yourself.

TANNER: Infamous, abandoned woman! Devil!

ANN: Boa-constrictor! Elephant!

TANNER: Hypocrite!

ANN [*softly*]: I must be, for my future husband's sake.

TANNER: For mine! [*Correcting himself savagely*] I mean for his.

ANN [*ignoring the correction*]: Yes, for yours. You had better marry what you call a hypocrite, Jack. Women who are not hypocrites go about in rational dress and are insulted and get into all sorts of hot water. And then their husbands get dragged in too, and live in continual dread of fresh complications. Wouldnt you prefer a wife you could depend on?

TANNER: No: a thousand times no: hot water is the revolutionist's element. You clean men as you clean milkpails, by scalding them.

ANN: Cold water has its uses too. It's healthy.

TANNER [*despairingly*]: Oh, you are witty: at the supreme moment the Life Force endows you with every quality. Well, I too can be a hypocrite. Your father's will appointed me your guardian, not your suitor. I shall be faithful to my trust.

ANN [*in low siren tones*]: He asked me who I would have as my guardian before he made that will. I chose you!

TANNER: The will is yours then! The trap was laid from the beginning.

ANN [*concentrating all her magic*]: From the beginning – from our childhood – for both of us – by the Life Force.

TANNER: I will not marry you. I will not marry you.

ANN: Oh, you will, you will.

TANNER: I tell you, no, no, no.

ANN: I tell you, yes, yes, yes.

TANNER: No.

ANN [*coaxing – imploring – almost exhausted*]: Yes. Before it is too late for repentance. Yes.

TANNER [*struck by the echo from the past*]: When did all this happen to me before? Are we two dreaming?

ANN [*suddenly losing her courage, with an anguish that she does not conceal*]: No. We are awake; and you have said no: that is all.

TANNER [*brutally*]: Well?

ANN: Well, I made a mistake: you do not love me.

TANNER [*seizing her in his arms*]: It is false. I love you. The Life Force enchants me. I have the whole world in my arms when I clasp you. But I am fighting for my freedom, for my honor, for my self, one and indivisible.

ANN: Your happiness will be worth them all.

TANNER: You would sell freedom and honor and self for happiness?

ANN: It will not be all happiness for me. Perhaps death.

TANNER [*groaning*]: Oh, that clutch holds and hurts. What have you grasped in me? Is there a father's heart as well as a mother's?

ANN: Take care, Jack; if anyone comes while we are like this, you will have to marry me.

TANNER: If we two stood now on the edge of a precipice, I would hold you tight and jump.

ANN [*panting, failing more and more under the strain*]: Jack: let me go. I have dared so frightfully – it is lasting longer than I thought. Let me go: I cant bear it.

TANNER: Nor I. Let it kill us.

ANN: Yes: I dont care. I am at the end of my forces. I dont care. I think I am going to faint.

> At this moment Violet and Octavius come from the villa with Mrs Whitefield, who is wrapped up for driving. Simultaneously Malone and Ramsden, followed by Mendoza and Straker, come in through the little gate in the paling. Tanner shamefacedly releases Ann, who raises her hand giddily to her forehead.

MALONE: Take care. Something's the matter with the lady.

RAMSDEN: What does this mean?

VIOLET [*running between Ann and Tanner*]: Are you ill?

ANN [*reeling, with a supreme effort*]: I have promised to marry Jack. [*She swoons. Violet kneels by her and chafes her hand Tanner runs round to her other hand, and tries to lift her head. Octavius goes to Violet's assistance, but does not know what to do. Mrs Whitefield hurries back into the villa. Octavius, Malone, and Ramsden run to Ann and crowd round her, stooping to assist. Straker coolly comes to Ann's feet, and Mendoza to her head, both upright and self-possessed.*]

STRAKER: Now then, ladies and gentlemen: she dont want a crowd round her: she wants air – all the air she can git. If you please, gents – [*Malone and Ramsden allow him to drive them gently past Ann and up the lawn towards the garden, where Octavius, who has already become conscious of his uselessness, joins them. Straker, following them up, pauses for moment to instruct Tanner.*] Dont lift er ed, Mr Tanner: let it go flat so's the blood can run back into it.

MENDOZA: He is right, Mr Tanner. Trust to the air of the Sierra. [*He withdraws delicately to the garden steps.*]

TANNER [*rising*]: I yield to your superior knowledge of physiology, Henry. [*He withdraws to the corner of the lawn; and Octavius immediately hurries down to him.*]

TAVY [*aside to Tanner, grasping his hand*]: Jack: be very happy.

TANNER [*aside to Tavy*]: I never asked her. It is a trap for me. [*He goes up the lawn towards the garden. Octavius remains petrified.*]

MENDOZA [*intercepting Mrs Whitefield, who comes from the villa with a glass of brandy*]: What is this, madam [*he takes it from her*]?

MRS WHITEFIELD: A little brandy.

MENDOZA: The worst thing you could give her. Allow me. [*He swallows it.*] Trust to the air of the Sierra, madam.

> For a moment the men all forget Ann and stare at Mendoza.

ANN [*in Violet's ear, clutching her round the neck*]: Violet: did Jack say anything when I fainted?

VIOLET: No.

ANN: Ah! [*With a sigh of intense relief she relapses.*]

MRS WHITEFIELD: Oh, she's fainted again.

> They are about to rush back to her; but Mendoza stops them with a warning gesture.

ANN [*supine*]: No, I havnt. I'm quite happy.

TANNER [*suddenly walking determinedly to her, and snatching her hand from Violet to feel her pulse*]: Why, her pulse is positively bounding. Come! get up. What nonsense! Up with you. [*He hauls her up summarily.*]

ANN: Yes: I feel strong enough now. But you very nearly killed me, Jack, for all that.

MALONE: A rough wooer, eh? Theyre the best sort, Miss Whitefield. I congratulate Mr Tanner; and I hope to meet you and him as frequent guests at the abbey.

ANN: Thank you. [*She goes past Malone to Octavius*] Ricky

Ticky Tavy: congratulate me. [*Aside to him*] I want to make you cry for the last time.

TAVY [*steadfastly*]: No more tears. I am happy in your happiness. And I believe in you in spite of everything.

RAMSDEN [*coming between Malone and Tanner*]: You are a happy man, Jack Tanner. I envy you.

MENDOZA [*advancing between Violet and Tanner*]: Sir: there are two tragedies in life. One is to lose your heart's desire. The other is to gain it. Mine and yours, sir.

TANNER: Mr Mendoza: I have no heart's desires. Ramsden: it is very easy for you to call me a happy man: you are only a spectator. I am one of the principals; and I know better. Ann: stop tempting Tavy, and come back to me.

ANN [*complying*]: You are absurd, Jack. [*She takes his proffered arm.*]

TANNER [*continuing*]: I solemnly say that I am not a happy man. Ann looks happy; but she is only triumphant, successful, victorious. That is not happiness, but the price for which the strong sell their happiness. What we have both done this afternoon is to renounce happiness, renounce freedom, renounce tranquillity, above all, renounce the romantic possibilities of an unknown future, for the cares of a household and a family. I beg that no man may seize the occasion to get half drunk and utter imbecile speeches and coarse pleasantries at my expense. We propose to furnish our own house according to our own taste; and I hereby give notice that the seven or eight travelling clocks, the four or five dressing cases, the carvers and fish slices, the copies of Patmore's Angel In The House in extra morocco, and the other articles you are preparing to heap upon us, will be instantly sold, and the proceeds devoted to circulating free copies of the Revolutionist's Handbook. The wedding will take place three days after our return to England, by special licence, at the office of the district superintendent registrar, in the presence of my solicitor and his clerk, who, like his clients, will be in ordinary walking dress –

VIOLET [*with intense conviction*]: You are a brute, Jack.

ANN [*looking at him with fond pride and caressing his arm*]: Never mind her, dear. Go on talking.

TANNER: Talking!

[*Universal laughter.*]

THE REVOLUTIONIST'S HANDBOOK AND POCKET COMPANION

BY JOHN TANNER, M.I.R.C.

(Member of the Idle Rich Class)

PREFACE TO THE REVOLUTIONIST'S HANDBOOK

'No one can contemplate the present condition of the masses of the people without desiring something like a revolution for the better.' *Sir Robert Giffen*. Essays in Finance, vol. ii. p. 393.

FOREWORD

A REVOLUTIONIST is one who desires to discard the existing social order and try another.

The constitution of England is revolutionary. To a Russian or Anglo-Indian bureaucrat, a general election is as much a revolution as a referendum or plebiscite in which the people fight instead of voting. The French Revolution overthrew one set of rulers and substituted another with different interests and different views. That is what a general election enables the people to do in England every seven years if they choose. Revolution is therefore a national institution in England; and its advocacy by an Englishman needs no apology.

Every man is a revolutionist concerning the thing he understands. For example, every person who has mastered a profession is a sceptic concerning it, and consequently a revolutionist.

Every genuine religious person is a heretic and therefore a revolutionist.

All who achieve real distinction in life begin as revolutionists. The most distinguished persons become more revolutionary as they grow older, though they are commonly supposed to become more conservative owing to their loss of faith in conventional methods of reform.

Any person under the age of thirty, who, having any knowledge of the existing social order, is not a revolutionist, is an inferior.

AND YET

Revolutions have never lightened the burden of tyranny: they have only shifted it to another shoulder.

JOHN TANNER.

THE REVOLUTIONIST'S HANDBOOK

I. ON GOOD BREEDING

If there were no God, said the eighteenth century Deist, it would be necessary to invent Him. Now this XVIII century god was *deus ex machina*, the god who helped those who could not help themselves, the god of the lazy and incapable. The nineteenth century decided that there is indeed no such god; and now Man must take in hand all the work that he used to shirk with an idle prayer. He must, in effect, change himself into the political Providence which he formerly conceived as god; and such change is not only possible, but the only sort of change that is real. The mere transfiguration of institutions, as from military and priestly dominance to commercial and scientific dominance, from commercial dominance to proletarian democracy, from slavery to serfdom, from serfdom to capitalism, from monarchy to republicanism, from polytheism to monotheism, from monotheism to atheism, from atheism to pantheistic humanitarianism, from general illiteracy to general literacy, from romance to realism, from realism to mysticism, from metaphysics to physics, are all but changes from Tweedledum to Tweedledee: *plus ça change, plus c'est la même chose*. But the changes from the crab apple to the pippin, from the wolf and fox to the house dog, from the charger of Henry V to the brewer's draught horse and the racehorse, are real; for here Man has played the god, subduing Nature to his intention, and ennobling or debasing Life for a set purpose. And what can be done with a wolf can be done with a man. If such monsters as the tramp and the gentleman can appear as mere by-products of Man's individual greed and folly, what might we not hope for as a main product of his universal aspiration?

This is no new conclusion. The despair of institutions, and

the inexorable 'ye must be born again,' with Mrs Poyser's stipulation, 'and born different,' recurs in every generation. The cry for the Superman did not begin with Nietzsche, nor will it end with his vogue. But it has always been silenced by the same question: what kind of person is this Superman to be? You ask, not for a super-apple, but for an eatable apple; not for a super-horse, but for a horse of greater draught or velocity. Neither is it of any use to ask for a Superman: you must furnish a specification of the sort of man you want. Unfortunately you do not know what sort of man you want. Some sort of goodlooking philosopher-athlete, with a handsome healthy woman for his mate, perhaps.

Vague as this is, it is a great advance on the popular demand for a perfect gentleman and a perfect lady. And, after all, no market demand in the world takes the form of exact technical specification of the article required. Excellent poultry and potatoes are produced to satisfy the demand of housewives who do not know the technical differences between a tuber and a chicken. They will tell you that the proof of the pudding is in the eating; and they are right. The proof of the Superman will be in the living; and we shall find out how to produce him by the old method of trial and error, and not by waiting for a completely convincing prescription of his ingredients.

Certain common and obvious mistakes may be ruled out from the beginning. For example, we agree that we want superior mind; but we need not fall into the football club folly of counting on this as a product of superior body. Yet if we recoil so far as to conclude that superior mind consists in being the dupe of our ethical classifications of virtues and vices, in short, of conventional morality, we shall fall out of the frying-pan of the football club into the fire of the Sunday School. If we must choose between a race of athletes and a race of 'good' men, let us have the athletes: better Samson and Milo than Calvin and Robespierre. But neither alternative is worth changing for: Samson is no more a Superman than Calvin. What then are we to do?

II. PROPERTY AND MARRIAGE

Let us hurry over the obstacles set up by property and marriage. Revolutionists make too much of them. No doubt it is easy to demonstrate that property will destroy society unless society destroys it. No doubt, also, property has hitherto held its own and destroyed all the empires. But that was because the superficial objection to it (that it distributes social wealth and the social labour burden in a grotesquely inequitable manner) did not threaten the existence of the race, but only the individual happiness of its units, and finally the maintenance of some irrelevant political form or other, such as a nation, an empire, or the like. Now as happiness never matters to Nature, as she neither recognizes flags and frontiers nor cares a straw whether the economic system adopted by a society is feudal, capitalistic, or collectivist, provided it keeps the race afoot (the hive and the anthill being as acceptable to her as Utopia), the demonstrations of Socialists, though irrefutable, will never make any serious impression on property. The knell of that overrated institution will not sound until it is felt to conflict with some more vital matter than mere personal inequities in industrial economy. No such conflict was perceived whilst society had not yet grown beyond national communities too small and simple to overtax Man's limited political capacity disastrously. But we have now reached the stage of international organization. Man's political capacity and magnanimity are clearly beaten by the vastness and complexity of the problems forced on him. And it is at this anxious moment that he finds, when he looks upward for a mightier mind to help him, that the heavens are empty. He will presently see that his discarded formula that Man is the Temple of the Holy Ghost happens to be precisely true, and that it is only through his own brain and hand that this Holy Ghost, formally the most nebulous person in the Trinity, and now become its sole survivor as it has always been its real Unity, can help him in any way. And so, if the Superman is to come, he must be born of Woman by Man's intentional and well-considered contrivance. Conviction of this will smash everything that opposes it. Even Property and Marriage, which laugh at the laborer's petty complaint that he is defrauded of 'surplus value,' and at the domestic miseries of the slaves of the wedding ring, will themselves be laughed aside as the lightest of trifles if they cross this conception when it becomes a fully realized vital purpose of the race.

That they must cross it becomes obvious the moment we acknowledge the futility of breeding men for special qualities as we breed cocks for game, greyhounds for speed, or sheep for mutton. What is really important in Man is the part of him that we do not yet understand. Of much of it we are not even conscious, just as we are not normally conscious of keeping up our circulation by our heart-pump, though if we neglect it we die. We are therefore driven to the conclusion that when we have carried selection as far as we can by rejecting from the list of eligible parents all persons who are uninteresting, unpromising, or blemished without any set-off, we shall still have to trust to the guidance of fancy (*alias* Voice of Nature), both in the breeders and the parents, for that superiority in the unconscious self which will be the true characteristic of the Superman.

At this point we perceive the importance of giving fancy the widest possible field. To cut humanity up into small cliques, and effectively limit the selection of the individual to his own clique, is to postpone the Superman for eons, if not for ever. Not only should every person be nourished and trained as a possible parent, but there should be no possibility of such an obstacle to natural selection as the objection of a countess to a navvy or of a duke to a charwoman. Equality is essential to good breeding; and equality, as all economists know, is incompatible with property.

Besides, equality is an essential condition of bad breeding also; and bad breeding is indispensable to the weeding out of the human race. When the conception of heredity took hold of the scientific imagination in the middle of the last century, its devotees announced that it was a crime to marry the lunatic to the lunatic or the consumptive to the consumptive. But pray are we to try to correct our diseased stocks by infecting our healthy stocks with them? Clearly the attraction which disease has for diseased people is beneficial to the race. If two really unhealthy people get married, they will, as likely as not, have a great number of children who will all die before they reach maturity. This is a far more satisfactory arrangement than the tragedy of a union between a healthy and an unhealthy person. Though more costly than sterilization of the unhealthy, it has the enormous advantage that in the event of our notions of health and unhealth being erroneous (which to some extent they most certainly are), the error will be corrected by experience instead of confirmed by evasion.

One fact must be faced resolutely, in spite of the shrieks of the romantic. There is no evidence that the best citizens are the offspring of congenial marriages, or that a conflict of temperament is not a highly important part of what breeders call crossing. On the contrary, it is quite sufficiently probable that good results may be obtained from parents who would be extremely unsuitable companions and partners, to make it certain that the experiment of mating them will sooner or later be tried purposely almost as often as it is now tried accidentally. But mating such couples must clearly not involve marrying them. In conjugation two complementary persons may supply one another's deficiencies: in the domestic partnership of marriage they only feel them and suffer from them. Thus the son of a robust, cheerful, eupeptic British country squire, with the tastes and range of his class, and of a clever, imaginative, intellectual, highly civilized Jewess, might be very superior to both his parents; but it is not likely that the Jewess would find the squire an interesting companion, or his habits, his friends, his place and mode of life congenial to her. Therefore marriage, whilst it is made an indispensable condition of mating, will delay the advent of the Superman as effectually as Property, and will be modified by the impulse towards him just as effectually.

The practical abrogation of Property and Marriage as they exist at present will occur without being much noticed. To the mass of men, the intelligent abolition of property would mean nothing except an increase in the quantity of food, clothing, housing, and comfort at their personal disposal, as well as a greater control over their time and circumstances. Very few persons now make any distinction between virtually complete property and property held on such highly developed public conditions as to place its income on the same footing as that of a propertyless clergyman, officer, or civil servant. A landed proprietor may still drive men and women off his land, demolish their dwellings, and replace them with sheep or deer; and in the unregulated trades the private trader may still spunge on the regulated trades and sacrifice the life and health of the nation as lawlessly as the Manchester cotton manufacturers did at the beginning of last century. But though the Factory Code on the one hand, and Trade Union organization on the other, have, within the lifetime of men still living, converted the old unrestricted property of the cotton manufacturer in his mill and the cotton spinner in his labor into a mere permission to trade or work on stringent public or collective conditions, imposed in the interest of the general welfare without any regard for individual hard cases, people in Lancashire still speak of their 'property' in the old terms, meaning nothing more by it than the things a thief can be punished for stealing. The total abolition of property, and the conversion of every citizen into a salaried functionary in the public service, would leave much more than 99 per cent of the nation quite unconscious of any greater change than now takes place when the son of a shipowner goes into the navy. They would still call their watches and umbrellas and back gardens their property.

Marriage also will persist as a name attached to a general custom long after the custom itself will have altered. For example, modern English marriage, as modified by divorce and by Married Women's Property Acts, differs more from early XIX century marriage than Byron's marriage did from

Shakespear's. At the present moment marriage in England differs not only from marriage in France, but from marriage in Scotland. Marriage as modified by the divorce laws in South Dakota would be called mere promiscuity in Clapham. Yet the Americans, far from taking a profligate and cynical view of marriage, do homage to its ideals with a seriousness that seems old fashioned in Clapham. Neither in England nor America would a proposal to abolish marriage be tolerated for a moment; and yet nothing is more certain than that in both countries the progressive modification of the marriage contract will be continued until it is no more onerous nor irrevocable than any ordinary commercial deed of partnership. Were even this dispensed with, people would still call themselves husbands and wives; describe their companionships as marriages; and be for the most part unconscious that they were any less married than Henry VIII. For though a glance at the legal conditions of marriage in different Christian countries shews that marriage varies legally from frontier to frontier, domesticity varies so little that most people believe their own marriage laws to be universal. Consequently here again, as in the case of Property, the absolute confidence of the public in the stability of the institution's name, makes it all the easier to alter its substance.

However, it cannot be denied that one of the changes in public opinion demanded by the need for the Superman is a very unexpected one. It is nothing less than the dissolution of the present necessary association of marriage with conjugation, which most unmarried people regard as the very diagnostic of marriage. They are wrong, of course: it would be quite as near the truth to say that conjugation is the one purely accidental and incidental condition of marriage. Conjugation is essential to nothing but the propagation of the race; and the moment that paramount need is provided for otherwise than by marriage, conjugation, from Nature's creative point of view, ceases to be essential in marriage. But marriage does not thereupon cease to be so economical, convenient, and comfortable, that the Superman might safely bribe the matrimonomaniacs by offering to revive all the old inhuman stringency and irrevocability of marriage, to abolish divorce, to confirm the horrible bond which still chains decent people to drunkards, criminals, and wasters, provided only the complete extrication of conjugation from it were conceded to him. For if people could form domestic companionships on no easier terms than these, they would still marry. The Roman Catholic, forbidden by his Church to avail himself of the divorce laws, marries as freely as the South Dakotan Presbyterians who can change partners with a facility that scandalizes the old world: and were his Church to dare a further step towards Christianity and enjoin celibacy on its laity as well as on its clergy, marriages would still be contracted for the sake of domesticity by perfectly obedient sons and daughters of the Church. One need not further pursue these hypotheses: they are only suggested here to help the reader to analyse marriage into its two functions of regulating conjugation and supplying a form of domesticity. These two functions are quite separable; and domesticity is the only one of the two which is essential to the existence of marriage, because conjugation without domesticity is not marriage at all, whereas domesticity without conjugation is still marriage: in fact it is necessarily the actual condition of all fertile marriages during a great part of their duration, and of some marriages during the whole of it.

Taking it, then, that Property and Marriage, by destroying Equality and thus hampering sexual selection with irrelevant conditions, are hostile to the evolution of the Superman, it is easy to understand why the only generally known modern experiment in breeding the human race took place in a community which discarded both institutions.

III. THE PERFECTIONIST EXPERIMENT AT ONEIDA CREEK

In 1848 the Oneida Community was founded in America to carry out a resolution arrived at by a handful of Perfectionist Communists 'that we will devote ourselves exclusively to the establishment of the Kingdom of God.'

Though the American nation declared that this sort of thing was not to be tolerated in a Christian country, the Oneida Community held its own for over thirty years, during which period it seems to have produced healthier children and done and suffered less evil than any Joint Stock Company on record. It was, however, a highly selected community; for a genuine communist (roughly definable as an intensely proud person who proposes to enrich the common fund instead of to spunge on it) is superior to an ordinary joint stock capitalist precisely as an ordinary joint stock capitalist is superior to a pirate. Further, the Perfectionists were mightily shepherded by their chief Noyes, one of those chance attempts at the Superman which occur from time to time in spite of the interference of Man's blundering institutions. The existence of Noyes simplified the breeding problem for the Communists, the question as to what sort of man they should strive to breed being settled at once by the obvious desirability of breeding another Noyes.

But an experiment conducted by a handful of people, who, after thirty years of immunity from the unintentional child slaughter that goes on by ignorant parents in private homes, numbered only 300, could do very little except prove that Communists, under the guidance of a Superman 'devoted exclusively to the establishment of the Kingdom of God,' and caring no more for property and marriage than a Camberwell minister cares for Hindoo Caste or Suttee, might make a much better job of their lives than ordinary folk under the harrow of both these institutions. Yet their Superman himself admitted that this apparent success was only part of the abnormal phenomenon of his own occurrence; for when he came to the end of his powers through age, he himself guided and organized the voluntary relapse of the Communists into marriage, capitalism, and customary private life, thus admitting that the real social solution was not what a casual Superman could persuade a picked company to do for him, but what a whole community of Supermen would do spontaneously. If Noyes had had to organize, not a few dozen Perfectionists, but the whole United States,

America would have beaten him as completely as England beat Oliver Cromwell, France Napoleon, or Rome Julius Caesar. Cromwell learnt by bitter experience that God himself cannot raise a people above its own level, and that even though you stir a nation to sacrifice all its appetites to its conscience, the result will still depend wholly on what sort of conscience the nation has got. Napoleon seems to have ended by regarding mankind as a troublesome pack of hounds only worth keeping for the sport of hunting with them. Caesar's capacity for fighting without hatred or resentment was defeated by the determination of his soldiers to kill their enemies in the field instead of taking them prisoners to be spared by Caesar; and his civil supremacy was purchased by colossal bribery of the citizens of Rome. What great rulers cannot do, codes and religions cannot do. Man reads his own nature into every ordinance: if you devise a superhuman commandment so cunningly that it cannot be misinterpreted in terms of his will, he will denounce it as seditious blasphemy, or else disregard it as either crazy or totally unintelligible. Parliaments and synods may tinker as much as they please with their codes and creeds as circumstances alter the balance of classes and their interests; and, as a result of the tinkering, there may be an occasional illusion of moral evolution, as when the victory of the commercial caste over the military caste leads to the substitution of social boycotting and pecuniary damages for duelling. At certain moments there may even be a considerable material advance, as when the conquest of political power by the working class produces a better distribution of wealth through the simple action of the selfishness of the new masters; but all this is mere readjustment and reformation: until the heart and mind of the people is changed the very greatest man will no more dare to govern on the assumption that all are as great as he than a drover dare leave his flock to find its way through the streets as he himself would. Until there is an England in which every man is a Cromwell, a France in which every man is a Napoleon, a Rome in which every man is a Caesar, a Germany in which every man is a Luther plus a Goethe, the world will be no more improved by its heroes than a Brixton villa is improved by the pyramid of Cheops. The production of such nations is the only real change possible to us.

IV. MAN'S OBJECTION TO HIS OWN IMPROVEMENT

But would such a change be tolerated if Man must rise above himself to desire it? It would, through his misconception of its nature. Man does desire an ideal Superman with such energy as he can spare from his nutrition, and has in every age magnified the best living substitute for it he can find. His least incompetent general is set up as an Alexander; his king is the first gentleman in the world; his Pope is a saint. He is never without an array of human idols who are all nothing but sham Supermen. That the real Superman will snap his superfingers at all Man's present trumpery ideals of right, duty, honor, justice, religion, even decency, and accept moral obligations beyond present human endurance, is a thing that contemporary Man does not foresee: in fact he does not notice it when our casual Supermen do it in his very face. He actually does it himself every day without knowing it. He will therefore make no objection to the production of a race of what he calls Great Men or Heroes, because he will imagine them, not as true Supermen, but as himself endowed with infinite brains, infinite courage, and infinite money.

The most troublesome opposition will arise from the general fear of mankind that any interference with our conjugal customs will be an interference with our pleasures and our romance. This fear, by putting on airs of offended morality, has always intimidated people who have not measured its essential weakness; but it will prevail with those degenerates only in whom the instinct of fertility has faded into a mere itching for pleasure. The modern devices for combining pleasure with sterility, now universally known and accessible, enable these persons to weed themselves out of the race, a process already vigorously at work; and the consequent survival of the intelligently fertile means the survival of the partizans of the Superman; for what is proposed is nothing but the replacement of the old unintelligent, inevitable, almost unconscious fertility by an intelligently controlled, conscious fertility, and the elimination of the mere voluptuary from the evolutionary process.* Even if this selective agency had not been invented, the purpose of the race would still shatter the opposition of individual instincts. Not only do the bees and the ants satisfy their reproductive and parental instincts vicariously; but marriage itself successfully imposes celibacy on millions of unmarried normal men and women. In short, the individual instinct in this matter, overwhelming as it is thoughtlessly supposed to be, is really a finally negligible one.

V. THE POLITICAL NEED FOR THE SUPERMAN

The need for the Superman is, in its most imperative aspect, a political one. We have been driven to Proletarian Democracy by the failure of all the alternative systems; for these depended on the existence of Supermen acting as despots or oligarchs; and not only were these Supermen not always or even often forthcoming at the right moment and in an eligible social position, but when they were forthcoming they could not, except for a short time and by morally suicidal coercive methods, impose superhumanity on those whom

---

*The part played in evolution by the voluptuary will be the same as that already played by the glutton. The glutton, as the man with the strongest motive for nourishing himself, will always take more pains than his fellows to get food. When food is so difficult to get that only great exertions can secure a sufficient supply of it, the glutton's appetite develops his cunning and enterprise to the utmost; and he becomes not only the best fed but the ablest man in the community. But in more hospitable climates, or where the social organization of the food supply makes it easy for a man to overeat, then the glutton eats himself out of health and finally out of existence. All other voluptuaries prosper and perish in the same way; and this is why the survival of the fittest means finally the survival of the self-controlled, because they alone can adapt themselves to the perpetual shifting of conditions produced by industrial progress.

they governed; so, by mere force of 'human nature,' government by consent of the governed has supplanted the old plan of governing the citizen as a public-schoolboy is governed.

Now we have yet to see the man who, having any practical experience of Proletarian Democracy, has any belief in its capacity for solving great political problems, or even for doing ordinary parochial work intelligently and economically. Only under despotisms and oligarchies has the Radical faith in 'universal suffrage' as a political panacea arisen. It withers the moment it is exposed to practical trial, because Democracy cannot rise above the level of the human material of which its voters are made. Switzerland seems happy in comparison with Russia; but if Russia were as small as Switzerland, and had her social problems simplified in the same way by impregnable natural fortifications and a population educated by the same variety and intimacy of international intercourse, there might be little to choose between them. At all events Australia and Canada, which are virtually protected democratic republics, and France and the United States, which are avowedly independent democratic republics, are neither healthy, wealthy, nor wise; and they would be worse instead of better if their popular ministers were not experts in the art of dodging popular enthusiams and duping popular ignorance. The politician who once had to learn how to flatter Kings has now to learn how to fascinate, amuse, coax, humbug, frighten, or otherwise strike the fancy of the electorate; and though in advanced modern States, where the artizan is better educated than the King, it takes a much bigger man to be a successful demagogue than to be a successful courtier, yet he who holds popular convictions with prodigious energy is the man for the mob, whilst the frailer sceptic who is cautiously feeling his way towards the next century has no chance unless he happens by accident to have the specific artistic talent of the mountebank as well, in which case it is as a mountebank that he catches votes, and not as a meliorist. Consequently the demagogue, though he professes (and fails) to readjust matters in the interests of the majority of the electors, yet stereotypes mediocrity, organizes intolerance, disparages exhibitions of uncommon qualities, and glorifies conspicuous exhibitions of common ones. He manages a small job well: he muddles rhetorically through a large one. When a great political movement takes place, it is not consciously led nor organized: the unconscious self in mankind breaks its way through the problem as an elephant breaks through a jungle; and the politicians make speeches about whatever happens in the process which, with the best intentions, they do all in their power to prevent. Finally, when social aggregation arrives at a point demanding international organization before the demagogues and electorates have learnt how to manage even a country parish properly much less internationalize Constantinople, the whole political business goes to smash; and presently we have Ruins of Empires, New Zealanders sitting on a broken arch of London Bridge, and so forth.

To that recurrent catastophe we shall certainly come again unless we can have a Democracy of Supermen; and the production of such a Democracy is the only change that is now hopeful enough to nerve us to the effort that Revolution demands.

VI. PRUDERY EXPLAINED

Why the bees should pamper their mothers whilst we pamper only our operatic prima donnas is a question worth reflecting on. Our notion of treating a mother is, not to increase her supply of food, but to cut it off by forbidding her to work in a factory for a month after her confinement. Everything that can make birth a misfortune to the parents as well as a danger to the mother is conscientiously done. When a great French writer, Emile Zola, alarmed at the sterilization of his nation, wrote an eloquent and powerful book to restore the prestige of parentage, it was at once assumed in England that a work of this character, with such a title as Fecundity, was too abominable to be translated, and that any attempt to deal with the relations of the sexes from any other than the voluptuary or romantic point of view must be sternly put down. Now if this assumption were really founded on public opinion, it would indicate an attitude of disgust and resentment towards the Life Force that could only arise in a diseased and moribund community in which Ibsen's Hedda Gabler would be the typical woman. But it has no vital foundation at all. The prudery of the newspapers is, like the prudery of the dinner table, a mere difficulty of education and language. We are not taught to think decently on these subjects, and consequently we have no language for them except indecent language. We therefore have to declare them unfit for public discussion, because the only terms in which we can conduct the discussion are unfit for public use. Physiologists, who have a technical vocabulary at their disposal, find no difficulty; and masters of language who think decently can write popular stories like Zola's Fecundity or Tolstoy's Resurrection without giving the smallest offence to readers who can also think decently. But the ordinary modern journalist, who has never discussed such matters except in ribaldry, cannot write a simple comment on a divorce case without a conscious shamefulness or a furtive facetiousness that makes it impossible to read the comment aloud in company. All this ribaldry and prudery (the two are the same) does not mean that people do not feel decently on the subject: on the contrary, it is just the depth and seriousness of our feeling that makes its desecration by vile language and coarse humor intolerable; so that at last we cannot bear to have it spoken of at all because only one in a thousand can speak of it without wounding our self-respect, especially the self-respect of women. Add to the horrors of popular language the horrors of popular poverty. In crowded populations poverty destroys the possibility of cleanliness; and in the absence of cleanliness many of the natural conditions of life become offensive and noxious, with the result that at last the association of uncleanliness with these natural conditions become so overpowering that among civilized people (that is, people massed in the labyrinths of slums we call cities), half their bodily life becomes a guilty secret, unmentionable except to the doctor in emergencies; and Hedda Gabler shoots herself because maternity is so unladylike. In short, popular prudery is only a mere incident of popular squalor: the subjects which it taboos remain the most interesting and earnest of subjects in spite of it.

VII. PROGRESS AN ILLUSION

Unfortunately the earnest people get drawn off the track of evolution by the illusion of progress. Any Socialist can convince us easily that the difference between Man as he is and Man as he might become, without further evolution, under millennial conditions of nutrition, environment, and training, is enormous. He can shew that inequality and iniquitous distribution of wealth and allotment of labor have arisen through an unscientific economic system, and that Man, faulty as he is, no more intended to establish any such ordered disorder than a moth intends to be burnt when it flies into a candle flame. He can shew that the difference between the grace and strength of the acrobat and the bent back of the rheumatic field laborer is a difference produced by conditions, not by nature. He can shew that many of the most detestable human vices are not radical, but are mere reactions of our institutions on our very virtues. The Anarchist, the Fabian, the Salvationist, the Vegetarian, the doctor, the lawyer, the parson, the professor of ethics, the gymnast, the soldier, the sportsman, the inventor, the political program-maker, all have some prescription for bettering us; and almost all their remedies are physically possible and aimed at admitted evils. To them the limit of progress is, at worst, the completion of all the suggested reforms and the levelling up of all men to the point attained already by the most highly nourished and cultivated in mind and body.

Here, then, as it seems to them, is an enormous field for the energy of the reformer. Here are many noble goals attainable by many of those paths up the Hill Difficulty along which great spirits love to aspire. Unhappily, the hill will never be climbed by Man as we know him. It need not be denied that if we all struggled bravely to the end of the reformers' paths we should improve the world prodigiously. But there is no more hope in that If than in the equally plausible assurance that if the sky falls we shall all catch larks. We are not going to tread those paths: we have not sufficient energy. We do not desire the end enough: indeed in most cases we do not effectively desire it at all. Ask any man would he like to be a better man; and he will say yes, most piously. Ask him would he like to have a million of money; and he will say yes, most sincerely. But the pious citizen who would like to be a better man goes on behaving just as he did before. And the tramp who would like the million does not take the trouble to earn ten shillings: multitudes of men and women, all eager to accept a legacy of a million, live and die without having ever possessed five pounds at one time, although beggars have died in rags on mattresses stuffed with gold which they accumulated because they desired it enough to nerve them to get it and keep it. The economists who discovered that demand created supply soon had to limit the proposition to 'effective demand,' which turned out, in the final analysis, to mean nothing more than supply itself; and this holds good in politics, morals, and all other departments as well: the actual supply is the measure of the effective demand; and the mere aspirations and professions produce nothing. No community has ever yet passed beyond the initial phases in which its pugnacity and fanaticism enabled it to found a nation, and its cupidity to establish and develop a commercial civilization. Even these stages have never been attained by public spirit, but always by intolerant wilfulness and brute force. Take the Reform Bill of 1832 as an example of a conflict between two sections of educated Englishmen concerning a political measure which was as obviously necessary and inevitable as any political measure has ever been or is ever likely to be. It was not passed until the gentlemen of Birmingham had made arrangements to cut the throats of the gentlemen of St James's parish in due military form. It would not have been passed to this day if there had been no force behind it except the logic and public conscience of the Utilitarians. A despotic ruler with as much sense as Queen Elizabeth would have done better than the mob of grown-up Eton boys who governed us then by privilege, and who, since the introduction of practically Manhood Suffrage in 1884, now govern us at the request of Proletarian Democracy.

At the present time we have, instead of the Utilitarians, the Fabian Society, with its peaceful, constitutional, moral, economical policy of Socialism, which needs nothing for its bloodless and benevolent realization except that the English people shall understand it and approve of it. But why are the Fabians well spoken of in circles where thirty years ago the word Socialist was understood as equivalent to cut-throat and incendiary? Not because the English have the smallest intention of studying or adopting the Fabian policy, but because they believe that the Fabians, by eliminating the element of intimidation from the Socialist agitation, have drawn the teeth of insurgent poverty and saved the existing order from the only method of attack it really fears. Of course, if the nation adopted the Fabian policy, it would be carried out by brute force exactly as our present property system is. It would become the law; and those who resisted it would be fined, sold up, knocked on the head by policemen, thrown into prison, and in the last resort 'executed' just as they are when they break the present law. But as our proprietary class has no fear of that conversion taking place, whereas it does fear sporadic cut-throats and gunpowder plots, and strives with all its might to hide the fact that there is no moral difference whatever between the methods by which it enforces its proprietary rights and the method by which the dynamitard asserts his conception of natural human rights, the Fabian Society is patted on the back just as the Christian Social Union is, whilst the Socialist who says bluntly that a Social revolution can be made only as all other revolutions have been made, by the people who want it killing, coercing, and intimidating the people who dont want it, is denounced as a misleader of the people, and imprisoned with hard labor to shew him how much sincerity there is in the objection of his captors to physical force.

Are we then to repudiate Fabian methods, and return to those of the barricader, or adopt those of the dynamitard and the assassin? On the contrary, we are to recognize that both are fundamentally futile. It seems easy for the dynamitard to say 'Have you not just admitted that nothing is ever conceded except to physical force? Did not Gladstone admit that the Irish Church was disestablished, not by the spirit of Liberalism, but by the explosion which wrecked Clerkenwell prison?' Well, we need not foolishly and timidly deny it. Let it be fully granted. Let us grant, further, that all this lies in the nature of things; that the most ardent Socialist, if he owns property, can by no means do otherwise than Conservative proprietors until property is forcibly abolished by the whole nation; nay, that ballots and parliamentaty divisions, in spite of their vain ceremony of discussion, differ from battles only as the bloodless surrender of an outnumbered force in the field differs from Waterloo or Trafalgar. I make a present of all these admissions to the Fenian who collects money from thoughtless Irishmen in America to blow up Dublin Castle; to the detective who persuades foolish young workmen to order bombs from the nearest ironmonger and then delivers them up to penal servitude; to our military and naval commanders who believe, not in preaching, but in an ultimatum backed by plenty of lyddite; and, generally, to all whom it may concern. But of what use is it to substitute the way of the reckless and bloodyminded for the way of the cautious and humane? Is England any the better for the wreck of Clerkenwell prison, or Ireland for the disestablishment of the Irish Church? Is there the smallest reason to suppose that the nation which sheepishly let Charles and Laud and Strafford coerce it, gained anything because it afterwards, still more sheepishly, let a few strongminded Puritans, inflamed by the masterpieces of Jewish revolutionary literature, cut off the heads of the three? Suppose the Gunpowder plot had succeeded, and set a Fawkes dynasty permanently on the throne, would it have made any difference to the present state of the nation? The guillotine was used in France up to the limit of human endurance, both on Girondins and Jacobins. Fouquier Tinville followed Marie Antoinette to the scaffold; and Marie Antoinette might have asked the crowd, just as pointedly as Fouquier did, whether their bread would be any cheaper when her head was off. And what came of it all? The Imperial France of the Rougon Macquart family, and the Republican France of the Panama scandal and the Dreyfus case. Was the difference worth the guillotining of all those unlucky ladies and gentlemen, useless and mischievous as many of them were? Would any sane man guillotine a mouse to bring about such a result? Turn to Republican America. America has no Star Chamber, and no feudal barons. But it has Trusts; and it has millionaires whose factories, fenced in by live electric wires and defended by Pinkerton retainers with magazine rifles, would have made a Radical of Reginald Front de Boeuf. Would Washington or Franklin have lifted a finger in the cause of American Independence if they had foreseen its reality?

No: what Caesar, Cromwell, and Napoleon could not do with all the physical force and moral prestige of the State in their mighty hands, cannot be done by enthusiastic criminals and lunatics. Even the Jews, who, from Moses to Marx and Lassalle, have inspired all the revolutions, have had to confess that, after all, the dog will return to his vomit and the sow that was washed to her wallowing in the mire; and we may as well make up our minds that Man will return to his idols and his cupidities, in spite of all 'movements' and all revolutions, until his nature is changed. Until then, his early successes in building commercial civilizations (and such civilizations, Good Heavens!) are but preliminaries to the inevitable later stage, now threatening us, in which the passions which built the civilization become fatal instead of productive, just as the same qualities which make the lion king in the forest ensure his destruction when he enters a city. Nothing can save society then except the clear head and the wide purpose: war and competition, potent instruments of selection and evolution in one epoch, become ruinous instruments of degeneration in the next. In the breeding of animals and plants, varieties which have arisen by selection through many generations relapse precipitously into the wild type in a generation or two when selection ceases; and in the same way a civilization in which lusty pugnacity and greed have ceased to act as selective agents and have begun to obstruct and destroy, rushes downwards and backwards with a suddenness that enables an observer to see with consternation the upward steps of many centuries retraced in a single lifetime. This has often occurred even within the period covered by history; and in every instance the turning point has been reached long before the attainment, or even the general advocacy on paper, of the levelling-up of the mass to the highest point attainable by the best nourished and cultivated normal individuals.

We must therefore frankly give up the notion that Man as he exists is capable of net progress. There will always be an illusion of progress, because wherever we are conscious of an evil we remedy it, and therefore always seem to ourselves to be progressing, forgetting that most of the evils we see are the effects, finally become acute, of long-unnoticed retrogressions; that our compromising remedies seldom fully recover the lost ground; above all, that on the lines along which we are degenerating, good has become evil in our eyes, and is being undone in the name of progress precisely as evil is undone and replaced by good on the lines along which we are evolving. This is indeed the Illusion of Illusions; for it gives us infallible and appalling assurance that if our political ruin is to come, it will be effected by ardent reformers and supported by enthusiastic patriots as a series of necessary steps in our progress. Let the Reformer, the Progressive, the Meliorist then reconsider himself and his eternal

ifs and ans which never become pots and pans. Whilst Man
remains what he is, there can be no progress beyond the
point already attained and fallen headlong from at every
attempt at civilization; and since even that point is but a
pinnacle to which a few people cling in giddy terror above
an abyss of squalor, mere progress should no longer charm
us.

VIII. THE CONCEIT OF CIVILIZATION

After all, the progress illusion is not so very subtle. We
begin by reading the satires of our fathers' contemporaries;
and we conclude (usually quite ignorantly) that the abuses
exposed by them are things of the past. We see also that
reforms of crying evils are frequently produced by the
sectional shifting of political power from oppressors to
oppressed. The poor man is given a vote by the Liberals in
the hope that he will cast it for his emancipators. The hope
is not fulfilled; but the lifelong imprisonment of penniless
men for debt ceases; Factory Acts are passed to mitigate
sweating; schooling is made free and compulsory; sanitary
by-laws are multiplied; public steps are taken to house the
masses decently; the bare-footed get boots; rags become
rare; and bathrooms and pianos, smart tweeds and starched
collars, reach numbers of people who once, as 'the un-
soaped,' played the Jew's harp or the accordion in mole-
skins and belchers. Some of these changes are gains: some of
them are losses. Some of them are not changes at all: all of
them are merely the changes that money makes. Still, they
produce an illusion of bustling progress; and the reading
class infers from them that the abuses of the early Victorian
period no longer exist except as amusing pages in the novels
of Dickens. But the moment we look for a reform due to
character and not to money, to statesmanship and not to
interest or mutiny, we are disillusioned. For example, we
remembered the maladministration and incompetence re-
vealed by the Crimean war as part of a bygone state of
things until the South African war shewed that the nation
and the War Office, like those poor Bourbons who have been

so impudently blamed for a universal characteristic, had learnt nothing and forgotten nothing. We had hardly recovered from the fruitless irritation of this discovery when it transpired that the officers' mess of our most select regiment included a flogging club presided over by the senior subaltern. The disclosure provoked some disgust at the details of this schoolboyish debauchery, but no surprise at the apparent absence of any conception of manly honour and virtue, of personal courage and self-respect, in the front rank of our chivalry. In civil affairs we had assumed that the sycophancy and idolatry which encouraged Charles I to undervalue the Puritan revolt of the XVII century had been long outgrown; but it has needed nothing but favorable circumstances to revive, with added abjectness to compensate for its lost piety. We have relapsed into disputes about transubstantiation at the very moment when the discovery of the wide prevalence of theophagy as a tribal custom has deprived us of the last excuse for believing that our official religious rites differ in essentials from those of barbarians. The Christian doctrine of the uselessness of punishment and the wickedness of revenge has not, in spite of its simple common sense, found a single convert among the nations: Christianity means nothing to the masses but a sensational public execution which is made an excuse for other executions. In its name we take ten years of a thief's life minute by minute in the slow misery and degradation of modern reformed imprisonment with as little remorse as Laud and his Star Chamber clipped the ears of Bastwick and Burton. We dug up and mutilated the remains of the Mahdi the other day exactly as we dug up and mutilated the remains of Cromwell two centuries ago. We have demanded the decapitation of the Chinese Boxer princes as any Tartar would have done; and our military and naval expeditions to kill, burn, and destroy tribes and villages for knocking an Englishman on the head are so common a part of our Imperial routine that the last dozen of them has not called forth as much pity as can be counted on by any lady criminal. The judicial use of torture to extort confession is sup-

posed to be a relic of darker ages; but whilst these pages
are being written an English judge has sentenced a forger
to twenty years' penal servitude with an open declaration
that the sentence will be carried out in full unless he confesses where he has hidden the notes he forged. And no
comment whatever is made either on this or on a telegram
from the seat of war in Somaliland mentioning that certain
information has been given by a prisoner of war 'under
punishment.' Even if these reports are false, the fact that
they are accepted without protest as indicating a natural
and proper course of public conduct shews that we are
still as ready to resort to torture as Bacon was. As to vindictive cruelty, an incident in the South African war, when
the relatives and friends of a prisoner were forced to witness his execution, betrayed a baseness of temper and character which hardly leaves us the right to plume ourselves on
our superiority to Edward III at the surrender of Calais.
And the democratic American officer indulges in torture in
the Philippines just as the aristocratic English officer did in
South Africa. The incidents of the white invasion of Africa
in search of ivory, gold, diamonds, and sport, have proved
that the modern European is the same beast of prey that
formerly marched to the conquest of new worlds under
Alexander, Antony, and Pizarro. Parliaments and vestries
are just what they were when Cromwell suppressed them
and Dickens derided them. The democratic politician remains exactly as Plato described him; the physician is still
the credulous impostor and petulant scientific coxcomb
whom Molière ridiculed; the schoolmaster remains at best
a pedantic child farmer and at worst a flagellomaniac;
arbitrations are more dreaded by honest men than lawsuits;
the philanthropist is still a parasite on misery as the doctor is
on disease; the miracles of priestcraft are none the less
fraudulent and mischievous because they are now called
scientific experiments and conducted by professors; witchcraft, in the modern form of patent medicines and prophyl-
actic inoculations, is rampant; the landowner who is no
longer powerful enough to set the mantrap of Rhampsinitis

improves on it by barbed wire; the modern gentleman who is too lazy to daub his face with vermilion as a symbol of bravery employs a laundress to daub his shirt with starch as a symbol of cleanliness; we shake our heads at the dirt of the middle ages in cities made grimy with soot and foul and disgusting with shameless tobacco smoking; holy water, in its latest form of disinfectant fluid, is more widely used and believed in than ever; public health authorities deliberately go through incantations with burning sulphur (which they know to be useless) because the people believe in it as devoutly as the Italian peasant believes in the liquefaction of the blood of St Januarius; and straight forward public lying has reached gigantic developments, there being nothing to choose in this respect between the pickpocket at the police station and the minister on the treasury bench, the editor in the newspaper office, the city magnate advertizing bicycle tyres that do not side-slip, the clergyman subscribing the thirty-nine articles, and the vivisector who pledges his knightly honor that no animal operated on in the physiological laboratory suffers the slightest pain. Hypocrisy is at its worst; for we not only persecute bigotedly but sincerely in the name of the curemongering witchcraft we do believe in, but callously and hypocritically in the name of the Evangelical creed that our rulers privately smile at as the Italian patricians of the fifth century smiled at Jupiter and Venus. Sport is, as it has always been, murderous excitement: the impulse to slaughter is universal; and museums are set up throughout the country to encourage little children and elderly gentlemen to make collections of corpses preserved in alcohol, and to steal birds' eggs and keep them as the red Indian used to keep scalps. Coercion with the lash is as natural to an Englishman as it was to Solomon spoiling Rehoboam: indeed, the comparison is unfair to the Jews in view of the facts that the Mosaic law forbade more than forty lashes in the name of humanity, and that floggings of a thousand lashes were inflicted on English soldiers in the XVIII and XIX centuries, and would be inflicted still but for the change in the balance of political power between the military caste and the commercial classes and the proletariat. In spite of that change, flogging is still an institution in the public school, in the military prison, on the training ship, and in that school of littleness called the home. The lascivious clamor of the flagellomaniac for more of it, constant as the clamor for more insolence, more war, and lower rates, is tolerated and even gratified because, having no moral ends in view, we have sense enough to see that nothing but brute coercion can impose our selfish will on others. Cowardice is universal: patriotism, public opinion, parental duty, discipline, religion, morality, are only fine names for intimidation; and cruelty, gluttony, and credulity keep cowardice in countenance. We cut the throat of a calf and hang it up by the heels to bleed to death so that our veal cutlet may be white; we nail geese to a board and cram them with food because we like the taste of liver disease; we tear birds to pieces to decorate our women's hats; we mutilate domestic animals for no reason at all except to follow an instinctively cruel fashion; and we connive at the most abominable tortures in the hope of discovering some magical cure for our own diseases by them.

Now please observe that these are not exceptional developments of our admitted vices, deplored and prayed against by all good men. Not a word has been said here of the excesses of our Neros, of whom we have the full usual percentage. With the exception of the few military examples, which are mentioned mainly to shew that the education and standing of a gentleman, reinforced by the strongest conventions of honor, *esprit de corps*, publicity and responsibility, afford no better guarantees of conduct than the passions of a mob, the illustrations given above are commonplaces taken from the daily practices of our best citizens, vehemently defended in our newspapers and in our pulpits. The very humanitarians who abhor them are stirred to murder by them: the dagger of Brutus and Ravaillac is still active in the hands of Caserio and Luccheni; and the pistol has come to its aid in the hands of Guiteau and Czolgosz. Our remedies are still limited to endurance or assassination; and the assassin is still judicially assassinated on the principle that two blacks make a white. The only novelty is in our methods: through the discovery of dynamite the over-loaded musket of Hamilton of Bothwellhaugh has been superseded by the bomb; but Ravachol's heart burns just as Hamilton's did. The world will not bear thinking of to those who know what it is, even with the largest discount for the restraints of poverty on the poor and cowardice on the rich.

All that can be said for us is that people must and do live and let live up to a certain point. Even the horse, with his docked tail and bitted jaw, finds his slavery mitigated by the fact that a total disregard of his need for food and rest would put his master to the expense of buying a new horse every second day; for you cannot work a horse to death and then pick up another one for nothing, as you can a laborer. But this natural check on inconsiderate selfishness is itself checked, partly by our shortsightedness, and partly by deliberate calculation; so that beside the man who, to his own loss, will shorten his horse's life in mere stinginess, we have the tramway company which discovers actuarially that though a horse may live from 24 to 40 years, yet it pays better to work him to death in 4 and then replace him by a fresh victim. And human slavery, which has reached its worst recorded point within our own time in the form of free wage labor, has encountered the same personal and commercial limits to both its aggravation and its mitigation. Now that the freedom of wage labor has produced a scarcity of it, as in South Africa, the leading English newspaper and the leading English weekly review have openly and without apology demanded a return to compulsory labor: that is, to the methods by which, as we believe, the Egyptians built the pyramids. We know now that the crusade against chattel slavery in the XIX century succeeded solely because chattel slavery was neither the most effective nor the least humane method of labor exploitation; and the world is now feeling its way towards a still more effective system which shall abolish the freedom of the worker without again making his exploiter responsible for him.

Still, there is always some mitigation: there is the fear of revolt; and there are the effects of kindliness and affection. Let it be repeated therefore that no indictment is here laid against the world on the score of what its criminals and monsters do. The fires of Smithfield and of the Inquisition were lighted by earnestly pious people, who were kind and good as kindness and goodness go. And when a negro is dipped in kerosene and set on fire in America at the present time, he is not a good man lynched by ruffians: he is a criminal lynched by crowds of respectable, charitable, virtuously indignant, high-minded citizens, who, though they act outside the law, are at least more merciful than the American legislators and judges who not so long ago condemned men to solitary confinement for periods, not of five months, as our own practice is, but of five years and more. The things that our moral monsters do may be left out of account with St Bartholomew massacres and other momentary outbursts of social disorder. Judge us by the admitted and respected practice of our most reputable circles; and, if you know the facts and are strong enough to look them in the face, you must admit that unless we are replaced by a more highly evolved animal – in short, by the Superman – the world must remain a den of dangerous animals among whom our few accidental supermen, our Shakespears, Goethes, Shelleys, and their like, must live as precariously as lion tamers do, taking the humor of their situation, and the dignity of their superiority, as a set-off to the horror of the one and the loneliness of the other.

IX. THE VERDICT OF HISTORY

It may be said that though the wild beast breaks out in Man and casts him back momentarily into barbarism under the excitement of war and crime, yet his normal life is higher than the normal life of his forefathers. This view is very acceptable to Englishmen, who always lean sincerely to virtue's side as long as it costs them nothing either in money or in thought. They feel deeply the injustice of foreigners, who allow them no credit for this conditional highmindedness. But there is no reason to suppose that our ancestors were less capable of it than we are. To all such claims for the existence of a progressive moral evolution operating visibly from grandfather to grandson, there is the conclusive reply that a thousand years of such evolution would have produced enormous social changes, of which the historical evidence would be overwhelming. But not Macaulay himself, the most confident of Whig meliorists, can produce any such evidence that will bear cross-examination. Compare our conduct and our codes with those mentioned contemporarily in such ancient scriptures and classics as have come down to us, and you will find no jot of ground for the belief that any moral progress whatever has been made in historic time, in spite of all the romantic attempts of historians to reconstruct the past on that assumption. Within that time it has happened to nations as to private families and individuals that they have flourished and decayed, repented and hardened their hearts, submitted and protested, acted and reacted, oscillated between natural and artificial sanitation (the oldest house in the world, unearthed the other day in Crete, has quite modern sanitary arrangements), and rung a thousand changes on the different scales of income and pressure of population, firmly believing all the time that mankind was advancing by leaps and bounds because men were constantly busy. And the mere chapter of accidents has left a small accumulation of chance discoveries, such as the wheel, the arch, the safety pin, gunpowder, the magnet, the Voltaic pile and so forth: things which, unlike the gospels and philosophic treatises of the sages, can be usefully understood and applied by common men; so that steam locomotion is possible without a nation of Stephensons, although national Christianity is impossible without a nation of Christs. But does any man seriously believe that the *chauffeur* who drives a motor car from Paris to Berlin is a more highly evolved man that the charioteer of Achilles, or that a modern Prime Minister is a more enlightened ruler than Caesar because he rides a tricycle, writes his dispatches by the electric light, and instructs his stockbroker through the telephone?

Enough, then, of this goose-cackle about Progress: Man, as he is, never will nor can add a cubit to his stature by any of its quackeries, political, scientific, educational, religious, or artistic. What is likely to happen when this conviction gets into the minds of the men whose present faith in these illusions is the cement of our social system, can be imagined only by those who know how suddenly a civilization which has long ceased to think (or in the old phrase, to watch and pray) can fall to pieces when the vulgar belief in its hypocrisies and impostures can no longer hold out against its failures and scandals. When religious and ethical formulae become so obsolete that no man of strong mind can believe them, they have also reached the point at which no man of high character will profess them; and from that moment until they are formally disestablished, they stand at the door of every profession and every public office to keep out every able man who is not a sophist or a liar. A nation which revises its parish councils once in three years, but will not revise its articles of religion once in three hundred, even when those articles avowedly began as a political compromise dictated by Mr Facing-Both-Ways, is a nation that needs remaking.

Our only hope, then, is in evolution. We must replace the man by the superman. It is frightful for the citizen, as the years pass him, to see his own contemporaries so exactly reproduced by the younger generation, that his companions of thirty years ago have their counterparts in every city crowd, where he has to check himself repeatedly in the act of saluting as an old friend some young man to whom he is only an elderly stranger. All hope of advance dies in his bosom as he watches them: he knows that they will do just what their fathers did, and that the few voices which will still, as always before, exhort them to do something else and be something better, might as well spare their breath to cool their porridge (if they can get any). Men like Ruskin and Carlyle will preach to Smith and Brown for the sake of preaching, just as St Francis preached to the birds and St Anthony to the fishes. But Smith and Brown, like the fishes and birds, remain as they are; and poets who plan Utopias and prove that nothing is necessary for their realization but that Man should will them, perceive at last, like Richard Wagner, that the fact to be faced is that Man does not effectively will them. And he never will until he becomes Superman.

And so we arrive at the end of the Socialist's dream of 'the socialization of the means of production and exchange,' of the Positivist's dream of moralizing the capitalist, and of the ethical professor's, legislator's, educator's dream of putting commandments and codes and lessons and examination marks on a man as harness is put on a horse, ermine on a judge, pipeclay on a soldier, or a wig on an actor, and pretending that his nature has been changed. The only fundamental and possible Socialism is the socialization of the selective breeding of Man: in other terms, of human evolution. We must eliminate the Yahoo, or his vote will wreck the commonwealth.

X. THE METHOD

As to the method, what can be said as yet except that where there is a will, there is a way? If there be no will, we are lost. That is a possibility for our crazy little empire, if not for the universe; and as such possibilities are not to be entertained without despair, we must, whilst we survive, proceed on the assumption that we have still energy enough to not only will to live, but to will to live better. That may mean that we must establish a State Department of Evolution, with a seat in the Cabinet for its chief, and a revenue to defray the cost of direct State experiments, and provide inducements to private persons to achieve successful results. It may mean a private society or a chartered company for the improvement of human live stock. But for the present it is far more likely to mean a blatant repudiation of such proposals as indecent and immoral, with, nevertheless, a general secret pushing of the human will in the repudiated direction; so that all sorts of institutions and public authorities will under some pretext or other feel their way furtively towards the Superman. Mr Graham Wallas has already ventured to suggest, as Chairman of the School Management Committee of the London School Board, that the accepted policy of the Sterilization of the Schoolmistress, however administratively convenient, is open to criticism from the national stock-breeding point of view; and this is as good an example as any of the way in which the drift towards the Superman may operate in spite of all our hypocrisies. One thing at least is clear to begin with. If a woman can, by careful selection of a father, and nourishment of herself, produce a citizen with efficient senses, sound organs, and a good digestion, she should clearly be secured a sufficient reward for that natural service to make her willing to undertake and repeat it. Whether she be financed in the undertaking by herself, or by the father, or by a speculative capitalist, or by a new department of, say, the Royal Dublin Society, or (as at present) by the War Office maintaining her 'on the strength' and authorizing a particular soldier to marry her, or by a local authority under a by-law directing that women may under certain circumstances have a year's leave of absence on full salary, or by the central government, does not matter provided the result be satisfactory.

It is a melancholy fact that as the vast majority of women and their husbands have, under existing circumstances, not enough nourishment, no capital, no credit, and no knowledge of science or business, they would, if the State would pay for birth as it now pays for death, be exploited by joint stock companies for dividends, just as they are in ordinary industries. Even a joint stock human stud farm (piously disguised as a reformed Foundling Hospital or something of that sort) might well, under proper inspection and regulation, produce better results than our present reliance on promiscuous marriage. It may be objected that when an ordinary contractor produces stores for sale to the Government, and the Government rejects them as not up to the required standard, the condemned goods are either sold for what they will fetch or else scrapped: that is, treated as waste material; whereas if the goods consisted of human beings, all that could be done would be to let them loose or send them to the nearest workhouse. But there is nothing new in private enterprise throwing its human refuse on the cheap labor market and the workhouse; and the refuse of the new industry would presumably be better bred than the staple product of ordinary poverty. In our present happy-go-lucky industrial disorder, all the human products, successful or not, would have to be thrown on the labor market; but the unsuccessful ones would not entitle the company to a bounty and so would be a dead loss to it. The practical commercial difficulty would be the uncertainty and the cost in time and money of the first experiments. Purely commercial capital would not touch such heroic operations during the experimental stage; and in any case the strength of mind needed for so momentous a new departure could not be fairly expected from the Stock Exchange. It will have to be handled by statesmen with character enough to tell our democracy and plutocracy that statecraft does not consist in flattering their follies or applying their suburban standards of propriety to the affairs of four continents. The matter must be taken up either by the State or by some organization strong enough to impose respect upon the State.

The novelty of any such experiment, however, is only in the scale of it. In one conspicuous case, that of royalty, the State does already select the parents on purely political grounds; and in the peerage, though the heir to a dukedom is legally free to marry a dairymaid, yet the social pressure on him to confine his choice to politically and socially eligible mates is so overwhelming that he is really no more free to marry the dairymaid than George IV was to marry Mrs Fitzherbert; and such a marriage could only occur as a result of extraordinary strength of character on the part of the dairymaid acting upon extraordinary weakness on the part of the duke. Let those who think the whole conception of intelligent breeding absurd and scandalous ask themselves why George IV was not allowed to choose his own wife whilst any tinker could marry whom he pleased? Simply because it did not matter a rap politically whom the tinker married, whereas it mattered very much whom the king married. The way in which all considerations of the king's personal rights, of the claims of the heart, of the sanctity of the marriage oath, and of romantic morality crumpled up before this political need shews how negligible all these apparently irresistible prejudices are when they come into conflict with the demand for quality in our rulers. We learn the same lesson from the case of the soldier, whose marriage, when it is permitted at all, is despotically controlled with a view solely to military efficiency.

Well, nowadays it is not the King that rules, but the tinker. Dynastic wars are no longer feared, dynastic alliances no longer valued. Marriages in royal families are becoming rapidly less political, and more popular, domestic, and romantic. If all the kings in Europe were made as free tomorrow as King Cophetua, nobody but their aunts and chamberlains would feel a moment's anxiety as to the consequences. On the other hand a sense of the social importance of the tinker's marriage has been steadily growing. We have made a public matter of his wife's health in the month after her confinement. We have taken the minds of his children out of his hands and put them into those of our State schoolmaster. We shall presently make their bodily nourishment independent of him. But they are still riff-raff; and to hand the country over to riff-raff is national suicide, since riff-raff can neither govern nor will let anyone else govern except the highest bidder of bread and circuses. There is no public enthusiast alive of twenty years' practical democratic experience who believes in the political adequacy of the electorate or of the bodies it elects. The overthrow of the aristocrat has created the necessity for the Superman.

Englishmen hate Liberty and Equality too much to understand them. But every Englishman loves and desires a pedigree. And in that he is right. King Demos must be bred like all other Kings; and with Must there is no arguing. It is idle for an individual writer to carry so great a matter further in a pamphlet. A conference on the subject is the next step needed. It will be attended by men and women who, no longer believing that they can live for ever, are seeking for some immortal work into which they can build the best of themselves before their refuse is thrown into that arch dust destructor, the cremation furnace.

MAXIMS FOR REVOLUTIONISTS

THE GOLDEN RULE

Do not do unto others as you would that they should do unto you. Their tastes may not be the same.

Never resist temptation: prove all things: hold fast that which is good.

Do not love your neighbour as yourself. If you are on good terms with yourself it is an impertinence: if on bad, an injury.

The golden rule is that there are no golden rules.

IDOLATRY

The art of government is the organization of idolatry.

The bureaucracy consists of functionaries; the aristocracy, of idols; the democracy, of idolaters.

The populace cannot understand the bureaucracy: it can only worship the national idols.

The savage bows down to idols of wood and stone: the civilized man to idols of flesh and blood.

A limited monarchy is a device for combining the inertia of a wooden idol with the credibility of a flesh and blood one.

When the wooden idol does not answer the peasant's prayer, he beats it: when the flesh and blood idol does not satisfy the civilized man, he cuts its head off.

He who slays a king and he who dies for him are alike idolaters.

ROYALTY

Kings are not born: they are made by artificial hallucination. When the process is interrupted by adversity at a critical age, as in the case of Charles II, the subject becomes sane and never completely recovers his kingliness.

The Court is the servant's hall of the sovereign.

Vulgarity in a king flatters the majority of the nation.

The flunkeyism propagated by the throne is the price we pay for its political convenience.

DEMOCRACY

If the lesser mind could measure the greater as a footrule can measure a pyramid, there would be finality in universal suffrage. As it is, the political problem remains unsolved.

Democracy substitutes election by the incompetent many for appointment by the corrupt few.

Democratic republics can no more dispense with national idols than monarchies with public functionaries.

Government presents only one problem: the discovery of a trustworthy anthropometric method.

IMPERIALISM

Excess of insularity makes a Briton an Imperialist.

Excess of local self-assertion makes a colonist an Imperialist.

A colonial Imperialist is one who raises colonial troops, equips a colonial squadron, claims a Federal Parliament sending its measures to the Throne instead of to the Colonial Office, and, being finally brought by this means into insoluble conflict with the insular British Imperialist, 'cuts the painter' and breaks up the Empire.

LIBERTY AND EQUALITY

He who confuses political liberty with freedom and political equality with similarity has never thought for five minutes about either.

Nothing can be unconditional: consequently nothing can be free.

Liberty means responsibility. That is why most men dread it.

The duke inquires contemptuously whether his game-keeper is the equal of the Astronomer Royal; but he insists that they shall both be hanged equally if they murder him.

The notion that the colonel need be a better man than the private is as confused as the notion that the keystone need be stronger than the coping stone.

Where equality is undisputed, so also is subordination.

Equality is fundamental in every department of social organization.

The relation of superior to inferior excludes good manners.

EDUCATION

When a man teaches something he does not know to somebody else who has no aptitude for it, and gives him a certificate of proficiency, the latter has completed the education of a gentleman.

A fool's brain digests philosophy into folly, science into superstition, and art into pedantry. Hence University education.

The best brought-up children are those who have seen their parents as they are. Hypocrisy is not the parent's first duty.

The vilest abortionist is he who attempts to mould a child's character.

At the University every great treatise is postponed until its author attains impartial judgment and perfect knowledge. If a horse could wait as long for its shoes and would pay for them in advance, our blacksmiths would all be college dons.

He who can, does. He who cannot, teaches.

A learned man is an idler who kills time with study. Beware of his false knowledge: it is more dangerous than ignorance.

Activity is the only road to knowledge.

Every fool believes what his teachers tell him, and calls his credulity science or morality as confidently as his father called it divine revelation.

No man fully capable of his own language ever masters another.

No man can be a pure specialist without being in the strict sense an idiot.

Do not give your children moral and religious instruction unless you are quite sure they will not take it too seriously. Better be the mother of Henri Quatre and Nell Gwynne than of Robespierre and Queen Mary Tudor.

MARRIAGE

Marriage is popular because it combines the maximum of temptation with the maximum of opportunity.

Marriage is the only legal contract which abrogates as between the parties all the laws that safeguard the particular relation to which it refers.

The essential function of marriage is the continuance of the race, as stated in the Book of Common Prayer.

The accidental function of marriage is the gratification of the amoristic sentiment of mankind.

The artificial sterilization of marriage makes it possible for marriage to fulfil its accidental function whilst neglecting its essential one.

The most revolutionary invention of the XIX century was the artificial sterilization of marriage.

Any marriage system which condemns a majority of the population to celibacy will be violently wrecked on the pretext that it outrages morality.

Polygamy, when tried under modern democratic conditions, as by the Mormons, is wrecked by the revolt of the mass of inferior men who are condemned to celibacy by it; for the maternal instinct leads a woman to prefer a tenth share in a first rate man to the exclusive possession of a third rate one. Polyandry has not been tried under these conditions.

The minimum of national celibacy (ascertained by dividing the number of males in the community by the number of females, and taking the quotient as the number of wives or husbands permitted to each person) is secured in England (where the quotient is 1) by the institution of monogamy.

The modern sentimental term for the national minimum of celibacy is Purity.

Marriage, or any other form of promiscuous amoristic monogamy, is fatal to large States because it puts its ban on the deliberate breeding of man as a political animal.

CRIME AND PUNISHMENT

All scoundrelism is summed up in the phrase 'Que Messieurs les Assassins commencent!'

The man who has graduated from the flogging block at Eton to the bench from which he sentences the garotter to be flogged is the same social product as the garotter who has been kicked by his father and cuffed by his mother until he has grown strong enough to throttle and rob the rich citizen whose money he desires.

Imprisonment is as irrevocable as death.

Criminals do not die by the hands of the law. They die by the hands of other men.

The assassin Czolgosz made President McKinley a hero by assassinating him. The United States of America made Czolgosz a hero by the same process.

Assassination on the scaffold is the worst form of assassination, because there it is invested with the approval of society.

It is the deed that teaches, not the name we give it. Murder and capital punishment are not opposites that cancel one another, but similars that breed their kind.

Crime is only the retail department of what, in wholesale, we call penal law.

When a man wants to murder a tiger he calls it sport: when the tiger wants to murder him he calls it ferocity. The distinction between Crime and Justice is no greater.

Whilst we have prisons it matters little which of us occupy the cells.

The most anxious man in a prison is the governor.

It is not necessary to replace a guillotined criminal: it is necessary to replace a guillotined social system.

TITLES

Titles distinguish the mediocre, embarrass the superior, and are disgraced by the inferior.

Great men refuse titles because they are jealous of them.

HONOR

There are no perfectly honorable men; but every true man has one main point of honor and a few minor ones.

You cannot believe in honor until you have achieved it. Better keep yourself clean and bright: you are the window through which you must see the world.

Your word can never be as good as your bond, because your memory can never be as trustworthy as your honor.

PROPERTY

Property, said Proudhon, is theft. This is the only perfect truism that has been uttered on the subject.

SERVANTS

When domestic servants are treated as human beings it is not worth while to keep them.

The relation of master and servant is advantageous only to masters who do not scruple to abuse their authority, and to servants who do not subscribe to abuse their trust.

The perfect servant, when his master makes humane advances to him, feels that his existence is threatened, and hastens to change his place.

Masters and servants are both tyrannical; but the masters are the more dependent of the two.

A man enjoys what he uses, not what his servants use.

Man is the only animal which esteems itself rich in proportion to the number and voracity of its parasites.

Ladies and gentlemen are permitted to have friends in the kennel, but not in the kitchen.

Domestic servants, by making spoiled children of their masters, are forced to intimidate them in order to be able to live with them.

In a slave state, the slaves rule; in Mayfair, the tradesman rules.

HOW TO BEAT CHILDREN

If you strike a child, take care that you strike it in anger, even at the risk of maiming it for life. A blow in cold blood neither can nor should be forgiven.

If you beat children for pleasure, avow your object frankly, and play the game according to the rules, as a foxhunter does; and you will do comparatively little harm. No foxhunter is such a cad as to pretend that he hunts the fox to teach it not to steal chickens, or that he suffers more acutely than the fox at the death. Remember that even in childbeating there is the sportsman's way and the cad's way.

RELIGION

Beware of the man whose god is in the skies.

What a man believes may be ascertained, not from his creed, but from the assumptions on which he habitually acts.

VIRTUES AND VICES

No specific virtue or vice in a man implies the existence of any other specific virtue or vice in him, however closely the imagination may associate them.

Virtue consists, not in abstaining from vice, but in not desiring it.

Self-denial is not a virtue: it is only the effect of prudence on rascality.

Obedience simulates subordination as fear of the police simulates honesty.

Disobedience, the rarest and most courageous of the virtues, is seldom distinguished from neglect, the laziest and commonest of the vices.

Vice is waste of life. Poverty, obedience, and celibacy are the canonical vices.

Economy is the art of making the most of life.

The love of economy is the root of all virtue.

FAIRPLAY

The love of fairplay is a spectator's virtue, not a principal's.

GREATNESS

Greatness is only one of the sensations of littleness.

In heaven an angel is nobody in particular.

Greatness is the secular name for Divinity: both mean simply what lies beyond us.

If a great man could make us understand him, we should hang him.

We admit that when the divinity we worshipped made itself visible and comprehensible we crucified it.

To a mathematician the eleventh means only a single unit: to the bushman who cannot count further than his ten fingers it is an incalculable myriad.

The difference between the shallowest routineer and the deepest thinker appears, to the latter, trifling; to the former, infinite.

In a stupid nation the man of genius becomes a god: everybody worships him and nobody does his will.

BEAUTY AND HAPPINESS, ART AND RICHES

Happiness and Beauty are by-products.

Folly is the direct pursuit of Happiness and Beauty.

Riches and Art are spurious receipts for the production of Happiness and Beauty.

He who desires a lifetime of happiness with a beautiful woman desires to enjoy the taste of wine by keeping his mouth always full of it.

The most intolerable pain is produced by prolonging the keenest pleasure.

The man with toothache thinks everyone happy whose teeth are sound. The poverty stricken man makes the same mistake about the rich man.

The more a man possesses over and above what he uses, the more careworn he becomes.

The tyranny that forbids you to make the road with pick and shovel is worse than that which prevents you from lolling along it in a carriage and pair.

In an ugly and unhappy world the richest man can purchase nothing but ugliness and unhappiness.

In his efforts to escape from ugliness and unhappiness the rich man intensifies both. Every new yard of West End creates a new acre of East End.

The XIX century was the Age of Faith in Fine Art. The results are before us.

THE PERFECT GENTLEMAN

The fatal reservation of the gentleman is that he sacrifices everything to his honor except his gentility.

A gentleman of our days is one who has money enough to do what every fool would do if he could afford it: that is, consume without producing.

The true diagnostic of modern gentility is parasitism.

No elaboration of physical or moral accomplishment can atone for the sin of parasitism.

A modern gentleman is necessarily the enemy of his country. Even in war he does not fight to defend it, but to prevent his power of preying on it from passing to a foreigner. Such combatants are patriots in the same sense as two dogs fighting for a bone are lovers of animals.

The North American Indian was a type of the sportsman warrior gentleman. The Periclean Athenian was a type of the intellectually and artistically cultivated gentleman. Both were political failures. The modern gentleman, without the hardihood of the one or the culture of the other, has the appetite of both put together. He will not succeed where they failed.

He who believes in education, criminal law, and sport, needs only property to make him a perfect modern gentleman.

MODERATION

Moderation is never applauded for its own sake.

A moderately honest man with a moderately faithful wife, moderate drinkers both, in a moderately healthy house: that is the true middle class unit.

THE UNCONSCIOUS SELF

The unconscious self is the real genius. Your breathing goes wrong the moment your conscious self meddles with it.

Except during the nine months before he draws his first breath, no man manages his affairs as well as a tree does.

REASON

The reasonable man adapts himself to the world: the unreasonable one persists in trying to adapt the world to himself. Therefore all progress depends on the unreasonable man.

The man who listens to Reason is lost: Reason enslaves all whose minds are not strong enough to master her.

DECENCY

Decency is Indecency's Conspiracy of Silence.

EXPERIENCE

Men are wise in proportion, not to their experience, but to their capacity for experience.

If we could learn from mere experience, the stones of London would be wiser than its wisest men.

TIME'S REVENGES

Those whom we called brutes had their revenge when Darwin shewed us that they are our cousins.

The thieves had their revenge when Marx convicted the bourgeoisie of theft.

GOOD INTENTIONS

Hell is paved with good intentions, not with bad ones.

All men mean well.

NATURAL RIGHTS

The Master of Arts, by proving that no man has any natural rights, compels himself to take his own for granted.

The right to live is abused whenever it is not constantly challenged.

FAUTE DE MIEUX

In my childhood I demurred to the description of a certain young lady as 'the pretty Miss So and So.' My aunt rebuked me by saying 'Remember always that the least plain sister is the family beauty.'

No age or condition is without its heroes. The least incapable general in a nation is its Caesar, the least imbecile statesman its Solon, the least confused thinker its Socrates, the least commonplace poet its Shakespear.

CHARITY

Charity is the most mischievous sort of pruriency.

Those who minister to poverty and disease are accomplices in the two worst of all the crimes.

He who gives money he has not earned is generous with other people's labor.

Every genuinely benevolent person loathes almsgiving and mendicity.

FAME

Life levels all men: death reveals the eminent.

DISCIPLINE

Mutiny Acts are needed only by officers who command without authority. Divine right needs no whip.

WOMEN IN THE HOME

Home is the girl's prison and the woman's workhouse.

CIVILIZATION

Civilization is a disease produced by the practice of building societies with rotten material.

Those who admire modern civilization usually identify it with the steam engine and the electric telegraph.

Those who understand the steam engine and the electric telegraph spend their lives in trying to replace them with something better.

The imagination cannot conceive a viler criminal than he who should build another London like the present one, nor a greater benefactor than he who should destroy it.

GAMBLING

The most popular method of distributing wealth is the method of the roulette table.

The roulette table pays nobody except him that keeps it. Nevertheless a passion for gaming is common, though a passion for keeping roulette tables is unknown.

Gambling promises the poor what Property performs for the rich: that is why the bishops dare not denounce it fundamentally.

THE SOCIAL QUESTION

Do not waste your time on Social Questions. What is the matter with the poor is Poverty: what is the matter with the rich is Uselessness.

STRAY SAYINGS

We are told that when Jehovah created the world he saw that it was good. What would he say now?

The conversion of a savage to Christianity is the conversion of Christianity to savagery.

No man dares say so much of what he thinks as to appear to himself an extremist.

Mens sana in corpore sano is a foolish saying. The sound body is a product of the sound mind.

Decadence can find agents only when it wears the mask of progress.

In moments of progress the noble succeed, because things are going their way: in moments of decadence the base succeed for the same reason: hence the world is never without the exhilaration of contemporary success.

The reformer for whom the world is not good enough finds himself shoulder to shoulder with him that is not good enough for the world.

Every man over forty is a scoundrel.

Youth, which is forgiven everything, forgives itself

nothing: age, which forgives itself everything, is forgiven nothing.

When we learn to sing that Britons never will be masters we shall make an end of slavery.

Do not mistake your objection to defeat for an objection to fighting, your objection to being a slave for an objection to slavery, your objection to not being as rich as your neighbor for an objection to poverty. The cowardly, the insubordinate, and the envious share your objections.

Take care to get what you like or you will be forced to like what you get. Where there is no ventilation fresh air is declared unwholesome. Where there is no religion hypocrisy becomes good taste. Where there is no knowledge ignorance calls itself science.

If the wicked flourish and the fittest survive, Nature must be the God of rascals.

If history repeats itself, and the unexpected always happens, how incapable must Man be of learning from experience!

Compassion is the fellow-feeling of the unsound.

Those who understand evil pardon it: those who resent it destroy it.

Acquired notions of propriety are stronger than natural instincts. It is easier to recruit for monasteries and convents than to induce an Arab woman to uncover her mouth in public, or a British officer to walk through Bond Street in a golfing cap on an afternoon in May.

It is dangerous to be sincere unless you are also stupid.

The Chinese tame fowls by clipping their wings, and women by deforming their feet. A petticoat round the ankles serves equally well.

Political Economy and Social Economy are amusing intellectual games; but Vital Economy is the Philosopher's Stone.

When a heretic wishes to avoid martyrdom he speaks of 'Orthodoxy, True and False' and demonstrates that the True is his heresy.

Beware of the man who does not return your blow: he

neither forgives you nor allows you to forgive yourself.

If you injure your neighbor, better not do it by halves.

Sentimentality is the error of supposing that quarter can be given or taken in moral conflicts.

Two starving men cannot be twice as hungry as one; but two rascals can be ten times as vicious as one.

Make your cross your crutch; but when you see another man do it, beware of him.

SELF-SACRIFICE

Self-sacrifice enables us to sacrifice other people without blushing.

If you begin by sacrificing yourself to those you love, you will end by hating those to whom you have sacrificed yourself.

MAN AND SUPERMAN

Composition begun in 1901 (scenario for the play begun 2 July 1901 and completed 8 October 1901); completed June 1902. Published 1903. Revised text in Collected Edition, 1930. Copyright reading at the Victoria Hall (Bijou Theatre), London, on 29 June 1903. First presented (without Act III, which includes the *Don Juan in Hell* dream scene) by the Stage Society at the Royal Court Theatre, London, for two performances on 21 May 1905. *Don Juan in Hell* first presented as a one-act play at the Royal Court Theatre, London, on 4 June 1907 for eight matinées.

Roebuck Ramsden   *Charles Goodhart*
Parlormaid   *Hazel Thompson*
Octavius Robinson   *Lewis Casson*
John Tanner   *Granville Barker*
Ann Whitefield   *Lillah McCarthy*
Mrs Whitefield   *Florence Haydon*
Miss Ramsden   *Agnes Thomas*
Violet Robinson   *Sarah Brooke*
Henry Straker   *Edmund Gwenn*
Hector Malone   *Hubert Harben*
Mr Malone   *J. D. Beveridge*
Mendoza
Anarchist
Duval
Rowdy Social-Democrat   } (omitted from 1905 production)
Sulky Social-Democrat
Goatherd
An Officer

Don Juan in Hell (1907 cast)

Don Juan   *Robert Loraine*
Doña Ana de Ulloa   *Lillah McCarthy*
The Statue   *Michael Sherbrooke*
The Devil   *Norman McKinnel*

Period – The Present

PRINCIPAL WORKS OF
BERNARD SHAW*

PLAYS

Widowers' Houses (1893)
Plays Pleasant and Unpleasant (1898) (including *Mrs Warren's Profession; Arms and the Man; Candida; You Never Can Tell*)
Three Plays for Puritans (1901) (including *The Devil's Disciple; Caesar and Cleopatra*)
Man and Superman (1903)
John Bull's Other Island (1907)
Major Barbara (1907)
The Doctor's Dilemma (1911)
Getting Married (1911)
Misalliance (1914)
Androcles and the Lion (1916)
Pygmalion (1916)
Heartbreak House (1919)
Back to Methuselah (1921)
Saint Joan (1924)
The Apple Cart (1930)
Too True to be Good (1934)
On the Rocks (1934)
The Millionairess (1936)
In Good King Charles's Golden Days (1939)

NOVELS AND OTHER FICTION

An Unsocial Socialist (1884)
Cashel Byron's Profession (1885–6)
The Irrational Knot (1885–7)
Love among the Artists (1887–8)
Immaturity (1830)
The Black Girl in Search of God (1932)

CRITICISM

Major Critical Essays (1930) (including *The Quintessence of Ibsenism*, 1891; *The Sanity of Art*, 1895 and 1908; *The Perfect Wagnerite*, 1898)
Music in London (1931; from serialization 1890–94)
Our Theatres in the Nineties (1931; from serialization 1895–98)

POLITICAL WRITINGS

Fabian Essays in Socialism (edited, 1893)
Common Sense about the War (1914)
The Intelligent Woman's Guide to Socialism and Capitalism (1928)
Everybody's Political What's What? (1944)

*Dates are of first English-language publication.
[NB This clarification is essential in Shaw, for some of his works appeared in translation two and three years before English publication.]

READ MORE IN PENGUIN

In every corner of the world, on every subject under the sun, Penguin represents quality and variety – the very best in publishing today.

For complete information about books available from Penguin – including Puffins, Penguin Classics and Arkana – and how to order them, write to us at the appropriate address below. Please note that for copyright reasons the selection of books varies from country to country.

In the United Kingdom: Please write to *Dept. EP, Penguin Books Ltd, Bath Road, Harmondsworth, West Drayton, Middlesex UB7 0DA*

In the United States: Please write to *Consumer Sales, Penguin Putnam Inc., P.O. Box 12289 Dept. B, Newark, New Jersey 07101-5289*. VISA and MasterCard holders call 1-800-788-6262 to order Penguin titles

In Canada: Please write to *Penguin Books Canada Ltd, 10 Alcorn Avenue, Suite 300, Toronto, Ontario M4V 3B2*

In Australia: Please write to *Penguin Books Australia Ltd, P.O. Box 257, Ringwood, Victoria 3134*

In New Zealand: Please write to *Penguin Books (NZ) Ltd, Private Bag 102902, North Shore Mail Centre, Auckland 10*

In India: Please write to *Penguin Books India Pvt Ltd, 11 Community Centre, Panchsheel Park, New Delhi 110017*

In the Netherlands: Please write to *Penguin Books Netherlands bv, Postbus 3507, NL-1001 AH Amsterdam*

In Germany: Please write to *Penguin Books Deutschland GmbH, Metzlerstrasse 26, 60594 Frankfurt am Main*

In Spain: Please write to *Penguin Books S. A., Bravo Murillo 19, 1° B, 28015 Madrid*

In Italy: Please write to *Penguin Italia s.r.l., Via Benedetto Croce 2, 20094 Corsico, Milano*

In France: Please write to *Penguin France, Le Carré Wilson, 62 rue Benjamin Baillaud, 31500 Toulouse*

In Japan: Please write to *Penguin Books Japan Ltd, Kaneko Building, 2-3-25 Koraku, Bunkyo-Ku, Tokyo 112*

In South Africa: Please write to *Penguin Books South Africa (Pty) Ltd, Private Bag X14, Parkview, 2122 Johannesburg*

READ MORE IN PENGUIN

THE BERNARD SHAW LIBRARY

'The most influential writer of his age . . . His plays can scarcely prove
other than lastingly delightful since they are the product of vigorous
intelligence joined to inexhaustible comic invention' J. I. M. Stewart
in the *Oxford History of English Literature*

Androcles and the Lion
The Apple Cart
Back to Methuselah
The Doctor's Dilemma
Heartbreak House
John Bull's Other Island
Last Plays
Major Barbara
Major Critical Essays
Man and Superman
Misalliance and the Fascinating Foundling
Plays Extravagant
(The Millionairess, Too True to be Good, The Simpleton of the
Unexpected Isles)
Plays Pleasant
(Arms and the Man, Candida, The Man of Destiny, You Never Can
Tell)
Plays Political
(The Apple Cart, On the Rocks, Geneva)
Plays Unpleasant
(Widowers' Houses, The Philanderer, Mrs Warren's Profession)
Pygmalion
Saint Joan
Selected Short Plays
(including The Admirable Bashville and Great Catherine)
Three Plays for Puritans
(The Devil's Disciple, Caesar and Cleopatra, Captain Brassbound's
Conversion)